New Legal Approaches to Studying the Court of Justice

Revisiting Law in Context

Edited by

CLAIRE KILPATRICK

and

JOANNE SCOTT

OXFORD
UNIVERSITY PRESS

OXFORD
UNIVERSITY PRESS

Great Clarendon Street, Oxford, OX2 6DP,
United Kingdom

Oxford University Press is a department of the University of Oxford. It furthers the University's objective of excellence in research, scholarship, and education by publishing worldwide. Oxford is a registered trade mark of Oxford University Press in the UK and in certain other countries

First Edition published in 2020

Published in the United States of America by Oxford University Press
198 Madison Avenue, New York, NY 10016, United States of America

British Library Cataloguing in Publication Data
Data available

Library of Congress Control Number: 2020941842

ISBN 978–0–19–887147–7

DOI: 10.1093/oso/9780198871477.003.0001

The manufacturer's authorised representative in the EU for product safety is Oxford University Press España S.A. of Parque Empresarial San Fernando de Henares, Avenida de Castilla, 2 – 28830 Madrid (www.oup.es/en or product.safety@oup.com). OUP España S.A. also acts as importer into Spain of products made by the manufacturer.

Contents

Table of Cases

CJEU CASES (IN NUMBER ORDER)

n = footnote

National and International Cases

CZECH REPUBLIC

DENMARK

UNITED KINGDOM

Table of Legislation

n = footnote

EUROPEAN LEGISLATION

Treaties and Conventions (in alphabetical order)

Directives (in chronological order)

Regulations (in chronological order)

Decisions (in chronological order)

Notes on Contributors

Anthony Arnull is Barber Professor of Jurisprudence at the University of Birmingham, UK. From 1989 to 1992, he was a *référendaire* at the European Court of Justice in the chambers of Advocate General FG Jacobs. He is Consultant Editor of the *European Law Review*, having been its co-editor from 1996 to 2007. He has given evidence to a number of UK Parliamentary Select Committees and acted as Specialist Adviser to the House of Lords EU Committee. His publications include *The European Union and its Court of Justice* (Oxford University Press, 2nd edn, 2006); *The Oxford Handbook of European Union Law* (Oxford University Press, 2015, co-edited with Damian Chalmers); and *European Union Law: A Very Short Introduction* (Oxford University Press, 2017).

Claire Kilpatrick is Professor of International and European Labour and Social Law at the European University Institute and Co-Director of the Academy of European Law at the EUI. She is also the EUI's Dean of Graduate Studies. Before coming to the EUI in 2011, she worked at LSE and before that at Cambridge University. Her interests lie mainly in the law and policy construction of Social Europe, especially the EU's roles. A focus of her recent work is EMU and Social Europe, with a particular focus on sovereign debt loan arrangements and legal challenges to those arrangements from those within debtor EU states. Professor Kilpatrick is involved in two research projects at present, concerning 'Equality Law in Europe—A New Generation' and 'The Court of Justice in the Archives'. These projects are hosted by the Academy of European Law at the EUI and involve the participation of many EUI researchers.

Jan Komárek is Professor of European Law at the Faculty of Law, University of Copenhagen, and a member of iCourts, Centre of Excellence for International Courts, at the same university. Previously he was Associate Professor at the London School of Economics and Political Science (LSE). Komárek obtained a PhD from the University of Oxford in 2011, and other degrees from the Charles University in Prague (Mgr, JUDr), and Stockholm University (LLM). He also worked as a legal counsellor at the Czech Ministry of Foreign Affairs and as a legal secretary to the President of the Czech Constitutional Court. He is a member of the editorial board of the *European Constitutional Law Review*. Komárek is the Principal Investigator of the ERC Starting Grant project, *IMAGINE: European Constitutional Imaginaries: Utopias, Ideologies and the Other*, running in 2019–2024.

Fernanda G. Nicola is Professor of Law at the Washington College of Law, American University, and she is the Director of the Program on International Organizations Law and Development. Her research and teaching interests are in European Union Law, Comparative Law, Constitutional Law, and Transnational Legal Theory. She received her PhD from Trento University and her SJD degree from Harvard Law School, where she was the recipient of the Mancini Prize and the Justice Welfare and Economics fellowship at the Weatherhead Center for International Affairs under the supervision of Amartya Sen.

Professor Nicola is a member of the American Society of Comparative Law (ASCL) and the International Academy of Comparative Law (IACL). She was a Fernand Braudel Senior Fellow at the European University Institute, Visiting Professor at LUISS in Rome, and she is a Permanent Visiting Professor at iCourts Centre of Excellence (University of Copenhagen). She co-edited with Bill Davies, *EU Law Stories: Contextual and Critical Histories of European Jurisprudence* (Cambridge University Press, 2017) and with Mikael Rask Madsen and Antoine Vauchez, *Researching the ECJ: New Approaches and Methodologies* (forthcoming, Cambridge University Press, 2020).

Urška Šadl is Professor of Law at the European University Institute and a Global Research Fellow at iCourts Centre of Excellence (University of Copenhagen). Her research focuses on the practices, mechanisms, and techniques which courts, and especially the Court of Justice of the European Union (the Court), use to change the law. Her most recent project, 'Judging under the influence' (financed by the Danish Research Council), examines how various participants in judicial proceedings influence judicial arguments, precedent citations, legal outcomes, and approaches to interpretation. Urška holds a BA degree from the Faculty of Law in Ljubljana and an LLM degree in Legal Studies from the College of Europe, Bruges. She received her PhD from the Faculty of Law in Copenhagen.

Joanne Scott is Professor of European Law and Co-Director of the Academy of European Law at the European University Institute. She is currently on leave from University College London, Faculty of Laws, where she taught from 2005 to 2017. Before that she taught at the University of Cambridge, Queen Mary University of London, and the University of Kent. Her research interests lie in the areas of environmental law and climate change law, EU extraterritoriality, new modes of EU governance, and the relationships between different legal orders. Among her recent publications is a co-edited book (with Marise Cremona) on *EU Law Beyond EU Borders: The Extraterritorial Reach of EU Law* (Oxford University Press, 2019). Professor Scott was elected as a Fellow of the British Academy in 2013 and a Fellow of the Royal Society of Edinburgh in 2012. Along with Professor Kilpatrick and Professor Marise Cremona, Professor Scott is currently involved in the Academy research project exploring 'The Court of Justice in the Archives', funded by the EUI Research Council.

Fabien Tarissan is a researcher at the French National Centre for Scientific Research (CNRS) and Adjunct Professor at Ecole Normale Supérieure de Paris-Saclay. He is also currently vice-president of the French Society for Computer Science (SIF), in charge of scientific mediation. His work mainly concerns the analysis and modelling of large networks encountered in practice, such as the internet, the web, social networks, or legal networks. These networks are typically represented by graphs, and a set of techniques stemming from graph theory has already proved to be very useful to characterize their structure and to model their behaviour. His work follows this approach by proposing new theoretical tools in order to identify non-trivial properties of these networks and to define new models able to capture these properties.

Antoine Vauchez is a CNRS Research Professor at the Centre européen de sociologie et de science politique (Université Paris 1-Sorbonne/CNRS) and a permanent Visiting Professor at iCourts Centre of Excellence (University of Copenhagen). Over the years, he has engaged in the critical sociology of law and historical sociology, researching extensively fields such as international courts, judicial politics, and lawyering in relation to transnational politics and the European Union. His most recent book, *Democratizing Europe* (published in French, German, and English), brings to a close a series of three books on law, politics, and democracy in the European Union, following an edited volume (with B. de Witte), *Lawyering Europe: European law as a Transnational Social Field* (Hart, 2014) and a monograph *Brokering Europe: Euro-lawyers and the Making of a Transnational Polity* (Cambridge University Press, 2015).

List of Abbreviations

CFI	Court of First Instance
CJEU	Court of Justice of the European Union
CST	EU Civil Service Tribunal
ECB	European Central Bank
ECHR	European Convention on Human Rights
ECJ	European Court of Justice
ECSC	European Coal and Steel Community
EMU	Economic and Monetary Union
EUI	European University Institute
Euratom	Treaty establishing the European Atomic Energy Community
FIDE	Fédération Internationale pour le Droit Européen
HAEU	Historical Archives of the European Union
ICJ	International Court of Justice
ILO	International Labour Organization
QMV	qualified majority voting
USSC	United States Supreme Court

Introduction

Claire Kilpatrick and Joanne Scott

This volume has its origins in the 2017 Academy of European Law summer course on the Law of the European Union which focused on new legal approaches to studying the Court of Justice of the European Union. The courses explored a number of innovative legal approaches to studying the Court. Each of these approaches differs from the classic, and still dominant, doctrinal work of understanding and systematizing the Court's jurisprudence. By developing critical, large data, historical, sociological, and reflective institutional approaches to the Court of Justice, the guest lecturers aimed to enrich our understanding of the Court of Justice and to expand our understanding of the range of approaches and sources available to study it. The chapters included in this volume are based on the classes that were offered as part of this summer course. They were revised following a 'meet the authors' workshop in Spring 2018 at which PhD researchers from the Law Department of the European University Institute served as discussants.

A core approach to the study of EU law, including the judgments of the Court of Justice, is the doctrinal endeavour, by which we mean the construction of an organized, and organizing, view of legal decisions. This involves the systematizing of a structured sphere of interaction of legal materials into various discrete bodies of EU law; for example, internal market law, EU administrative law, EU migration law, and the law of the Economic and Monetary Union (EMU). This volume seeks to sharpen our appreciation of that doctrinal endeavour as active, iterative, and interpretative, rather than being an automatic product of the legal materials themselves. It does this primarily by stepping outside that doctrinal endeavour, whilst not denying its usefulness or intellectual value. The volume includes five chapters which analyse the activities of the Court of Justice from a highly diverse range of non-doctrinal perspectives.

We take inspiration from Neil MacCormick's 1994 analysis of the 'Four Quadrants of Jurisprudence', these being identified as raw law, doctrinal law, law in social science, and fundamental values and principles.[1] Raw law is a mainly

[1] MacCormick, 'Four Quadrants of Jurisprudence', in W. Krawietz, N. MacCormick, and G. H. von Wright (eds), *Prescriptive Formality and Normative Rationality in Modern Legal Systems. Festschrift for Robert S. Summers* (1994) 53.

Claire Kilpatrick and Joanne Scott, *Introduction*. In: *New Legal Approaches to Studying the Court of Justice*. First edition. Edited by Claire Kilpatrick and Joanne Scott, Oxford University Press (2020).
DOI: 10.1093/oso/9780198871477.003.0001

heuristic category; 'the unexamined substratum of brute fact (if any) that gives theorized, scholarly law-constructs whatever anchoring they have in the real world'.[2] The principal function of its inclusion is to underline that we do not approach law pre-theoretically. The other three quadrants then offer three different ways of theorizing legal understanding, each of which relies on distinct goals and methods.

MacCormick's primary goal is to show how the second quadrant—doctrinal law—does not flow mechanically from the legal materials themselves, but is the result of a transformative practice. 'The system-quality of law depends essentially upon the existence of a scholarly practice of rationally systematising legal experience'.[3] And this doctrinal-generating transformative practice has important interactions with the final two quadrants, namely law in social science and fundamental values and principles. On the one hand, those interested in law in social science have no direct access to 'raw law' so that '[a] sociology of law or an economics of law or a history or anthropology of law would then aim to account for the systematisers and their systematisations as well as that which they systematise'.[4] On the other, those interested in fundamental values and principles, 'the "ought" by which we finally criticise whatever is',[5] need to consider what the relationship between their work and doctrinal scholarship is.

The contributions to this volume show how innovative, recent scholarship can sharpen and extend what we mean by 'law in context' significantly beyond what MacCormick noted when he characterized the 'Four Quadrants of Jurisprudence' towards the end of the twentieth century, with specific regard to the field of EU law and the role of the Court of Justice. In its extended version, law in context does not simply imply that other disciplines 'are drawn into the process of constructing coherent accounts of legal values and their developments'.[6] On the contrary, as this volume exemplifies, legal scholars looking at EU law and courts have taken a deep dive into non-doctrinal approaches, methods, conventions, and literatures. For example, they pay close attention to the actors and processes that construct and reconstruct the law. At times, legal scholars are even working with and within other disciplines, albeit with a view to shedding light on legal institutions. Thus, EU legal scholars are much more fully and consciously operating within the other two quadrants identified by MacCormick, namely law in social science and fundamental values and principles. At the same time, the volume also demonstrates how non-lawyers are deeply knowledgeable of how EU lawyers and courts consider legal sources from an 'internal' point of view.

The chapters in this volume are interesting because they exemplify the flourishing of new legal approaches to studying the Court of Justice. However, they also highlight significant new developments at the Court itself which attract our

[2] Ibid. 55. [3] Ibid. 57. [4] Ibid. 61. [5] Ibid. 61. [6] Ibid. 67.

attention and deserve analysis. Thus, the idea behind this volume is to make available new tools and approaches through which the activities of the Court of Justice can be studied.

We tend to think of the Court of Justice as a unified institution, over time and space, and indeed this is part of its claim to authority and legitimacy (it is and always has been 'We the Court'). However, its composition, structure, management, and organization have changed dramatically over time. And so too have the Coal and Steel Community, European Economic Community, European Community, and European Union, whose texts and actions it must interpret and apply in cases brought before it. There has been a turn to history in the study of the Court of Justice in recent years. What stimulated such a turn is itself an interesting question. Regardless, it has been a fruitful time to develop such approaches, as the Court of Justice at the beginning of 2015 opened its archives which are deposited at the Historical Archives of the EU at the European University Institute (EUI) in Florence. This has created a new and challenging primary source for those studying the Court of Justice: the *dossiers de procédure*, which contain much more than the contemporary documents published by the Court.

Ethnographic or sociological analysis of the Court and its legal communities can also shed light on the making of EU law and the legal entrepreneurs who played key roles: the lawyers, the legal services of the institutions, the *référendaires*, and so on. Similarly, network citation analysis is emerging as a valuable tool to understand the case law of the Court of Justice. By using data techniques to trace the importance and uses of cases by the Court of Justice of the European Union (CJEU) and contrasting their use by other participants in the making of EU law, for instance Advocates General and EU law textbooks, such work can generate interesting and sometimes surprising findings, and promising new avenues for research.

The volume opens with a chapter by Anthony Arnull (Chapter 1). This offers an engaging and sweeping overview of the role, structure, and composition of the CJEU; from the time of the birth of the Court of Justice of the European Coal and Steel Community (ECSC) to the present day. Arnull brings the CJEU alive with his attentiveness to the role and importance of people, personalities, and politics in its history.

Originating in an 'enigmatic sentence' at the end of the Schuman Declaration, the Court of Justice of the ECSC was shaped by the hand of Maurice Lagrange and deeply influenced by French administrative law. The first Court of Justice of the ECSC brought together 'a group of people whose experiences of the previous decades had been markedly different': from people who had lived under Nazi occupation to individuals who had been active in the Vichy Government. '[T]he war was never discussed in the Court.' In important respects, the judgments of the ECSC Court 'foreshadowed ideas that would later emerge under the Treaty of Rome', including the principle of sincere cooperation and the doctrines of primacy and direct effect. In other respects, it adopted what turned out to be a distinctive approach, including in relation to its open stance to the admissibility of annulment actions.

When the new European Court of Justice (ECJ) took up its duties on 7 March 1958 following the entry into force of the Treaty of Rome, continuity of membership from the ECSC Court was ensured by the presence of six members of that Court; four judges and Advocates General Lagrange and Roemer. While the new Court was hamstrung by the inclusion of more restrictive rules on individual standing in annulment actions in the EEC Treaty, it was also empowered by a preliminary ruling mechanism that gave it jurisdiction over questions relating to the interpretation as well as the validity of EEC law. Arnull describes the early case law of the ECJ as 'a puzzling mix of deference to the Member States and buccaneering constitutionalism'. Arnull argues that this buccaneering constitutionalism should be understood in its historical context which was characterized by dramatic geopolitical tensions and the ascendance within the EEC of a paralysing intergovernmentalism.

Arnull argues that the early constitutionalizing case law of the ECJ ensured that when the 'empty chair crisis' came along, the ECJ was 'forearmed' though not 'forewarned'. '[T]he Court deployed the weapons with which it had equipped itself to compensate for the Member States' failure to ensure that the common market was completed by end of the transitional period'; particularly the flexible and expanding doctrine of direct effect. While the ECJ was sensitive to the danger of negative political reactions to its judgments, its role in facilitating the establishment of the common market during this period generated tensions between the ECJ and some higher national courts.

Over time, tensions also emerged within the CJEU and in particular between the Court and the General Court (previously the Court of First Instance). These tensions were played out in a public and embarrassing way, and Arnull suggests that '[t]his sorry tale highlights some of the Union's worst features'. 'The intergovernmental instincts of some of the Member States and the way the Union diffuses responsibility for spending public money rendered most of the Member States incapable of focusing on the main issue: did the General Court need to be reinforced and, if so, what was the most economical way in which that could be done?'

Arnull's chapter concludes with some brief reflections on the future of the CJEU. He considers how we might arrive at the point where the Court of Justice 'is less defensive, less deferential to the Union institutions, and better at managing internal dissent. In short, a Court comfortable in its own skin'.

The title of Antoine Vauchez's chapter (Chapter 2) nicely evokes its approach to the Court of Justice by taking both a 'close up' and a 'long shot'. Vauchez is a leading exponent of the new turn to sociologically informed political science analyses of the Court of Justice with this body of work being distinctive from the earlier generation of political science studies on the Court of Justice in a number of ways. Rather than considering the Court of Justice within large-scale integration hypotheses based on power and interests such as supranationalization versus intergovernmentalism, or the empowerment of lower national courts via the preliminary reference procedure, this body of work looks instead at EU law as something produced in concrete and situated historical processes and practices. Such a shift also requires a turn to very different methods: focusing on how Eurolawyers create practices of Eurolawyering, examining localized contexts, and considering how they interact with the potential production or effects of EU law.

In this contribution, he reflects on the growing politicization of the Court of Justice from the 1990s and the challenges of developing an intellectual apparatus adequate for the analysis of this phenomenon. Noting the limits of characterizations of the Court as engaging in 'judicial activism' or being 'neo-liberal', he considers how a focus on practices might open productive new angles to grasping the Court of Justice as a political object.

Taking a 'long shot', it is suggested that that we depart from fixating on locating the 'political' exclusively or primarily in the moment of the decision made by the Court of Justice. The Court, and any judgment it makes, does not stand alone. Rather it is one point in a large co-production of EU law with multiple participants connecting before, during, and after it. He suggests this allows us to consider the Court of Justice's projection of the political through dominant stances and concepts developed in its case law, such as the 'autonomy' of the EU legal order, the meaning of 'restrictions' to free movement, the definition of a 'worker', and how these contribute to positioning actors in sectors of the economy and society. The important counterpart to this is considering the non-production of EU law, that is to say, the rare configurations in which these actors and groups translate their issue into an 'EU law' case which, in an even smaller and more specialized subset, comes before the Court of Justice.

Looking 'close up', the invitation is to open up the Court of Justice not just to look at the members of the Court or even the broader cast of *référendaires*, but rather to consider the constraining and shaping of the roles and orientations of those crafting EU judgments by conventions, routines, procedures, and the socialization of ideas of what constitutes best practice.

The aim of Fernanda Nicola's rich and engaging chapter (Chapter 3) is to offer 'methodological insights' for those who wish to conduct legal-historical research into the case law of the CJEU, using the Historical Archives of the European Union (HAEU). The HAEU were opened in Villa Salviati at the EUI in 2014. The archives house the historical records of many of the EU institutions, including those of the CJEU following a voluntary decision by the Court to open its archives to the public. Included in the archives are *dossiers de procédure* relating to CJEU cases. These *dossiers* enable a researcher to 'trace the entire procedure of a judgment', including the arguments presented by parties and intervenors in the relevant case. The Court's administrative archive will also soon be made available following the process of digitalization by the HAEU.

Nicola situates her chapter at the crossroads of important research conducted by comparative lawyers on legal transplants/influences and the work of 'the new legal historians'. Consistent also with the observations of Arnull, she argues that this research 'has challenged the notion of an accepted and necessary constitutionalization of EU law'. Rather, the constitutional trajectory was a contested one, promoted and resisted by different categories of legal entrepreneurs. Research by the new legal historians has brought the study of CJEU case law alive, by shining a spotlight on actors—including judges, civil servants, and lawyers—and processes.

Building on this earlier research, Nicola's chapter offers an engaging viewpoint on the process of conducting legal-historical research using the HAEU. She explains that the *dossiers de procédure* relating to CJEU cases become available 30 years after the proceedings before the Court ended. A researcher interested in a particular case is required to send a request for access to the HAEU. The file will only be released some months later, following the digitalization of the file and redaction of some parts by the CJEU. Nicola offers a sensitive and thoughtful critique of the Court's current approach to redaction, asking, for example, at what point access to documents shedding light on the deliberations of the judges should become available. Pragmatically, she warns that linguistic limitations will often restrict the usefulness of particular *dossiers* because although the working language of the Court is French, French translations of documents in other official languages are not included in the file. In the same way, the comparative research notes that helped the judges to better understand the legal systems of the original six and later in 1973 nine Member States of the European Community are not included in the files. The CJEU is, however, beginning to grant access to such notes.

Nicola's chapter also illustrates the value of the *dossiers de procedure* by reference to four cases that appear in the EU law canon as *grands arrêts* for the primacy or direct effect of EC law. For example, she observes that the *dossier* relating to the landmark case of *Costa v. ENEL* well-known for the primacy of EC law, in reality offers 'very important insights on the Italian political economy' related to the case. This concerns the nationalization of Italian electricity and how to reconcile a state monopoly with rules prohibiting anticompetitive conduct. It also offers insights into which actors, including individual 'Eurolawyers', and which arguments exerted influence on the final judgment of the Court. Nicola also uses the *dossiers* relating to three early cases involving the UK to show 'how British lawyers and politicians alike [learnt] to present their arguments in Luxembourg' in order to gain traction before the Court. For example, we see from the *dossier* in *Defrenne II*, a quintessential case for direct effect of EU law, in reality shows the influence of the economic arguments about the implementation of equal pay measures presented by the UK and Irish governments.

Nicola is, however, realistic about what archival research on the CJEU might be expected to achieve. On the one hand, she argues that unearthing European legal history through archival research can help us to understand better 'the acceptance and resistance to EU law and its institutions' and the role played by transnational professional networks in the evolution of EU law. On the other, she suggests exploring other archives beyond the CJEU and she admits that '[a]t the end of my own voyage inside the ECJ archives, I humbly realized that working on archival documents is harder than expected and that often the promise of finding the white truffles in an unexplored forest can remain unfulfilled'. Like Coetzee's novel, which forms the inspiration for the title of Nicola's chapter, the *dossiers de procédure* are 'full of gaps, absences and uncertainties'.[7] It is the scholars pushing for fuller access who are the barbarians banging (politely in Nicola's case) on the CJEU's door.

Chapter 4, by Urška Šadl and Fabien Tarissan, explores how network analysis is or could become relevant for studying the case law of the CJEU. As applied to CJEU case law, network analysis explores relations between cases and the patterning of these relations. This is labelled citation network analysis. 'The cases become nodes (the dots) and the relations become links (lines or arrows).' The patterning of these relations is often presented in graphic form such as in the striking figure which illustrates the network of citations to different paragraphs in three landmark judgments, including the extraction of implicit citations.[8] In the chapter, Šadl and Tarissan seek both to refute two common criticisms of network analysis and to present three case studies to demonstrate the relevance of this approach.

In relation to the criticisms, Šadl and Tarissan argue that network analysis is not inherently quantitative as has often been suggested and, indeed, that it has its roots in the more qualitative social sciences such as sociology, anthropology, and social psychology. Thus, this methodology can be integrated in quantitative, qualitative, as well as mixed methods, approaches. While Šadl and Tarissan acknowledge that citation network analysis can be reductionist in its approach to evaluating the *legal* relevance of a case, they argue that 'one can re-imagine the network approach' by introducing modifications that enable it to reveal more clearly the 'true' nature of the jurisprudence under investigation. They seek to test and exemplify this claim in the presentation of their three case studies.

The first case study tests whether citation patterns reflect the legal importance of cases. Šadl and Tarissan take the CJEU's own compilation of 'landmark cases' as their starting point and use citation network analysis to test the hypothesis that cases were included in this list due not only to their contribution to providing practical solutions to emerging legal problems, but also as a result of their

[7] Van Zanten Gallagher, 'Torture and the Novel: J.M. Coetzee's *Waiting for the Barbarians*', 29 *Contemporary Literature* (1988) 277.

[8] See Figure 4.3, in Chapter 4 Section C.

historical significance and symbolic status. They evaluated to what 'extent the selection of the Court matched the "objective" importance [of cases] according to the network metrics'. They find that while a good match exists in relation to cases that have or had a practical importance, they do not serve to identify cases that are of more symbolic importance.

The second case study builds on the first, deploying a modification to their network methodology. It explores the evolution of citation networks to ascertain how cases gain and maintain authority over time. This case study offers an illustration of an innovative re-imagining of network analysis and shows how this methodological addition can help to use network analysis to identify historically important cases and to identify different pathways to case 'immortality' over time.

The final case study asks what citation networks can tell us about the 'real' importance of cases and links back to their critical engagement with the issue of whether network analysis can be relevant in shedding light on the legal relevance of a case. Here, Šadl and Tarissan conclude that the results of their 'objective-quantitative analysis' is in line with scholarly perceptions of the importance of cases. For example, while *Dassonville* is essentially a single issue case, *Francovich* stands for judicial innovation and *Defrenne* is of importance for the development of a number of different areas of EU law.

Šadl and Tarissan's chapter is situated at the cutting edge of new methodologies for studying law. While their approach is empirical in the sense that it seeks to describe relations between cases, it also draws upon a close reading and analysis of the relevant cases and requires the exercise of interpretative judgment reading these cases. It is only by combining the 'objective-quantitative' and the 'subjective-qualitative' that the relevance, or indeed added value, of evolving network approaches can be tested. While the methodological dimensions of this chapter may be challenging for those unfamiliar with a network approach, the authors conclude by offering a clear summary of their findings and reflections on the role and limitations of this form of analysis.

Jan Komárek concludes this volume (with Chapter 5) on new legal approaches to studying the Court of Justice by revisiting and casting important new light on a perennial topic of scholarship on courts: how to evaluate their work. Specifically, he adjusts the recent claim of Joseph Weiler[9] that legitimacy is not useful for this evaluation, arguing that it can be a useful lens but only if we respect certain conditions in its deployment. It is essential to be clear and explicit and detailed on its meaning and mode of use. This would avoid using legitimacy in the manner that Weiler argues renders it without value, namely as a shorthand for approving or disapproving of a particular court or case.

[9] Weiler, 'Epilogue: Judging the Judges—Apology and Critique', in M. Adams *et al.* (eds), *Judging Europe's Judges. The Legitimacy of the Case Law of the European Court of Justice* (2013) 235.

Komárek then makes good on this claim by engaging in the illuminating and challenging task of reviewing existing patterns of use to characterize and clarify the role played by legitimacy analyses in relation to courts in general, and the Court of Justice more specifically. He argues, in particular, that all accounts of legitimacy of political authority contain normative elements so that it is not sustainable, although often done, to draw a bright line between sociological accounts of legitimacy based on people's beliefs or empirical consent and normative accounts based on some benchmark of acceptability. The bridge between these two consists of identifying and evaluating, through competing discourses and semantic struggles, what count as good reasons for accepting political authority.

Drawing in particular on influential recent work on legitimating international law and courts[10] and linking this to public law theory, analyses of judicial interpretation, and features of the EU as oscillating between relying on the consent of its states and of its citizens, he builds a frame for considering the legitimacy of the Court of Justice. In the EU, traditionally the dominant discourse was democracy while more recently other contenders such as constitutionalism and justice have appeared. To apply this to the specific case of courts, he suggests distinguishing between two functions: the effects of a specific case for those directly involved and the broader effects of the case law of the Court, with tension arising between these individual and common interests. Crucially, while consent (to laws) underpins the democratic legitimacy of courts with compulsory jurisdiction, the interpretative freedom courts necessarily exercise when deciding cases escapes such consent.

With this important ground-clearing exercise as its backdrop, the chapter turns to consider 'the perennial problem of judicial legitimacy in the Western legal tradition: how to legitimize creative moments of judicial interpretation of law'. Following a rich and thoughtful assessment of the existing positions, he explores in more detail his most promising contender, the Court as interstitial interpreter which knows it must interpret with an eye to the past and future and to its interpretive community, and considers how this sociological basis for legitimacy combines with normative justifications such as democracy.

To conclude this introduction, it is important to stress that the selection in this volume is only that. Our aim is to show through a series of illuminating worked-through examples the considerable interest of stepping outside hermeneutic and 'internal coherence' analysis of legal arguments. One can, however, easily imagine other productive directions in which such a point of departure can lead and it is our hope that this volume will encourage and help to link such endeavours. We offer two brief additional examples to reinforce this point.

[10] Most centrally, M. Koskenniemi, *From Apology to Utopia: The Structure of International Legal Argument: Reissue with a New Epilogue* (2005); I. Venzke, *How Interpretation Makes International Law: On Semantic Change and Normative Twists* (2012).

First, by stepping outside the legal arguments being made and considering instead who is making them, we can shed light on and begin to better understand, situate, and evaluate an important phenomenon in the making of EU law, namely the writing by members of the Court of Justice as academics about the judgments of their Court. Members of the Court (most notably perhaps Pescatore and Mancini) have been foundational in constructing Community law as an area of study. However, this is still a central feature of contemporary EU law scholarship, with judges such as Allan Rosas and the President of the Court Koen Lenaerts as central exponents of EU academic scholarship. This opens up a range of interesting lines of inquiry. On the one hand, it is surely unsurprising that intense interactions between legal scholarship and judges exist. As MacCormick notes:

> Judges write opinions in the manner of law review articles, and law review articles do the return compliment of playing back a judge-centred view of the law. Judges indeed are often distinguished legal scientists in their own right. And academics brought into judging can make distinguished contributions, nowhere more noticeably than in the European Community, whose law has been developed by a strongly academic Court of Justice from the very partial materials of the foundation Treaties.[11]

On the other hand, while acknowledging this interactive to-and-fro between high courts and doctrinal scholarship, we can also usefully ask whether the functions and our assessments of such contributions to EU law scholarship vary according both to the period of EU development and the particular issues on which EU Court members are reflecting as 'academics'.

A second, and very different, illustration is to consider the Court of Justice from the perspective of public interest lawyering. In such a perspective, the Court and the 'legal stock' of the relevant EU substantive law and access rules and options become a legal opportunity structure, to be assessed by activist lawyers and civil society groups against other possible options for achieving legal, political, or social change.[12] In this perspective we, for instance, look at unions taking annulment actions against EU sovereign debt measures in a different light, or at national judges as gate-keepers in accessing the Court of Justice by using the preliminary reference procedure.

We finish by putting on the table an important and obvious question that such departures from doctrinal scholarship raise, namely the role or contribution legal scholars can make to new approaches of this kind. One could imagine a position

[11] MacCormick (n. 1) 67.

[12] See e.g. Hilson, 'New Social Movements: The Role of Legal Opportunity', 9 *Journal of European Public Policy* (2002) 238; Vanhala, 'Legal Opportunity Structures and the Paradox of Legal Mobilisation Structures by the Environmental Movement in the UK', 46 *Law and Society Review* (2012) 523.

in which legal scholars are assigned the role of doing the doctrinal work, with that work being viewed as both falling within their unique sphere of competence and constituting their exclusive specialization. In this division of labour, EU lawyers would undertake doctrinal analysis while scholars from other social science disciplines—history, sociology, anthropology, political science, or philosophers and political theorists when it comes to questions of fundamental values—would develop and explore new legal approaches. A variant, and one considered by MacCormick in his 'Four Quadrants of Jurisprudence', is that legal scholars could also undertake various kinds of 'law in context'. Here, what is essentially doctrinal work is supplemented, usually to its benefit, by historical, economic, political, and social science as well as philosophy and political theory. At the same time, as he rightly notes, such scholarship remains very different from scholarship that is situated in the other quadrants.

As already noted, it seems to us that neither of these alternatives fully reflects the kinds of work done in this volume and more generally across the new wave of scholarship that it exemplifies. This shows a more intense engagement with scholars across disciplines to reflect on law and courts, with the Court of Justice as a central focus, and new methods (such as network citation analysis) and sources (such as the Court's archives) being discovered and developed. It also shows a more intense and deeply knowledgeable engagement with EU law and the Court of Justice by non-legal scholars, such as the new sociologies and histories of the Court of Justice. Thus, these and other new approaches have spawned productive and ongoing conversations across disciplines.

1

The Many Ages of the Court of Justice of the European Union

*Anthony Arnull**

1. Introduction

This chapter examines the role, structure, and composition over time of the Court of Justice of the European Union ('CJEU' or 'the Court').[1] The discussion comprises three substantive sections. Section 2 considers the birth of the Court of Justice of the European Coal and Steel Community (ECSC), the individuals entrusted with making it function, and the powers with which it was equipped. Section 3 looks at the effect of the Rome Treaties on the Court and the role it played in the difficult early years of the general common market that those Treaties set out to construct. Section 4 examines a major problem that confronted the Court once it had reached cruising speed: how to cope with its mounting case load. Section 5 concludes with some suggestions about the future shape of the EU's judicial architecture.

2. A Court is Born

A. The Origins of the Court and its Jurisdiction

A visitor to the CJEU in its grandiose home in Luxembourg, a 'palais' in more than just name, might be surprised to learn of its humble origins. These are to be found in a throwaway sentence in the Schuman Declaration of 9 May 1950, which led to the signing in Paris less than a year later of the ECSC Treaty. The centrepiece of the Schuman Declaration was the proposal to place Franco-German production

* I am grateful to Sophia Ayada, Dimitri Persoz, and the other participants at the Authors' Workshop in Florence on 23 February 2018 for their comments. Any errors are mine.

[1] The term 'Court of Justice of the European Union' comprises both the Court of Justice and the General Court (see Art. 19(1) TEU). The Court of Justice is the modern incarnation of the Court of Justice of the European Communities, which took the place of the Court of Justice of the European Coal and Steel Community in late 1958 (see Arts 3 and 4(1), Convention on Certain Institutions Common to the European Communities (25 March 1957)).

Anthony Arnull, *The Many Ages of the Court of Justice of the European Union*. In: *New Legal Approaches to Studying the Court of Justice*. First edition. Edited by Claire Kilpatrick and Joanne Scott, Oxford University Press (2020).
 DOI: 10.1093/oso/9780198871477.003.0002

of coal and steel under a High Authority, whose decisions would bind France, Germany, and other European countries who chose to participate in a venture intended to 'lead to the first concrete foundation of a European federation indispensable to the preservation of peace'. Towards the end of the Declaration, the following statement appeared: 'Appropriate measures will be provided for means of appeal against the decisions of the Authority.'

With the benefit of hindsight, it is easy to recognize in that enigmatic sentence the origins of the CJEU, but at the time there were differing views about how 'means of appeal' might be provided.[2] Jean Monnet and colleagues who had helped draft the Schuman Declaration discussed among themselves a mechanism in which the High Authority would be asked to review its own decisions if they were contested. If that did not settle the matter, it might then go before an arbitral tribunal, with recourse to the International Court of Justice (ICJ) in The Hague as a last resort.

The jurisdiction of the ICJ in contentious proceedings is open only to states, yet it was clear that the activities of the High Authority would affect not just states but also private parties. By the time the Paris Conference opened, the French had therefore abandoned the idea of involving the ICJ, and a two-stage review mechanism was presented to the other states that had decided to take part: Germany, Italy, and the three Benelux countries. The right to appeal to the High Authority would extend to any Member State whose interests were affected by one of its measures and to undertakings which were individually concerned by them. The arbitral tribunal would comprise judges appointed on a case-by-case basis as and when necessary.

Monnet, anxious to ensure the effectiveness of the High Authority and avoid a 'gouvernement des juges', was attracted by these arrangements. However, Germany and the Benelux countries took the view that the new Community would need a permanent court with jurisdiction to review acts of the High Authority. Opinions differed on the form any such court should take. While the preference of the Benelux countries was for an international tribunal for resolving disputes between Member States, Germany favoured a constitutional court along the lines of the US Supreme Court, with access extended to private applicants.

Monnet was eventually persuaded that a court of limited jurisdiction could reinforce rather than weaken the High Authority. In the autumn of 1950, he appointed Maurice Lagrange, a member of France's highest court in administrative law matters, the Conseil d'Etat, to help with the drafting of the Treaty articles

[2] See Boerger-De Smedt, 'La Cour de Justice dans les Négotiations du Traité de Paris Instituant la CECA', 14 *Journal of European Integration History* (2008) 7; Boerger-De Smedt, 'Negotiating the Foundations of European Law, 1950–57: The Legal History of the Treaties of Paris and Rome', 21 *Contemporary European History* (2012) 339; Rasmussen, 'Constructing and Deconstructing "Constitutional" European Law: Some Reflections on How to Study the History of European Law', in H. Koch *et al.* (eds), *Europe: The New Legal Realism* (2010) 639.

on the new court.[3] In this exercise, Lagrange played a central role. He later wrote that 'the judicial system set up under the Treaty draws directly on French administrative law', incorporating 'virtually the entire range of procedures available in the French administrative courts, including actions for annulment, action[s] for failure to act and non-contractual liability'.[4]

The French influence was reinforced by two factors. First, only the French text of the ECSC Treaty was authentic, although there were official translations into Dutch, German, and Italian. Second, French emerged from the outset as the working language of the Court. It is true that Article 27 of the Rules of Procedure of the ECSC Court provided that its official languages were French, German, Italian, and Dutch. However, according to Valentine,[5] the discussions on what the Court's official languages should be were conducted entirely in French. Lagrange later observed of that language: 'one of the Court's official languages was spoken fluently by all its Members. No interpreter was ever needed in the deliberation room. That invaluable asset remains, . . . It may even have acquired the status of a tradition.'[6] The Court's decision to adopt French as its working language, a status it still enjoys today, had important implications for the style of its judgments and its mode of reasoning.[7] Mancini and Keeling observed that, throughout the 1950s and early 1960s, judgments of the ECJ 'looked like a carbon copy of the judgments of the great French courts'.[8] That may no longer be true, but the influence on the CJEU of French legal thinking remains significant.[9]

Lagrange noted that the action for annulment was more restrictive than comparable remedies in most of the Member States. Article 33 ECSC gave the Member States and the Council automatic standing before the Court 'to have decisions or recommendations of the High Authority declared void on grounds of lack of competence, infringement of an essential procedural requirement, infringement of this Treaty or of any rule of law relating to its application, or misuse of powers'. That list of grounds is now contained in Article 263 TFEU, under which the Member States and the Council continue to have automatic standing to bring proceedings. When it came to undertakings or associations of undertakings, however, Article 33, like Article 263 TFEU, was more restrictive. They could only challenge: (a) decisions or recommendations concerning them which were

[3] See D. G. Valentine, *The Court of Justice of the European Coal and Steel Community* (1955).

[4] *Mélanges Fernand Dehousse* (Vol. 2, 1979), available at http://www.cvce.eu/content/publication/1999/1/1/30dbbb02-97f2-46ad-898c-49b074cb2ab2/publishable_en.pdf, at 4 (accessed 18 July 2018).

[5] Valentine (n. 3) 147, at fn. 6.

[6] *Mélanges Dehousse* (n. 4) 6.

[7] See Arnull, 'The Working Language of the CJEU: Time for a Change?' 43 *European Law Review* (2018) 904.

[8] Mancini and Keeling, 'Language, Culture and Politics in the Life of the European Court of Justice', 1 *Columbia Journal of European Law* (1995) 397, 399.

[9] See Bobek, 'Epilogue: Searching for the European Hercules', in M. Bobek (ed.), *Selecting Europe's Judges: A Critical Review of the Appointment Procedures to the European Courts* (2015) 309.

individual in character; or (b) general decisions or recommendations which they considered to involve a misuse of powers affecting them.

In other respects, the Court's powers exceeded those usually conferred on administrative courts. For example, Article 38 enabled the Court, on application by a Member State or the High Authority, to declare an act of the Assembly or the Council void. Article 88 ECSC established an infringement procedure under which the High Authority would record the failure of a Member State to fulfil a Treaty obligation in a reasoned decision which set the State concerned a time limit for compliance. That State would then have the right to challenge the High Authority's decision before the Court. If the State failed to comply with its obligation within the time limit set, or was unsuccessful before the Court, the High Authority would be entitled to impose sanctions on it. These could involve suspending payments due under the Treaty to the State concerned or taking or authorizing measures 'to correct the effects of the infringement of the obligation'. Another example is Article 95 ECSC, which required the approval of the Court for changes to the High Authority's powers if, after the end of the transitional period, unforeseen difficulties or fundamental economic or technical changes directly affecting the common market in coal and steel made this necessary. The way in which the Court exercised some of these powers is considered later.

Lagrange also drew attention to the office of Advocate General, 'a proposal directly inspired by the French *Conseil d'État* which . . . includes "*commissaires du gouvernement*" [now *rapporteurs publics*]',[10] an office which did not then exist in most of the Member States. The decision to provide for Advocates General ended a debate over whether judges should be permitted to give dissenting opinions. It was concluded that this was unnecessary, since Advocates General would be in a position both to contribute to the doctrinal development of Community law and to protect the independence of judges. We will return to the question of dissenting opinions in Section 5.

B. The Members of the New Court

Article 32 ECSC said that the Court was to be composed of seven judges. The purpose of the extra judge was to fulfil a pledge by the six Member States to the trade union movement to include in the Court a member who was sensitive to the interests of workers. A seventh judge would also have the advantage of allowing the Court to sit *in plenum* without risk of deadlock.[11] Judges would be

[10] *Mélanges Dehousse* (n. 4) 4.

[11] Art. 18 of the ECSC Statute provided that decisions of the Court were to be valid only when an uneven number of its members were sitting.

appointed for six years[12] by agreement between the national governments from among persons of recognized independence and competence. They were to be eligible for reappointment. Agreement on the inclusion of Advocates General having been reached only at a late stage of the negotiations, provision for them was made in Articles 11–13 of the ECSC Statute. Article 12 of the Statute said that they were to be appointed under the same conditions as the judges. Like the judges, they would be eligible for reappointment. The Statute referred to Advocates General in the plural, suggesting that there had to be more than one, but it did not specify a precise number. The number of both judges and Advocates General could be increased by unanimous vote of the Council on a proposal from the Court.

The distribution of roles within the new Court was not agreed until the last minute. One of the reasons for this was Italy's desire to have an Advocate General and its nomination of a candidate for the post of seventh judge.[13] It failed to secure either, but its judge (Massimo Pilotti) was appointed President of the Court by the Council of Ministers.[14] The other two large Member States, France and Germany, each had one judge (Jacques Rueff and Otto Riese respectively) and one Advocate General (Lagrange and Karl Roemer respectively). Belgium and Luxembourg, the smallest Member States, had one judge each (Louis Delvaux and Charles Hammes respectively).[15] There were two judges of Dutch nationality, but only one of them (Adrianus Van Kleffens) had the active support of the Dutch government. The other (Petrus Serrarens, a former Secretary General of the International Confederation of Christian Trade Unions) was appointed to fulfil the Member States' pledge that due account would be taken of the interests of workers.[16]

Thus the new Court brought together a group of people whose experiences of the previous decades had been markedly different.[17] Riese had been a member of the Swiss Nazi Party; Roemer had been heavily engaged in the administration of occupied France; Lagrange had been closely involved in the implementation of the Vichy Government's anti-Jewish policy; Pilotti had used his position as Deputy Secretary-General of the League of Nations from 1932 to 1937 to protect Italy from criticism of its designs on Abyssinia (now Ethiopia). Others had lived under occupation or been prisoners of war. However, according to a former

[12] Reservations about the effect of this on judicial independence were expressed in Luxembourg and Belgium. See Valentine (n. 3) 12.

[13] See V. Fritz, *Juges et avocats généraux de la Cour de Justice de l'Union européenne (1952–1972): Une approche biographique de l'histoire d'une revolution juridique* (2018) 81.

[14] He was appointed on 1 December 1952 (Valentine (n. 3) 3) and re-elected by his peers in 1955 (Fritz (n. 13) 100–101).

[15] The first and only Registrar of the Court, Albert Van Houtte, was Belgian. After the entry into force of the Rome Treaties, he became the first Registrar of the Court of Justice of the European Communities, a post he held until 9 February 1982.

[16] See Fritz (n. 13) 89–91.

[17] Ibid. 47–53.

référendaire of Serrarens quoted by Fritz,[18] the war was never discussed in the Court, even if discreet questions were occasionally asked about the role played in it by some members. Be that as it may, the capacity of these individuals to work together offered a small sign that the aspirations set out in the preamble to the ECSC Treaty might be realized.

A striking feature of the provisions applicable to the appointment of members of the ECSC Court is that candidates did not require legal qualifications. Although the initial desire of the Member States seems to have been to nominate jurists of high repute,[19] when this was not possible the flexibility of the Treaty proved useful. Five of the judges were indeed legally qualified but two, Serrarens and Rueff, respectively a distinguished civil servant and economist, were not.[20] Of the others, all except Delvaux seem to have held judicial appointments in their countries of origin. Delvaux had practised at the bar in Belgium and been active in politics and journalism. That they were all white men of a certain age would not at the time have attracted much comment.

Serrarens served only until the ECSC Court was replaced by the Court of Justice of the European Communities on 7 October 1958 following the entry into force of the Rome Treaties on 1 January of that year. Rueff continued to serve in the new Court until 18 May 1962 (and therefore just missed the start of the most momentous period in its history). In the late 1950s, Rueff combined his work as a judge with a role in economic and financial policy-making in Paris. Although this seemed to contravene the Statute of the Court[21] and attracted criticism from the Assembly, the Council declined to intervene.[22] Rueff's case did, however, expose a loophole. Because the Treaties of Paris and Rome all said that retiring judges were eligible for reappointment, it was possible for judges appointed under the ECSC Treaty, and who wished to continue when the Rome Treaties entered into force, to avoid scrutiny of whether they satisfied the more exacting criteria for appointment laid down by the latter. These are considered in more detail later.

Without any formal decision on the seat of the institutions having been taken, the members of the Court were sworn in and held their first meeting on 10 December 1952 in the Villa Vauban in Luxembourg, the city where the High Authority under the Presidency of Monnet had established itself some four months previously. Pilotti gave a speech in which he emphasized the responsibility of the Court for protecting the rights of litigants where the institutions of the

[18] Ibid. 54. [19] Ibid. 93.

[20] See A. Vauchez, *Brokering Europe: Euro-Lawyers and the Making of a Transnational Polity* (2015), at 54 and 93. Brief biographical details of current and former members of the Court may be found on its website, at http://curia.europa.eu/jcms/jcms/j_6/en/ (accessed 18 July 2018).

[21] See Art. 4, ECSC Statute, and Art. 4 EEC Statute, both of which prevented judges from holding any political or administrative office.

[22] Vauchez (n. 20) 93–94.

Community exceeded their powers.[23] This was a task that would later slip down the Court's list of priorities.

There had been an unresolved debate about whether the independence of the ECSC Court might be compromised if it were co-located with the Commission. Lagrange later observed: 'there was no question of the judges' independence being undermined. In fact, they undoubtedly benefited from the personal contacts they immediately established with the Members of the High Authority. This very quickly encouraged a genuine Community spirit'.[24] The Court would later demonstrate its independence from the High Authority.[25] On the eve of the entry into force of the Rome Treaties, however, the view that it would be better if the two institutions were geographically separated seemed to be supported by Pilotti. Consulted about the seat of the institutions, he said that, if there were to be more than one seat, separating the Court geographically from the others would not entail any major disadvantages.[26] The Commission now has its seat in Brussels, while the seat of the Court continues to be located in Luxembourg.[27]

C. The Work of the New Court

The first judgment of the ECSC Court was given on 21 December 1954 in a case launched on 9 February of that year.[28] Lagrange claimed that the members of the Court had used the intervening period to familiarize themselves with the Treaty and monitor the activities of the High Authority, draw up the Rules of Procedure and the Court's budget, and recruit officials in accordance with the Staff Regulations.[29] They also apparently spent time studying comparative law, a reflection of their previous careers as specialists largely in domestic law.[30] This was significant. When the ECSC Treaty was agreed, public international lawyers had tended to see the Court it established as an international court. However, the disputes the ECSC Court was destined to hear would mainly concern challenges to the validity of measures taken by the High Authority.[31] To a group of lawyers with expertise in national law, these disputes resembled challenges to national measures. The Treaty itself outlined the law that was to be applied, but it left many

[23] Valentine (n. 3) 4. [24] *Mélanges Dehousse* (n. 4) 6.

[25] See e.g. Case 20/59, *Italy v. High Authority* (EU:C:1960:33).

[26] Pennera, 'The Beginnings of the Court of Justice and its Role as a Driving Force in European Integration', 1 *Journal of European Integration History* (1995) 111, at 117.

[27] See Protocol No. 6 on the location of the seats of the institutions and of certain bodies, offices, agencies and departments of the European Union, annexed to the TEU and the TFEU.

[28] Case 1/54, *France v. High Authority* (EU:C:1954:7). [29] *Mélanges Dehousse* (n. 4) 6.

[30] Cohen, '"Ten Majestic Figures in Long Amaranth Robes": the Formation of the Court of Justice of the European Communities', in A. Vauchez and B. de Witte (eds), *Lawyering Europe: European Law as a Transnational Social Field* (2013) 21, 41 (quoting Lagrange, 'Une réalité européenne. La Cour de justice de la CECA', *Cahiers Chrétiens de la fonction publique* (28 April 1955) 16, at 21).

[31] Pennera (n. 26) 113.

questions unanswered. It was therefore natural for the Court to turn to the legal systems with which its members were most familiar, in order to devise solutions using the comparative method to the problems raised by the cases brought before them. Advocate General Lagrange explained in *Fédération Charbonnière Belgique v. High Authority*:[32]

> our Court is not an international court but the court of a Community created by six States on a model which is more closely related to a federal than to an international organization . . . although the Treaty which the Court has the task of applying was concluded in the form of an international treaty . . . it is nevertheless, from a material point of view, the charter of the Community, since the rules of law which derive from it constitute *the internal law of that Community.*

Cohen[33] revealingly calls this 'a sort of "third way" between international law and internal law'. The Court's sense of itself not as an international court but the domestic court of an entity that constituted 'a first step in the federation of Europe' (as the Schuman Declaration put it) helps to explain the subsequent development of the case law and anticipated the birth in 1963 of the 'new legal order'.[34]

The ECSC Treaty did not prove well-adapted to the evolution of the European coal and steel sectors in the 1950s.[35] The detailed rules on the operation of the common market in coal and steel were dry and technical and the reports of the disputes to which they gave rise are largely neglected nowadays. However, when given the opportunity, the ECSC Court delivered several judgments that foreshadowed ideas and debates that would later emerge under the Treaties of Rome.

The Court could only deal with the cases that came before it. The ECSC Treaty lacked a case generator comparable to the preliminary rulings procedure in the form it would later assume in the EEC Treaty. Under Article 41 ECSC, the right of national courts to seek preliminary rulings seemed to be confined to questions of validity and was apparently designed to protect the monopoly of the Court to rule on such questions.[36] It was not until 1990 that the Court, ruling *contra legem*, held that it also covered questions of interpretation.[37] Be that as it may, the Court took the opportunities presented by several direct actions to develop the law and indicate its general approach.

[32] Case 8/55, *Fédération Charbonnière Belgique v. High Authority* (EU:C:1956:6), at 277 (emphasis in the original).

[33] Cohen (n. 30) 42.

[34] See Case 26/62, *Van Gend en Loos v. Netherlands Inland Revenue Administration* (EU:C:1963:1).

[35] See Boerger and Rasmussen, 'The Making of European Law: Exploring the Life and Work of Michel Gaudet', 57 *American Journal of Legal History* (2017) 51, at 62.

[36] See Boerger-De Smedt, 'La Cour de Justice' (n. 2) 28–30; Valentine (n. 3) 122–124.

[37] Case C-221/88, *Busseni* (EU:C:1990:84) 135. See Arnull, 'The Legal Order of the ECSC', 15 *European Law Review* (1990) 321.

Take *Industries Sidérurgiques Luxembourgeoises v. High Authority*,[38] an action for failure to act under Article 35 ECSC. The applicant argued that an implied decision of refusal of the High Authority was incompatible with Article 4 ECSC. That provision declared certain types of measure 'incompatible with the common market for coal and steel' and required them to be 'abolished and prohibited within the Community, *as provided in this Treaty*' (emphasis added). It might have been inferred that the italicized words meant that Article 4 had effect only in so far as other provisions of the Treaty elaborated on it. However, the Court had already ruled that Article 4 had a fundamental status. It followed that 'the provisions of Article 4 are sufficient of themselves and are directly applicable when they are not restated in any part of the Treaty'.[39] So the applicant could in principle rely on Article 4 against the respondent institution. The idea that an individual might rely directly on a Treaty provision in legal proceedings would within a decade have transformed Europe's legal landscape.

Yet more was to come. *Humblet v. Belgium*[40] arrived at the Court in April 1960, after the entry into force of the Rome Treaties. The Court was now presided over by Andreas Donner, a Dutch professor of public law. Donner was 40 years old when he was nominated and brought to his task an energy that was beyond his experienced but elderly predecessor.[41] The *Humblet* case involved a dispute over the interpretation of the Protocol on the Privileges and Immunities of the ECSC. That Protocol gave the Court jurisdiction to rule on such disputes. The essential question was whether a Member State was entitled to take into account the remuneration of an official of the ECSC, which according to the Protocol was exempt from tax, in determining the rate of tax applicable to the income of his wife, who was not a Community official.

In the course of rejecting a challenge to its jurisdiction, the Court invoked Article 86 ECSC, the forerunner of the principle of sincere cooperation now set out in Article 4(3) TEU. It declared:[42]

> if the Court rules in a judgment that a legislative or administrative measure adopted by the authorities of a Member State is contrary to Community law, that Member State is obliged, by virtue of Article 86 of the ECSC Treaty, to rescind the measure in question and to make reparation for any unlawful consequences which may have ensued. This obligation is evident from the Treaty and from the Protocol which have the force of law in the Member States following their ratification and which take precedence over national law.

[38] Joined Cases 7 and 9/54, *Industries Sidérurgiques Luxembourgeoises v. High Authority of the ECSC* (EU:C:1956:2).

[39] Ibid. 195.

[40] Case 6/60, *Humblet v. Belgium* (EU:C:1960:48) 569.

[41] Fritz (n. 13) 61–62. Pilotti was 73 when appointed and 79 when he retired from the Court.

[42] *Humblet v. Belgium* (n. 40) 569.

> Consequently if in the present dispute the Court were to rule that the tax assessment in question was unlawful, it would necessarily follow that the Belgian government would be obliged to adopt the requisite measures to cancel it and to reimburse to the applicant any amounts which were wrongfully collected.

Thus, over two years before *Van Gend en Loos* and over three years before *Costa v. ENEL*, the Court had recognized the capacity of the ECSC Treaty to confer on individuals rights which would take precedence over inconsistent provisions of national law. It will be noticed also that the order in which these qualities were recognized—rights followed by primacy—was the same under both the ECSC and the EEC Treaties. This could have been happenstance but it might be taken to imply that the Court saw primacy as a consequence of direct effect.[43] It is even possible to read into the Court's reference in *Humblet* to making 'reparation for any unlawful consequences which may have ensued' a harbinger of the principles of effectiveness and equivalence, which govern the enforcement of EU rights before national courts, and even of state liability.

Some of the Court's early case law also manifested a liberal approach to the admissibility of actions for annulment under Article 33 ECSC. This was perhaps a reflection of Pilotti's speech when the Court was sworn in. An example is *Assider v. High Authority*,[44] where the applicant challenged a number of decisions adopted by the High Authority. The applicant argued that they were vitiated by misuse of powers and an infringement of the Treaty. The High Authority challenged the admissibility of the application on the basis that the applicant had failed to prove that a misuse of powers had been committed. The Court rejected the High Authority's argument. At the admissibility stage, it was enough for the applicant merely to allege that a misuse of powers had taken place. Proof was not necessary until the substance of the case was considered.[45]

A good illustration of the use by the Court of the comparative method is provided by *Algera v. Common Assembly*.[46] The central issue in that case was the extent to which administrative measures giving rise to individual rights could be revoked. The Court[47] declared that this was a possibility which was:

> familiar in the case-law and learned writing of all the countries of the Community, but for the solution of which the Treaty does not contain any rules.

[43] The point assumed particular importance in relation to the case law on so-called 'incidental effect'. See P. Craig and G. de Búrca, *EU Law* (6th ed., 2015) 276–277.

[44] Case 3/54, *Assider v. High Authority* (EU:C:1955:2). See also Case 4/54, *ISA v. High Authority* (EU:C:1955:3).

[45] See also *Industries Sidérurgiques Luxembourgeoises* (n. 38).

[46] Joined Cases 7/56 and 3/57 to 7/57, *Algera v. Common Assembly* (EU:C:1957:7). See also Case 8/57, *Aciéries Belges v. High Authority* (EU:C:1958:9) 256 ('equality of treatment in the matter of economic rules').

[47] Ibid. 55.

> Unless the Court is to deny justice it is therefore obliged to solve the problem by reference to the rules acknowledged by the legislation, the learned writing and the case-law of the member countries.

The Court stated that 'a comparative study of this problem of law . . . in the six Member States' showed that a lawful administrative measure conferring individual rights could not in principle be withdrawn, whereas the law of all the Member States permitted the revocation of an unlawful administrative measure. It proceeded to examine in some detail the position in French, German, and Italian law and made a passing reference to Belgian, Luxembourg, and Netherlands law. It accepted 'the principle of the revocability of illegal measures at least within a reasonable period of time'. The applicants' claims were partly successful.[48]

The *Algera* case also provides an early example of the application of a general principle of law. The case required the Court to take a decision of principle on which the Treaty did not provide any guidance. The principle was one on which the national laws of the Member States had much to say. Given their backgrounds, it was natural for the members of the Court to look to that rich body of law for guidance on the most appropriate approach to take to the case under consideration. The judgment of the Court underlined the Court's self-perception as a domestic, not an international, tribunal. Recourse to the national laws of the Member States as a source of general principles would later become well established in the case law, though the comparative analysis is now rarely set out in the judgment, as it was in *Algera*.

In *Meroni v. High Authority*,[49] a case decided by the ECSC Court after the entry into force of the Rome Treaties but before its successor court had been constituted, the Court drew on a different source for a general principle: the Rome Treaties themselves. One of the questions it needed to decide was the extent to which a plea of illegality was available under the ECSC Treaty. Such a plea could be invoked under Articles 184 EEC and 156 Euratom but the corresponding provision of the ECSC Treaty, Article 36, was more limited in scope and did not apply on the facts of *Meroni*. The Court observed: '[A]n illegal general decision ought not to be applied to an undertaking and no obligations affecting the said undertaking must be deemed to arise therefrom.'[50] Article 36 was not a special rule applicable only in the particular circumstances to which it referred, but 'the application of a general principle'.[51] Otherwise, the Court pointed out, it would be difficult for undertakings 'to exercise their right to bring actions, because it would oblige them to scrutinize every general decision upon publication thereof for provisions which might later adversely affect them or be considered as involving a misuse of powers affecting them'.[52]

[48] Ibid. 56. [49] Case 9/56, *Meroni v. High Authority* (EU:C:1958:7). [50] Ibid. 139–140.
[51] Ibid. 140. [52] Ibid.

The issue for which *Meroni* is most famous was the extent to which the High Authority was entitled to delegate its powers. The sophisticated principle laid down by the Court became part of the Union's constitutional orthodoxy and continued to be applied for several decades, although there are now signs that it is becoming less influential in the context of the Union's increasing recourse to agencies that it has itself established.[53] Its ruling also contained[54] an early reference to what is now called institutional balance—a principle which remains fundamental to the governance of the Union. This was the judgment of an increasingly assertive and self-confident court.

3. The Rome Treaties

A. Une Procession Dansante d'Echternach?

On 25 March 2017, European heads of state and government gathered in Rome to celebrate the 60th anniversary of the signing of the Treaties of Rome. In the late 1950s, however, some considered those Treaties a retrograde step. For one thing, there were concerns that the proliferation of Communities might lead to internecine quarrelling. True, the Convention on Certain Institutions Common to the European Communities signed alongside the Rome Treaties had created a single Assembly and Court for all three Communities, but agreement on a single Council and Commission would not materialize until 1965.[55] In the meantime, the Rome Treaties enhanced significantly the powers of the Member States through the Council(s) at the expense of the now three European Executives (as the High Authority and two Commissions came collectively to be known). Moreover, the ECSC Court's attempts to open up access to individuals were peremptorily reversed by the Member States, which introduced strict standing rules for individuals wishing to launch annulment proceedings under the Rome Treaties. This remains a subject of controversy to the present day.[56] In addition, the infringement procedure was weakened by removing from the Commission, when acting under the Rome Treaties, the power to issue decisions declaring Member States to be in breach of their Treaty obligations and to impose sanctions in the event of continuing non-compliance. A sanctions regime for the Rome Treaties would not be added until Maastricht.

[53] R. Schütze, *European Union Law* (2015) 326–327, referring to Case C-270/12, *United Kingdom v. Parliament and Council* (EU:C:2014:18).

[54] *Meroni v. High Authority* (n. 49) 152.

[55] Treaty establishing a Single Council and a Single Commission of the European Communities (8 April 1965).

[56] Arnull, 'Judicial review in the European Union', in A. Arnull and D. Chalmers (eds), *The Oxford Handbook of European Union Law* (2015) 376.

However, an innovation whose full significance was not initially appreciated was introduced following an initiative by Nicola Catalano, formerly legal adviser to the High Authority and a member of the Italian delegation during the negotiations that led to the Rome Treaties. Catalano's proposal concerned the preliminary rulings procedure. He suggested that the new treaties should give the Court jurisdiction to give preliminary rulings on questions, not only of the validity of Community acts, but also of the proper interpretation of Community law. That proposal was accepted and was to have momentous consequences, giving the Court an opportunity to rule on a host of questions which might not otherwise have reached it and enabling it to influence directly the application of Community law in the Member States.

B. Membership

In accordance with Articles 244 EEC and 212 Euratom, the new single Court took up its duties on 7 October 1958, as soon as its members had been appointed. Four of the judges of the ECSC Court—Riese, Delvaux, Rueff, and Hammes—as well as Advocates General Lagrange and Roemer, continued in office. Lingering doubts about whether a judge representing the interests of workers could be genuinely independent led to the departure of Serrarens. Reluctant to go, he was persuaded to do so by a substantially increased pension.[57] This meant that Italy's long-held desire for a second member of the Court could be satisfied. Accordingly, Catalano and Rino Rossi, a member of the Italian Court of Cassation, were appointed.

More significantly, the continued presence on the Court of members who had been involved in negotiating the Community's founding Treaties—Lagrange, Roemer, and Van Kleffens in the case of the ECSC Treaty and Catalano in the case of the Rome Treaties—must have had an effect on the culture of the Court. These individuals 'could legitimately claim to know the spirit and the philosophy of the founding Treaties'[58] and would have reinforced a collective sense that it was the task of the Court to contribute to the attainment of the Community's objectives.[59] In this, the Court was encouraged by the EEC Commission, presided over by the distinguished German lawyer Walter Hallstein, who had chaired the German delegations at both the Paris and Rome conferences and had also been involved in the negotiations which led to the European Convention on Human Rights. Other members of the Commission had also been involved in the Treaty negotiations, as had the head of its legal service, Michel Gaudet.[60] Originally recruited, like

[57] Fritz (n. 13) 102–109. [58] Vauchez (n. 20) 111.
[59] *Mélanges Dehousse* (n. 4) 8–9. [60] Cohen (n. 30) 34.

Lagrange, from the French Conseil d'Etat, Gaudet was a disciple of Monnet and had cultivated strong links with the US legal profession. This gave him an Anglo-Saxon appreciation of the role courts might play.[61] He would soon have his moment in the sun.

The Rome Treaties had strengthened the criteria for appointment to the Court so that they now required members to be 'chosen from persons whose independence is beyond doubt and who possess the qualifications required for appointment to the highest judicial offices in their respective countries or who are jurisconsults of recognized competence'.[62] Much therefore depended on the qualifications required in each Member State for appointment to the highest judicial offices. The Treaties did not say anything about the nationality of members of the Court, it probably having been assumed that they would have the nationality of the Member State which nominated them. None the less, the Court might theoretically have been composed of, say, nine Russians.[63]

According to Fritz,[64] the appointments process was conducted without formal recruitment exercises. This effectively meant that it was confined to the great and the good in the Member States who were aware of vacancies. No thought was given by governments of the time to the effect a particular candidate might have on the ideology of the Court. Once appointed, the main concern of members was not that governments would object to the case law, but that they personally would be ousted from the Court because they no longer enjoyed the political support of their Member States. Political factors therefore seem to have been more important than the case law or legal competence in securing a lengthy tenure.

It was, however, necessary for the Member States to be realistic about the likely profile of candidates. They rightly assumed that each Member State needed to be represented on the Court and that all members of the Court would be formally of equal status. They must have known also that membership of what was still a little known entity might be regarded as unattractive or at least entailing a degree of professional risk. It is known that many who were originally approached by the French government about membership of the Court declined the opportunity.[65] Rueff resigned from the Court in 1959 having been asked by the French government to join a committee to examine reforms to the French economy. Article 5 of the Statute provided that a judge who resigned should 'continue to hold office until his successor takes up his duties'. After a delay of five months, Rueff was reappointed even though he had made clear that his preference was to

[61] See Boerger and Rasmussen (n. 35) 61.

[62] Arts 167 EEC and 139 Euratom.

[63] The idea of a Court composed entirely of Russians (presumably French-speaking) is attributed to Lord Mackenzie-Stuart, President of the Court 1984–1988. See Kennedy, 'Thirteen Russians! The composition of the European Court of Justice', in A. Campbell and M. Voyatzi (eds), *Legal Reasoning and Judicial Interpretation of European Law: Essays in Honour of Lord Mackenzie-Stuart* (1996) 69.

[64] Fritz (n. 13) 123–124, 136–137.

[65] Vauchez (n. 20) 94; Fritz (n. 13) 85–86.

return to Paris.[66] He did not finally leave the Court until 1962. He was succeeded by Robert Lecourt, a former minister and known Europhile who had been unsuccessful in securing an alternative post in France. It almost certainly remains the case that the professional attractions of life in Luxembourg depend, at least in part, on an individual's career prospects at home and the lure of life in other capitals. But once there, many have been reluctant to leave.[67]

C. Case Law and Context

The new Court's early decisions were a puzzling mix of deference to the Member States and buccaneering constitutionalism. *Producteurs de Fruits v. Council*,[68] decided on 14 December 1962, was an action for the annulment under Article 173 EEC of a Council regulation on the establishment of a common organization of the market in fruit and vegetables. It was dismissed as inadmissible on the basis that the regulation was not of individual concern to the applicants. Advocate General Lagrange emphasized that there were 'important differences' between the EEC Treaty and the ECSC Treaty 'which have obviously been intended by the authors of the Treaty of Rome'.[69] The EEC Treaty was 'more strict than the ECSC Treaty with regard to the conditions which must be fulfilled before certain measures may be challenged'.[70] He reminded the Court that:

> these [legislative] texts have been arrived at only after considerable difficulty, and sometimes after a compromise reached in the Council, still wedded to the rule of unanimity . . . we are presented here, by the authors of the Treaty, with a considered choice which it cannot be for the Court to correct.[71]

The Court accepted that the system established by the Rome Treaties laid down:

> more restrictive conditions than does the ECSC Treaty for the admissibility of applications for annulment by private individuals. However, it would not be appropriate for the Court to pronounce on the merits of this system which appears clearly from the text under examination.[72]

The Court confirmed its restrictive approach to individual standing the following year in the 'clementines case', *Plaumann v. Commission*.[73]

[66] Fritz (n. 13) 109–111. [67] Ibid. 134–135.
[68] Joined Cases 16 and 17/62, *Producteurs de Fruits v. Council* (EU:C:1962:47). [69] Ibid. 482.
[70] Ibid. [71] Ibid. 486–487. [72] Ibid. 478.
[73] Case 25/62, *Plaumann v. Commission* (EU:C:1963:17).

These cases established a pattern of reluctance to entertain challenges to Community/Union acts by individuals that has endured to the present day. It reflects the strength of the Court's conviction that its task—perhaps even its principal task—is to help secure the achievement of the Community/Union's objectives. It has not been prepared to accept that, in the long run, shielding the institutions from review might undermine the EU's legitimacy by weakening the principles of conferral and ultimately the rule of law.

In the early 1960s, however, the Court probably had little choice but to go along with the manifest intention of the Member States to make it more difficult to bring annulment actions under the Rome Treaties than under the Paris Treaty. What is surprising is that at almost exactly the same time it was delivering judgments that ran counter to what also seems likely to have been the intention of the Member States. The story of how this came about begins with Hallstein's appointment in 1958 as first President of the EEC Commission. A federalist and proponent of a constitutional reading of the Community Treaties, he found in Gaudet a willing and highly able lieutenant. In 1958, Gaudet secured the establishment of a single Legal Service to advise all three European Executives 'in order to make sure that the same "constructive" interpretations of the treaties would be put before the Court in each case'.[74] He headed the Legal Service of the European Executives, and subsequently that of the Commission of the European Communities, until 1969.

Anxious to avoid a loss of momentum on the journey towards a federal Europe, Gaudet set out to persuade the Court 'to act as the federal Court of one single Community, considering the three different treaties all together as its "constitution" '.[75] One of his early initiatives was to promote the establishment of a learned society dedicated to the study of Community law with a view to creating doctrinal support for a constitutional reading of the Treaties. Gaudet also encouraged the publication in each Member State of academic journals devoted to Community law.[76]

One result of Gaudet's activities was FIDE, the Fédération Internationale pour le Droit Européen, whose founding congress in Brussels in 1961 was sponsored by the European Executives. Alter has claimed that FIDE and the growing number of national associations dedicated to the study of European law created 'an impression of a momentum favoring the ECJ's doctrinal creations' and 'critically defined what European legal integration became'.[77] M. Rasmussen observes,

[74] Bailleux, 'Michel Gaudet, a Law Entrepreneur: The Role of the Legal Service of the European Executives in the Invention of EC Law and the Birth of the Common Market Law Review', 50 *Common Market Law Review* (2013) 359, at 363–364.

[75] Ibid. 362.

[76] The first example of such a journal, the *Common Market Law Review*, was launched in 1963. See Byberg, 'The History of *Common Market Law Review* 1963–1993', 23 *European Law Journal* (2017) 45.

[77] K. Alter, *The European Court's Political Power* (2009) 73.

however, that FIDE and the national associations 'did not quite achieve the impact . . . that Gaudet had initially hoped for'.[78] That view is supported by Byberg, who maintains that 'neither organisationally nor ideologically did FIDE and the "Euro-law associations" constitute a cohesive network in the ideological confrontation with sceptical national actors; FIDE was itself an arena of contestation'.[79] The communication strategy later implemented by Lecourt, when he became President of the Court in 1967, to encourage national courts to make use of the preliminary rulings procedure seems to have been more effective in raising awareness of the possibilities offered by Community law.[80]

It was in 1961 that the Dutch section of FIDE began a project to identify self-executing provisions of the EEC Treaty. Two Dutch lawyers, H. G. Stibbe and L. F. D. ter Kuile, persuaded the Tariefcommissie, Amsterdam, to refer to the Court, using the new preliminary rulings procedure, two cases which raised the question whether Article 12 EEC had direct application within the territory of a Member State. One of them was *Van Gend en Loos*.[81] Advocate General Roemer and the three Member States that took part in the proceedings (the Netherlands, Belgium, and Germany) urged the Court to give a negative response to the question referred to it. However, the Court preferred the submissions of the Commission and endorsed the argument of the claimant.

There was an element of serendipity in the outcome. M. Rasmussen observes that the replacement of Rueff by the Europhile Lecourt 'clearly testifies to the extent to which the French leadership did not consider the Court of Justice an important actor in the Communities'.[82] Together with Alberto Trabucchi, an Italian judge who had replaced Catalano,[83] Lecourt opposed Hammes, Riese, and Donner, who were minded to follow Advocate General Roemer. Ultimately, Rossi and Delvaux sided with Lecourt and Trabucchi to form a 4:3 majority in the claimant's favour.[84]

[78] Rasmussen, 'Establishing a Constitutional Practice of European Law: The History of the Legal Service of the European Executive, 1962–65', 21 *Contemporary European History* (2012) 375, 384.

[79] Byberg, 'A Miscellaneous Network: The History of FIDE 1961–94', 57 *American Journal of Legal History* (2017) 142.

[80] Fritz (n. 13) 148–150.

[81] Case 26/62, *Van Gend en Loos v. Netherlands Inland Revenue Administration* (EU:C:1963:1) (n. 34). See Rasmussen, 'Revolutionizing European Law: A History of the *Van Gend en Loos* Judgment', 12 *International Journal of Constitutional Law* (2014) 136. The other case was Joined Cases 28, 29 and 30/62, *da Costa en Schaake* (EU:C:1963:6).

[82] Rasmussen, 'Constructing and Deconstructing' (n. 2) 648.

[83] Catalano, who had been an ally of Gaudet in the Treaty negotiations, was forced to resign shortly after being reappointed because the Italian government wished to replace him with Alberto Trabucchi, whose brother, Giuseppe, was the Italian Finance Minister: Fritz (n. 13) 113 and 200–201.

[84] Rasmussen, 'Constitutional Practice' (n. 78) 153–154. See also Pescatore, 'Robert Lecourt (1908–2004). Eloge funèbre prononcé par Pierre Pescatore, ancient Juge de la Cour, à l'audience solennelle du 7 mars 2005', 41 *Revue Trimestrielle de Droit Européen* (2005) 589, 590–591; Phelan, 'The Revolutionary Doctrines of European Law and the Legal Philosophy of Robert Lecourt', 28 *European Journal of International Law* (2017) 935 (who finds a link between Lecourt's approach at the Court and his thesis on French property law completed in 1931).

The case was a ringing endorsement of the constitutional reading of the Treaties espoused by Hallstein and Gaudet. True, the Court had left some gaps in its reasoning which made it possible to argue that the implications of the case were limited. How important was it that the dispute was a vertical one, between a private company and the state? How much significance should be attributed to the emphasis placed by the Court on the negative character of Article 12 EEC? Was the Court implying that directly effective provisions of the Treaty might take precedence over incompatible rules of national law? What about acts of secondary law?

Nothing could be taken for granted, but hindsight shows that some at least of these questions were easily answered. The Court said that the negative character of Article 12 was one of a number of features that made it 'ideally adapted to produce direct effects'. This clearly did not exclude the possibility that a provision with different characteristics might also have direct effect. It did indeed seem to follow from the judgment that directly effective provisions of Community law would take precedence over inconsistent rules of national law for otherwise a finding of direct effect might not make any practical difference. The reason the Court did not address the issue in *Van Gend en Loos* was simply that it was settled by Dutch law and the national judge therefore did not feel it necessary to put a question on the matter to the Court. Donner, who had been in the minority, later maintained that if the Court 'had been competent to do so it would presumably have ruled that the EEC Treaty has precedence over local law but it held that the determination at law of this priority belonged in this case . . . to the competence of the domestic courts'.[85] As for secondary law, it was widely assumed that regulations, described by the Treaties as 'directly applicable' and as entering into force on the date specified or 20 days after publication in the *Official Journal*, were capable of conferring rights directly on individuals. It was also assumed that directives were not. That assumption proved to be false, although the issue of the extent to which directives might have direct effect would in due course cause the Court more difficulty than the question of whether Treaty articles might do so.

The Court's decision encouraged the advocates of a constitutional reading of the Treaties to pursue their attempts to enlist the support of the Court. Its decision in *Van Gend en Loos* was brought to the attention of professional circles and the wider public at every opportunity by judges, *référendaires*, lawyers involved in the case, and others, in an attempt to ensure that its potential implications were widely understood.[86]

[85] Donner, 'National Law and the Case Law of the Court of Justice of the European Communities', 1 *Common Market Law Review* (1963) 8, at 14.

[86] Ibid. 13.

An opportunity to add the next piece of the jigsaw arose in *Costa v. ENEL*,[87] a reference made by the *Giudice Conciliatore*, Milan, on 16 January 1964. In the main action, the claimant was challenging a demand that he pay a bill issued by ENEL, the recently nationalized Italian electricity company. The claimant alleged that the Law establishing ENEL infringed Articles 102, 93, 53, and 37 EEC. Because of the small amount of money involved, the referring court, which was relatively junior, was the court of first and last resort and was therefore subject to the obligation to refer under the third paragraph of Article 177 EEC.

The case has become famous because of its relationship with *Van Gend en Loos*, decided less than a year before the reference was made, yet it also had major implications for Italian energy policy. The referring court provided little information about the background to the case, however, merely transmitting a copy of the case file to the Court and noting that the Italian legislation nationalizing the distribution of electricity had been alleged to contravene the articles of the Treaty mentioned in the previous paragraph.[88] It did not ask what the consequences might be if that allegation were to be wholly or partly upheld and in particular whether any of the provisions in question would take precedence over the contested national legislation.

In parallel with the reference to the Court of Justice, the *Giudice Conciliatore* also referred the case to the Italian Constitutional Court under a domestic procedure which had partly inspired Article 177. The Italian Constitutional Court (perhaps wishing to pre-empt the Court of Justice) responded so quickly that Advocate General Lagrange was able to comment on its ruling in his Opinion, delivered on 25 June 1964.[89] As he explained, the Constitutional Court held that, since the Treaty had been ratified by an ordinary Law not having constitutional status, it would be expressly or impliedly repealed by a later Law that was inconsistent with it. There was therefore no need to consider whether the first Law was compatible with the Treaty or to make a reference to the Court of Justice. In the proceedings before the Court of Justice, the Italian government accordingly argued that the referring court's task was simply to apply the applicable domestic Law. If Italy was in breach of its Treaty obligations, this could be brought before the Court of Justice only pursuant to the infringement procedure under Articles 169 and 170 EEC.

This argument illustrated perfectly why primacy was the necessary corollary of direct effect. Advocate General Lagrange underlined the issues at stake by

[87] Case 6/64, *Costa v. ENEL* (EU:C:1964:66).

[88] However, Nicola, in Chapter 3 of this volume, reveals that the Court had the benefit of an extensive submission by Professor G. Stendardi on behalf of Mr Costa setting out the political and economic implications of the Law nationalizing the production of electricity. Nicola also notes that a file relating to ENEL's industrial policy has been removed from the records on *Costa v. ENEL* at the Historical Archives of the EU at the EUI in Florence, available at https://www.eui.eu/Research/HistoricalArchivesOfEU (accessed 18 July 2018).

[89] Case 6/64, *Costa v. ENEL*, Opinion of AG Lagrange (EU:C:1964:51) 605.

insisting on 'the disastrous consequences (and I do not think this expression is too strong)' that the precedent set by the Italian Constitutional Court, if endorsed, 'would risk having as regards the functioning of the system of institutions established by the Treaty and, as a consequence, the very future of the Common Market'. Although he did not use the term, Advocate General Lagrange therefore maintained that directly effective provisions of Community law should be accorded precedence over inconsistent provisions of national law, a view which the Court famously and explicitly endorsed.[90]

Whatever the legal niceties, it is possible that the outcome in *Van Gend en Loos* and *Costa* was affected by the political and geopolitical backdrop. This would undoubtedly have been weighing on the governments of the Member States, with which the members of the Court had close connections.[91] The period was one of great global tension. On 1 May 1960, an American U-2 spy plane was shot down in Soviet airspace and its pilot, Gary Powers, captured. On 17 April 1961, a paramilitary group backed by the CIA embarked on an ill-fated invasion of Cuba at the Bay of Pigs in a doomed attempt to overthrow the regime of Fidel Castro, which was backed by the Soviet Union. On 13 August 1961, the long-running crisis over the status of Berlin came to a head when the German Democratic Republic started building the infamous Berlin Wall in an attempt to stop emigration to the West. From 16 to 28 October 1962, the world seemed on the brink of nuclear war over the surreptitious deployment by the Soviet Union in Cuba of nuclear missiles capable of hitting targets in the continental US. These linked incidents underlined the fragility of the post-war international order.

The failure of the European Defence Community Treaty in 1954, following a negative vote in the French National Assembly and the subsequent abandonment of the related European Political Community Treaty, meant that the EEC Treaty needed to succeed. However, the idea that Europe could be constructed through a project led by the Commission to harmonize the national laws of the Member States was running into difficulty and intergovernmentalism seemed to be gaining ground.[92] The election in June 1958 of the eurosceptic Charles de Gaulle as French President further blighted the development of the Communities until his resignation in 1969.

Soon after his election, de Gaulle set in motion a process that would seek to shift the development of Europe away from the supranational model on which

[90] Phelan (n. 84), links *Van Gend en Loos* and *Costa* with the refusal of the Court to allow Member States to take the law into their own hands. See Joined Cases 90 and 91/63, *Commission v. Luxembourg and Belgium* (EU:C:1964:80); Case 232/78, *Commission v. France* (EU:C:1979:215).

[91] See the discussion of Harold Macmillan's unsuccessful efforts to take the UK into the European Community in the early 1960s in H. Young, *This Blessed Plot: Britain and Europe from Churchill to Blair* (1999) ch. 4. Archival research might reveal the extent, if any, to which the Court was influenced by that context. See generally Nicola (n. 88).

[92] Vauchez, 'The Transnational Politics of Judicialization. *Van Gend en Loos* and the Making of EU Polity', 16 *European Law Journal* (2010) 1, at 6–7.

the Communities were based to an intergovernmental model—a 'Europe of Nation States'[93]—more conducive to enhancing France's international profile. That process began with the so-called first Fouchet Plan of November 1961, which envisaged[94] the creation of a union of states with the aim of adopting common foreign and defence policies and cooperation in the scientific and cultural fields. It was envisaged that this would ultimately absorb the European Communities. The plan unmasked disagreement among the six about the balance between intergovernmentalism and supranationalism; the role of the Atlantic alliance and NATO; and the possible involvement of the UK, which had applied for membership the previous August.

With the negotiations becoming acrimonious, France produced a second Fouchet Plan in January 1962.[95] Teasdale observes:[96] 'this text was characterized . . . by a significant hardening of position . . . accentuating the intergovernmental character of the proposed Union and enhancing its ability to act independently of the United States'. The effect was to unite the other five Member States against France and the following month they produced a counterproposal. However, it proved impossible to find common ground and negotiations collapsed in April 1962. In May, de Gaulle attacked the Community's institutions and underlying philosophy at a press conference, prompting five of his ministers to resign.[97] In January 1963, de Gaulle vetoed UK membership of the Communities. Teasdale concludes:[98]

> The stalemate over the Fouchet Plan gradually became endemic . . . Unable to secure agreement to his intergovernmental design, de Gaulle resolved to stall the Community and prevent any who opposed his institutional vision (Belgium and the Netherlands) or who might challenge France's geopolitical interests (those states plus Britain) from getting their way. In this, he succeeded.

It was in that febrile context that the Court was asked to decide *Van Gend en Loos* and *Costa*, a context in which a new and potentially devastating world war was not a remote possibility and the most powerful Member State was seeking to unpick Treaties on which the ink had only just dried. It is not perhaps surprising that the Court felt that it was incumbent on it to do what it could to ensure that Member States complied with the obligations they had so recently accepted. It

[93] The phrase 'l'Europe des patries' is often associated with de Gaulle, though at a press conference at the Elysée Palace on 15 May 1962 he denied ever having used it.

[94] The text is available at http://www.cvce.eu/obj/draft_treaty_fouchet_plan_i_2_november_1961-en-485fa02e-f21e-4e4d-9665-92f0820a0c22.html (accessed 18 July 2018).

[95] The text is available at http://www.cvce.eu/content/publication/1999/1/1/c9930f55-7d69-4edc-8961-4f12cf7d7a5b/publishable_en.pdf (accessed 18 July 2018).

[96] Teasdale, 'The Fouchet Plan: De Gaulle's Intergovernmental Design for Europe', LSE 'Europe in Question' Discussion Paper Series, No. 117/2016, October 2016, at 36.

[97] Ibid. 49. [98] Ibid. 52–53.

was, after all, its duty to ensure that in the application of the Treaties the law was observed.

Though the Court could not have predicted it, France was to trigger a new crisis less than a year after *Costa v. ENEL* when de Gaulle told his ministers not to attend Council meetings during the last six months of 1965, effectively paralysing the Community's legislative process.[99] A particular sticking point for France was the increased use of qualified majority voting envisaged by the Treaty from the start of the third stage of the transitional period on 1 January 1966.[100] The crisis was resolved on 29 January 1966 by the so-called Luxembourg Compromise. A classic agreement to disagree, the Luxembourg Compromise came to be understood as conferring a veto over Community legislation on any Member State which considered its vital national interests to be at stake, whatever the Treaties might say about how the legislation concerned was to be adopted. The result was the adoption by the Council of a practice of consensus, with legislation not being adopted until all Member States were content with it. This had the effect of slowing down the process and diluting the content of the measures adopted. It played a major role in the failure of the Community to complete the common market by the end of the transitional period on 31 December 1969 (though it did succeed in completing the customs union 18 months ahead of schedule on 1 July 1968).[101]

The empty chair crisis also brought Hallstein into conflict with de Gaulle. There could only be one winner, and Hallstein resigned in 1967 when the 1965 Merger Treaty, which created a single Council and a single Commission of the European Communities, took effect. Gaudet's position was also undermined and he resigned in 1969.[102]

It was not until the 1980s that the practice of consensus started to break down. It was delivered a mortal blow by the Single European Act, when all Member States accepted the need for qualified majority voting if the 'internal' market was to be completed by 31 December 1992.

[99] For a good short account, see S. Weatherill and P. Beaumont, *EU Law* (3rd edition, 1999) 85–87.

[100] In a number of important areas of Community competence, qualified majority voting (QMV) was introduced progressively during the course of the transitional period. The use of QMV in the field of establishment and services, for example, was intended to take effect at the start of the second stage of the transitional period for some aspects (see Arts 54(2) and 63(2) EEC) and the start of the third stage for others (see Art. 56(2) EEC). The start of the third stage was also intended to mark the introduction of QMV in connection with the common agricultural policy (see Art. 43(2) EEC), the free movement of capital (see Art. 69 EEC), the common transport policy (see Art. 75(1) EEC) and the common commercial policy (see Arts 111(3) and 112(1) EEC).

[101] Decision 66/532 concerning the abolition of customs duties, the prohibition of quantitative restrictions as between Member States and the application of the Common Customs Tariff duties for products other than those set out in Annex II to the Treaty, JO 1966, p. 2971 (known as 'the Acceleration Decision'); D. Edward and R. Lane, *Edward and Lane on European Union Law* (2013) 446.

[102] Boerger and Rasmussen (n. 35) 73–74.

D. Completing the Common Market

The Court was not asked to intervene over the empty chair crisis and studiously ignored the Luxembourg Compromise.[103] Donner later argued that, had it been asked to intervene, the Communities might have collapsed since their legal framework was not then sufficiently robust to secure compliance with whatever the Court might have said the Treaties required.[104] That does not, however, mean that the Court did not respond indirectly. As Lagrange explained, the Court viewed itself as under a duty, 'in securing observance of the law, to give priority to the attainment of the fundamental objectives of the Treaty, in the face of any obstacle, and, more particularly, where the Community legislative authority has failed to act within the prescribed time-limit'. Where that happened, the Court was led 'to assume responsibilities it would not have had to shoulder, had the institutions been functioning properly'.[105]

The Luxembourg Compromise inflicted a career-threatening injury on the Community. The Court had not been forewarned, but the decisions in *Van Gend en Loos* and *Costa* meant that it was forearmed. In the 1970s, against a background of worsening economic conditions following steep rises in the price of oil, the Court deployed the weapons with which it had equipped itself to help compensate for the Member States' failure to ensure that the common market was completed by the end of the transitional period. Particularly notable rulings from this period included *Reyners*,[106] *van Binsbergen*,[107] and *Defrenne II*,[108] in which it held that Treaty provisions which might have been thought to require implementation by the Community legislature were capable, in certain circumstances, of producing direct effect. In *Express Dairy Foods*,[109] the Court was openly critical of the Community legislature, speaking of 'the regrettable absence of Community provisions harmonizing procedure and time limits'[110] in the national courts.

It is hard to deny that the Court's case law of the 1960s and 1970s made a difference to the development of the Community. Indeed, in his famous book, *L'Europe des Juges*, published in 1976, Lecourt argued that it would have been

[103] Though it has made it clear that mere resolutions or declarations by the Member States cannot derogate from the rules laid down in the Treaties or in secondary law. See e.g. Case 68/86, *United Kingdom v. Council* (EU:C:1988:85) para. 38; Case C-292/89, *Antonissen* (EU:C:1991:80) para. 18.

[104] Quoted in Vauchez (n. 20) 48–49.

[105] *Mélanges Dehousse* (n. 4) 11. Lagrange acknowledged that there were limits to what the Court could do to compensate for the shortcomings of the legislature.

[106] Case 2/74, *Reyners v. Belgium* (EU:C:1974:68) (right of establishment).

[107] Case 33/74, *Van Binsbergen v. Bedrijfsvereniging Metaalnijverheid* (EU:C:1974:131) (right to provide services).

[108] Case 43/75, *Defrenne v. SABENA* (EU:C:1976:56) (equal pay).

[109] Case 130/79, *Express Dairy Foods* (EU:C:1980:155).

[110] Ibid., at para. 12 of the judgment.

impossible to establish the common market without the judges of the Court of Justice and their colleagues in the national courts.[111]

Does this mean that Jean Monnet's fear of a *gouvernement des juges* had come to pass? Not entirely. The appointments process, and particularly the fate of Catalano, as well as ongoing contacts with the Member States, made the judges very sensitive to the limits of what was politically acceptable.[112] The Court was seeking during this time to help the Community navigate what was a tempestuous early period, both internally and externally. Views may—and do—differ about whether or not the Court went too far in *Van Gend en Loos* and *Costa*. Certainly there is a reasonable argument that, when dealing with a framework Treaty (*traité cadre*) such as the EEC Treaty, it is sensible, perhaps even unavoidable, to approach its interpretation through consideration of its spirit and its general scheme as well as its wording. It also seems self-evident that the common market would simply not have worked in the way intended in the absence of direct effect and primacy, as Lecourt points out. Once the die was cast in the early 1960s, much of the later case law simply represented a working out of the consequences.

Moreover, Fritz has shown that the ideological direction of the Court was not uppermost in the minds of the Member States, who were preoccupied in the 1960s with more overtly national concerns.[113] Even in the 1970s, the Member States did not seek to use the nomination process to influence the Court's case law. A potential successor to Lecourt refused to go to Luxembourg on the basis that he disagreed with the direction of the case law and would be wasting his time by constantly expressing resistance.[114] The person finally chosen to succeed Lecourt was Adolphe Touffait, who had played such an important role in persuading the French Cour de Cassation to accept the doctrine of primacy.[115] So governments continued to nominate and renominate judges who were unlikely to question the direction of the case law.

However, it was undoubtedly relevant that Lecourt, a convinced European, was joined on his appointment to the Presidency by so many like-minded judges. They included Josse Mertens de Wilmars (President himself from 1980 to 1984) and Pierre Pescatore, described by Fritz as '*la troupe d'assaut*' of supranationalism.[116] Trabucchi, who had helped swing *Van Gend en Loos*, and Walter Strauss, who succeeded Riese, were other proponents of an activist Court.[117]

[111] See also R. Lecourt, 'Qu'eut été le droit des Communautés sans les arrêts de 1963 et 1964?', in *Mélanges Jean Boulouis: l'Europe et le droit* (1991) 350.

[112] See Fritz (n. 13) 167. [113] Ibid. 124–127. [114] Ibid. 127–128.

[115] See *Directeur Général des Douanes v. Société Vabre* [1975] 2 CMLR 336, 363; Mancini, 'The Making of a Constitution for Europe', 24 *Common Market Law Review* (1989) 595, at 605.

[116] Pescatore's enthusiasm for closer integration was particularly evident in his involvement in the negotiations over the Fouchet Plan, where he led the Luxembourg delegation: Fritz (n. 13) 151–152.

[117] For a trenchant and wide-ranging assault on the Court's alleged activism, see H. Rasmussen, *On Law and Policy in the European Court of Justice* (1986). The extent to which the Court plays a political role is considered by Vauchez in Chapter 2 of this volume.

But if national governments seemed sanguine about the direction of the case law, some apex national courts were beginning to cavil at the idea that Community law might take precedence over fundamental rights and values enshrined in national constitutions. The standard-bearers in this development were the German courts, particularly the Bundesverfassungsgericht,[118] whose case law reflected what Davies calls 'a broad swath of West German intellectual and public discourse [that] was dedicated to analysing critically, comparing, and ultimately rejecting the path chosen by the ECJ for the European legal system'.[119]

The resistance grew following the great enlargement of 2004 and 2007, with several courts of the new Member States showing reluctance to allow their newly recovered judicial freedom to be limited by the CJEU.[120] In May 2020, the Bundesverfassungsgericht openly defied the CJEU[121] in a decision with potentially far-reaching implications.[122]

4. The Price of Success

A. Growing Pains

When the single Court of Justice opened for business on 7 October 1958, its members must have felt a mixture of excitement and trepidation: excitement, because the integration project had become much larger in scope and the Court could be expected to play a correspondingly enhanced role; trepidation, because it would be working with an elegantly drafted but often imprecise Treaty for which precedents set by the ECSC Court would have only limited application.

The Court might, however, have been reassured by two factors. The shortage of useful precedents meant that it would often be called upon to rule *de novo*, unencumbered by previous case law. The light case load meant that each case could be given the Court's full attention and decided fairly quickly. *Van Gend en Loos* and

[118] See e.g. *Internationale Handelsgesellschaft v. Einfuhr- und Vorratsstelle für Getreide und Futtermittel* ('*Solange I*') [1974] 2 CMLR 540; '*Solange II*' [1987] 3 CMLR 225; *Brunner v. European Union Treaty* [1994] 1 CMLR 57; *Re Ratification of the Treaty of Lisbon* [2010] 3 CMLR 13.

[119] B. Davies, *Resisting the European Court of Justice: West Germany's Confrontation with European Law, 1949–1979* (2012) 201.

[120] See e.g. the decision of the Czech Constitutional Court in the so-called 'Slovak Pensions' case, Pl. ÚS 5/12, 31 January 2012; Zbíral, 'A Legal Revolution or Negligible Episode? Court of Justice Decision Proclaimed *Ultra Vires*', 49 *Common Market Law Review* (2012) 1475.

[121] See the *PSPP* ruling, 5 May 2020 – 2 BvR 859/15.

[122] See D. Sarmiento and J. Weiler, 'The EU Judiciary After *Weiss*: Proposing a New Mixed Chamber of the Court of Justice', *Verfassungsblog* (2 June 2020), available at https://verfassungsblog.de/the-eu-judiciary-after-weiss/ (accessed 19 September 2020). Cf. the ruling of the Danish Supreme Court in Case No. 15/2014, 6 December 2016; Case C-619/18 *Commission v. Poland* (EU:C:2019:531).

Costa were both decided in around six months. Indeed, the workload was initially so light that Rueff was not the only member of the Court who felt able to take on outside activities. Riccardo Monaco of Italy, a judge of the Court from 8 October 1964 to 3 February 1976, had previously held senior posts in the Italian Ministry of Foreign Affairs and later wrote that his workload at the Court enabled him to return to the Ministry quite frequently.[123]

Until 1969, the Court's annual output could be accommodated comfortably in a single volume of the European Court Reports. In 1970, when there were six Member States, two volumes were needed for the first time (see Table 1.1).

The increasing case load of the Court had a number of fairly obvious consequences. First, membership of the Court became a full-time occupation. Second, the growing case load meant a growing body of case law, which had to be taken into account when new cases were decided. This made judgments harder to draft at a time when successive enlargements had themselves made deliberations more difficult.[124] Third, proceedings before the Court began to take longer (see Table 1.2).

Table 1.1 The increasing case load of the CJEU

	1970	1980	1988
Number of Member States	6	9	12
New cases	79	279	373
Judgments	64	132	238

Source: T. Millett, *The Court of First Instance of the European Communities* (1990) 2.

Table 1.2 Length of proceedings (months)

	1975	1980	1988
Preliminary rulings	6	9	18
Direct actions	9	18	24

Source: T. Millett, *The Court of First Instance of the European Communities* (1990) 2. Figures for the length of proceedings in 1970 are not available.

[123] See Vauchez (n. 20) 110. Many judges continued to be involved in activities outside the Court notwithstanding Art. 4 of the Statute: Fritz (n. 13) 161–167.

[124] See the Address of Judge T. Koopmans on the occasion of the retirement of Lord Mackenzie Stuart, 14 *European Law Review* (1989) 1, at 2.

B. The Advent of the General Court

To address growing concern about the Court's workload, the Single European Act added to the EEC Treaty a new provision, Article 168a, authorizing the Council to establish a court of first instance.[125] Created by the Council in 1988,[126] the Court of First Instance (CFI) quickly established its credentials among practitioners and academics. Its jurisdiction was initially limited, but over time the limits were whittled away. The result is that Article 256 TFEU now confers on what is, since the Treaty of Lisbon, now called the General Court a potentially broad first instance jurisdiction, leaving much of the detail to be worked out in the Statute. It currently deals with all direct actions brought by natural or legal persons as well as certain direct actions brought by Member States.[127] Although Article 168a EEC had said it could not hear preliminary references, Article 256(3) TFEU now permits it to do so 'in specific areas laid down in the Statute'. No such areas have yet been specified.

In 2001, the Treaty of Nice introduced into the Union judicial system a third tier of tribunals below the CFI. Known as judicial panels, they would be created by the Council to deal at first instance with cases brought in certain specific areas.[128] The first (and so far only) judicial panel to be created was the EU Civil Service Tribunal (CST), set up in 2004 to deal with staff cases. These then formed a significant proportion of the new cases brought before the CFI, which was starting to face workload problems of its own. The CST comprised seven judges appointed by the Council. This gave grounds for optimism that, if the CFI continued to struggle with workload problems, the appointment of a small number of extra judges might be feasible. While the number of judges in the Court of Justice has, since the Treaty of Nice, been fixed by the Treaty at one per Member State, the number of judges in the CFI was and remains specified in the Statute, the relevant part of which may be amended without a Treaty change.[129]

In March 2011, the Court submitted a request to the European Parliament and the Council under Article 281 TFEU for the number of judges in the General Court to be increased by 12, from 27 to 39.[130] Member States seemed sympathetic to the idea in principle, but were unable to agree on how the extra judges should

[125] Corresponding provisions were inserted in the other Treaties: see Art. 32d ECSC; Art. 140a Euratom.

[126] Decision 88/591, OJ 1989 C 215/1 (corrected version). See Kennedy, 'The Essential Minimum: The Establishment of the Court of First Instance', 14 *European Law Review* (1989) 7 and 15 *European Law Review* (1990) 54.

[127] See Art. 51 of the Statute.

[128] Art. 225a EC.

[129] Art. 245 EC/Art. 281 TFEU.

[130] See *The Workload of the Court of Justice of the European Union* (House of Lords European Union Committee, Session 2010–11, 14th Report, HL Paper 128) para. 53.

be chosen.[131] By the first half of 2014 and notwithstanding the precedent of the CST, the Greek Presidency was driven to the conclusion that any solution involving less than one additional judge per Member State would be unlikely to secure agreement in the Council. In September 2014, the Court was therefore invited by the Italian Presidency of the Council to present new proposals on how an increase in the number of General Court judges might be agreed.

The following month, the Court took the hint and proposed a phased increase in the number of General Court judges to two per Member State. It also proposed the abolition of the CST and the return of staff cases to the General Court. The proposal noted that this had been discussed internally and that the General Court had expressed a 'preference for the establishment of a specialized trade mark court and for the status quo to be maintained as regards the CST'.[132]

For the Court, one of the main advantages of its preferred course was that it would enable greater flexibility in dealing with cases. The Court was also worried about alleged failures by the General Court to adjudicate within a reasonable time, thereby exposing the Union to potentially substantial claims for damages. However, this was an uncomfortable situation for the Union to find itself in.[133] As Table 1.3 shows, there had been no significant deterioration in the position since the 2011 request and in some respects the position had improved. This made a plan for 28 new judges when 12 had previously been thought sufficient objectively unsustainable.

Table 1.3 Workload of the General Court (2011–2018)

	2011	2012	2013	2014	2015	2016	2017	2018
New cases	722	617	790	912	831	974	917	834
Completed cases	714	688	702	814	987	755	895	1009
Pending cases	1308	1237	1325	1423	1267	1486	1508	1333
Duration*	26.7	24.8	26.9	23.4	20.6	18.7	16.3	20
Number of judges at year end	27	27	28	28	40	47	47	47

*Months and tenths of months.

Source: CJEU Statistics of Judicial Activity, available at https://curia.europa.eu/jcms/jcms/Jo2_7032/en/.

[131] See *Workload of the Court of Justice of the European Union: Follow-Up Report* (House of Lords European Union Committee, Session 2012–13, 16th Report, HL Paper 163) para. 61.

[132] The CST had been widely considered a success: Alemanno and Pech, 'Thinking Justice Outside the Docket: a Critical Assessment of the Reform of the EU's Court System', 54 *Common Market Law Review* (2017) 137.

[133] See F. Dehousse, 'The Reform of the EU Courts (II): Abandoning the Management Approach by Doubling the General Court' (Egmont Paper 83, March 2016). The title refers to an earlier paper by the same author: 'The Reform of the EU Courts: The Need of a Management Approach' (Egmont Paper 53, December 2011). Dehousse was a member of the General Court from 7 October 2003 to 19 September 2016.

Be that as it may, the proposals were eventually adopted by the European Parliament and the Council[134] in the form of two regulations. Regulation 2015/2422[135] amended the Statute of the Court to provide for a progressive increase in the membership of the General Court to 40 on 25 December 2015 and 47 on 1 September 2016. It was due to reach two judges per Member State as from 1 September 2019, although there was a delay in the appointment of the Slovak and Slovene judges. Regulation 2016/1192[136] transferred first instance jurisdiction in staff cases back to the General Court and dissolved the CST.

The position taken by the Council seemed all the more difficult to defend given the budgetary pressures under which the legal systems of many Member States were operating in the wake of the 2008 financial crisis. It was not as if there were no other ways to address the General Court's problems. One possibility would have been to introduce court fees, which are standard in the national systems.[137] Another would have been to increase the number of *référendaires*, who undertake much of the time-consuming work of sifting and synthesizing the often voluminous case files. This option had proved successful in the past. Instead, the Council suggested reducing the number of *référendaires* and assistants per judge in the final stage of the reform as a cost-saving measure.

The Court's 2014 proposal stated that its President and Vice-President had been 'able to explain to the members of the General Court why the Court of Justice is proceeding with the current proposal'. That bland sentence conveyed little of the strength of the opposition to the proposal in the General Court. The opposition became public when the European Parliament began to consider the Court's proposal, which Article 281 TFEU required to be adopted under the ordinary legislative procedure.

In April 2015, the Legal Affairs Committee of the European Parliament invited a number of members of the General Court to assist it in considering the proposal. This prompted the President of the Court of Justice to write to the President of the Legal Affairs Committee to say that judges were not entitled to attend a meeting of the Committee without his prior authorization and that no judge other than the President of the General Court should attend.

The meeting went ahead on 28 April 2015, when four judges of the General Court,[138] who had been invited as 'individual experts', presented a paper entitled 'Doubling the General Court's Judges: Why Progressive, Reversible and More Economical Solutions Are Far Better'. They revealed that the President of the Court of Justice had 'commenced an official disciplinary procedure' against the

[134] The UK voted against the proposals while Belgium and the Netherlands abstained: Alemanno and Pech (n. 132) 138.

[135] OJ 2015 L 341/14.

[136] OJ 2016 L 200/137.

[137] While the proposal was under consideration in the Council, Germany invited the Court to consider the possibility of introducing fees: Dehousse (n. 133) 30, at fn. 60.

[138] Judges G. Berardis, A. Collins, F. Dehousse, and I. Pelikanova.

General Court 'with the aim of preventing the communication of any previously uncensored information to the legislative authorities'. They insisted that the last thing the General Court needed was 'the creation of a Mexican army of new judges, supported by a reduced number of qualified personnel, which will inevitably lead to a serious reduction in the productivity per personnel unit'.

In June 2015, the European Parliament rapporteur issued a press release in which he said that there was 'no urgent need to reform the General Court' and that 'targeted increases of personnel at the level of legal secretaries [i.e. *référendaires*], registry staff and in the translation service . . . give better results, are cheaper and are reversible'. According to Dehousse, this led the President of the Court of Justice to make a complaint to the President of the European Parliament. If this is true, it represents an extraordinary attempt to interfere in the democratic process of the Union.

The controversy to which the proposals had given rise was reflected in Article 3(1) of Regulation 2015/2422. This required the Court of Justice to draw up by 26 December 2020 a report, using an external consultant, on the functioning of the General Court. The report was to 'focus on the efficiency of the General Court, the necessity and effectiveness of the increase to 56 Judges, the use and effectiveness of resources and the further establishment of specialized chambers and/or other structural changes'.

This sorry tale highlights some of the Union's worst features. The intergovernmental instincts of the Member States and the way the Union diffuses responsibility for spending public money rendered most of the Member States incapable of focusing on the main issue: did the General Court need to be reinforced and, if so, what was the most economical way in which that could be done? Instead, those who supported the reforms seem to have allowed themselves to be distracted by self-interest.[139] Against that background, the risk that the reforms might make the General Court more difficult and more expensive to run proved to be a consideration that few were public-spirited enough to entertain.

Dehousse argues that consideration should be given to withdrawing the 'exorbitant prerogative'[140] enjoyed by the Court of Justice—not the Court of Justice of the European Union—to request changes to the Statute. The original versions of the three Community Treaties[141] contained no such provision, meaning that changes to the Statute would require recourse to the full Treaty amendment procedure. Provisions allowing the Court to request amendments to certain

[139] Dehousse (n. 133), at fns 101 and 125, argues that Luxembourg, the seat of the CJEU, had an economic interest in the enlargement of the General Court and reducing the risk that any further specialized courts might be located in other Member States. The Commission may have wished to reduce the risk that a specialized competition court would be created that might subject its own decisions in that field to even closer scrutiny. Member States that were net beneficiaries of the Union budget might have seen an opportunity to secure well paid and influential jobs for their own nationals.

[140] Dehousse (n. 133) 6. Cf. Alemanno and Pech (n. 132) 146.

[141] See Art. 45 ECSC; Art. 188 EEC; Art. 160 Euratom.

provisions of the Statute were introduced by the Single European Act, which empowered the Council to act unanimously after consulting the Commission and the European Parliament. The Treaty of Nice permitted changes to be requested by the Commission, but it was not until the Treaty of Lisbon that the Parliament acquired a role in adopting proposed amendments.[142]

Given the difficulty of amending the Treaties in a Union of its current size, it seems right that a simplified procedure should be available for amending the Statute of the Court. It also seems right that the Court should be able to initiate the procedure, because otherwise it would have to rely on the Commission, which is regularly a party to proceedings before the Court, to do so. The involvement of the Council and the Parliament in principle confers a degree of democratic legitimacy on the outcome. The authors of the Treaties are unlikely to have contemplated the collective failure of leadership among both the Member States and the Union Courts which characterized the process by which it was decided to double the size of the General Court.

Be that as it may, there is merit in Dehousse's suggestion[143] that Article 281 TFEU should be reformed at the next available opportunity. However, the right to submit a formal request could not simply be attributed to the CJEU as a whole, as he proposes, if that means giving the General Court a veto or permitting it to submit a request with which the Court of Justice disagrees. A reformed procedure should seek to encourage consensus within the institution but give the General Court (or any future specialized courts) a formal opportunity to submit their views to the Union legislator if overruled by the Court of Justice. This would help ensure that the legislator and the public had a complete picture of the issues at stake.[144] Ultimately, however, the effectiveness of any process depends on the honesty, openness, professionalism, and good sense of the individuals responsible for conducting it. These qualities seem to have been in short supply in the saga of the 28 judges.

5. The Future of the Court?

The Court has come a long way since that distant day in 1952 when it met for the first time in Luxembourg. The intimacy which once characterized the institution was swept away with the great enlargement of 2004 and 2007, when the EU fulfilled its inescapable moral duty to the countries of central and Eastern Europe. The Court is now a legal leviathan, almost certainly the largest international court

[142] Art. 281 TFEU was foreshadowed by Arts III-381 and I-34 of the Constitutional Treaty.

[143] Dehousse (n. 133) 66–67.

[144] See further Keppenne, 'Les procédures de révision du cadre réglementaire des juridictions de l'Union', 53 *Cahiers de Droit Européen* (2017) 343.

in the world. With seven female members in the Court of Justice and 16 female members in the General Court, it is no longer exclusively male, though it remains exclusively white.

However, the configuration of the Court is unstable. Once the General Court has recovered from the trauma of being force-fed 27 extra judges, it may find itself with spare capacity. The legislator may think that a good way of providing it with extra work would be by transferring to it a significant proportion of the preliminary rulings which dominate the docket of the Court of Justice. Article 3(2) of Regulation 2015/2422 required the Court of Justice to draw up by 26 December 2017 a report 'on possible changes to the distribution of competence for preliminary rulings under Article 267 TFEU'. That report was to be 'accompanied, where appropriate, by legislative requests'. The Court produced a short report concluding, perhaps predictably, that there was 'no need, at this time . . . to transfer to the General Court part of the jurisdiction that the Court exercises in preliminary ruling cases'.[145] The Court added, however, that its present view 'should not at all be understood as a definitive position on the question'.[146] The Court's report was followed in March 2018 by a request for infringement actions under Articles 108(2), 258, and 259 TFEU to be transferred to the General Court and for certain categories of appeal from the General Court to be allowed to proceed only with the permission of the Court of Justice. In return, the Court asked to be given responsibility for annulment actions connected with the failure of a Member State to comply with a judgment under Article 260 TFEU.[147]

These measures, if implemented, could leave the Court of Justice with time on its hands, a dangerous position to be in when budgets are tight. Would the Member States dare to contemplate a reduction in the size of the Court of Justice itself? The recent reforms to the General Court show that there is unlikely to be any political appetite for unequal national representation in the Court of Justice. However, an interesting precedent is offered by the European Commission. A convention dating from the Merger Treaty gave the larger Member States two commissioners, but following the Treaty of Nice the Commission has comprised just one national from each Member State.[148]

Might we perhaps contemplate a streamlined Court consisting of just one member per Member State, either a judge or an Advocate General? If the present Court were to be reconfigured in this way, it would be the same size as the

[145] 'Report submitted pursuant to Art. 3(2) of Regulation (EU, Euratom) 2015/2422 of the European Parliament and of the Council amending Protocol No 3 on the Statute of the Court of Justice of the European Union' (December 2017) 8. Weiler describes the Court's determination to cling on to its monopoly over the preliminary rulings procedure as 'its most cherished article of faith': Weiler, Editorial, 14 *International Journal of Constitutional Law* (2016) 321, at 323.

[146] 'Report submitted pursuant to Art. 3(2)' (n. 145) 9.

[147] Interinstitutional file 2018/0900 (COD), Brussels, 28 March 2018.

[148] Plans to reduce the size of the Commission further have come to nought: see A. Dashwood *et al.*, *Wyatt and Dashwood's European Union Law* (6th ed., 2011) 51–52.

Bundesverfassungsgericht. There would of course need to be discussion on the right balance between judges and Advocates General and how those roles might be allocated. The Court and the Member States might also wish to consider whether the Court has the right mix of expertise to enable it to deal effectively with the increasingly diverse disputes brought before it. But is it too much to hope that this simple solution to the problem of over-capacity in the Court of Justice, should it arise, might appeal to the Member States? It would, after all, merely require them to accept the practical reality of the formal equality of status enjoyed by judges and Advocates General.

A smaller Court with a lighter case load would have a number of advantages. It would be able to address the growing criticism of the quality of its judgments.[149] This is in part a consequence of the growth in its case load, which means that less time is available for thinking and deliberating, resulting in judgments that are too often gnomic in style. The arguments of the Advocate General are almost never addressed; little attempt is made to explain changes of direction in the case law;[150] and hardly any effort is made to persuade the reader of the correctness of the outcome. This dogmatic approach seems out of keeping with modern demands for transparency and inadequate to maintain the confidence of the national courts.

One way of addressing these problems would be to introduce dissenting opinions with a view to enabling the majority to express itself more clearly and analyse previous case law more thoroughly. The Court should also reinstate its former practice of having an Advocate General's Opinion in every (or nearly every) case. It should make clear in its judgments when it is following the advice of its Advocate General. More importantly, it should give reasons when it decides not to do so.[151]

The result might be a Court of Justice that is less defensive, less deferential to the Union institutions, and better at managing internal dissent. In short, a Court comfortable in its own skin.

[149] See e.g. Weiler, 'Epilogue: The Judicial Après Nice', in G. de Búrca and J. Weiler (eds), *The European Court of Justice* (2001) 215, at 219 and 225.

[150] A notorious illustration is Case C-144/04, *Mangold* (EU:C:2005:709), which led to the decision of the Danish Supreme Court of 6 December 2016 (n. 122). Holdgaard, Elkan, and Schaldemose (n. 122) 36, observe: 'the ECJ's *Mangold* jurisprudence is one of the most criticized lines of case law in the Court's recent history'.

[151] The UK Supreme Court has repeatedly criticized the Court of Justice for delivering judgments which fail to address issues raised by the Advocate General. See e.g. *Patmalniece v. Secretary of State* [2011] UKSC 11; *Aimia Coalition Loyalty* [2013] UKSC 15; *R (HS2 Action Alliance Ltd) v. Secretary of State for Transport* [2014] UKSC 3; *HMRC v. Pendragon* [2015] UKSC 37; *Cavendish Square Holding v. Talal El Makdessi* [2015] UKSC 67.

2

From Close-Ups to Long Shot

In Search of the 'Political Role' of the Court of Justice of the European Union

*Antoine Vauchez**

1. Introduction

Engaging in a discussion on the political role of any given court is always a risky task. To say of a court that it is 'political' is not only giving an abstract definition of its role; it also directly impinges on one of the most sensitive elements for courts' legitimacy, i.e. their capacity to convince scholars and the general public of the intrinsically *judicial* quality of their acts and of the ontologically *jurisdictional* nature of the institutions themselves. Unsurprisingly, courts are very concerned by their reputation in this regard—and the Court of Justice of the European Union (CJEU) probably even more than its national counterparts given the more recent and more contested nature of its jurisdiction. In their public appearances—from CJEU press releases to the judges' Jubilees, from judicial Festschriften to public interviews with its president—members of the CJEU keep emphasizing that they are 'exterior' to politics.[1] Examining the various ways and formats through which the CJEU exhibits its apolitical reputation and avoids politics would probably require a whole research study of its own. Among them are: the insistence on the Court's *judicial* origin through the appeal of the founding cases rather than on its political origin (the intergovernmental negotiations and related treaties from Paris (1951) to Lisbon (2010) that have continuously redesigned the court); the distance from politics, with EU politics marked symbolically with a geographical location far away from Brussels; and the continuous denial on the part of the judges of sensitivity to political or intellectual junctures of any given type.[2]

* I am grateful to Claire Kilpatrick, Joanne Scott, and all participants at the Workshop on New Approaches to Studying the Court of Justice (February 2018) for their many useful remarks and insights.

[1] Vauchez, 'Keeping the Dream Alive: The Transnational Fabric of Integrationist Jurisprudence', 5(1) *European Political Science Review* (2012) 51.

[2] Questioned on whether 'l'histoire de la Cour (laissait) apparaître des personnalités qui ont particulièrement influencé sa jurisprudence' [the history of the Court (reveals) the role of personalities

Antoine Vauchez, *From Close-Ups to Long Shot: In Search of the 'Political Role' of the Court of Justice of the European Union.* In: *New Legal Approaches to Studying the Court of Justice.* First edition. Edited by Claire Kilpatrick and Joanne Scott, Oxford University Press (2020). © Antoine Vauchez.
DOI: 10.1093/oso/9780198871477.003.0003

While the CJEU is committed to remaining under the political radar, this position has proved harder and harder to maintain over time. The first reason relates to the basic fact that the CJEU has to defend itself 'as an institution' in the context of EU polity where its position is far from settled once and for all. One has only to think about the hard negotiations it has to undertake every year with the Parliament and the Council in the framework of budget preparation;[3] or, even more dramatically, in the context of intergovernmental conferences, or during the Convention for the future of Europe,[4] when the founding treaties are re-drafted and risk undermining the pivotal position acquired by the CJEU and its case law.[5] Most recently, the President of the Court and the Court's administration have been drawn into a long and bitter conflict—both internal and external—about the reform of its organization, leading to heated discussions at the European Parliament.[6]

Yet, beyond the institutional dimension, there is another element that continuously threatens the capacity of the CJEU to appear as an *apolitical* actor: the public discourse about the 'political role' of the Court has become more and more diffuse and banal—to a point that it is almost mainstream today. While we are still short of a study that would delineate the progressive rise of the CJEU critics since the 1990s, it is possible to point at both the enlargement of the circles/milieu involved and the diversification of the types of *registre* mobilized (doctrinal, political, media, economic, etc.). This is not to say that there was no criticism of the CJEU before that period but—with very few exceptions[7]—this remained essentially contained in semi-public circles, from bureaux of national ministries to specific segments of national legal doctrine in the area of international public

which particularly influenced its case law], Koen Lenaerts (at that time a judge at the Court of First Instance) answered: 'je ne pense pas que ce soit le cas... le principe retenu étant celui de la collégialité: il n'est pas question pour chaque magistrat de se démarquer par une conception personnelle de l'issue à donner à l'espèce dont la Cour est saisie' [I do not think that this is the case... the principle is that of collegiality: this is not about each judge distinguishing him/herself by giving his/her personal view on the issue at stake in a given case]: Lenaerts, 'Entretien. La Cour assure surtout le respect des droits que les justiciables tirent du droit communautaire', 4 *Europe* (2007).

[3] Krenn, 'The European Court of Justice's Financial Accountability: How the European Parliament Incites and Monitors Judicial Reform through the Budgetary Process', 13(3) *European Constitutional Law Review* (2017) 453.

[4] Granger, 'The Future of Europe: Judicial Interference and Preferences', 3 *Comparative European Politics* (2005) 155.

[5] See on the Lisbon Treaty, the discussions over the desirability of affirming the principle of 'supremacy' in the treaty itself or in a mere protocol.

[6] On this long and conflictual saga, see Alemanno and Pech, 'Thinking Justice Outside the Dock: A Critical Assessment of the Reform of the EU's Court System', 54(1) *Common Market Law Review* (2017) 129. In terms of press coverage, see the well-informed blog of French journalist Jean Quatremer, 'Les coulisses de Bruxelles': 'Copinage et clientélisme à la Cour de justice européenne', *Blog Libération* (8 June 2015); 'La réforme de la Cour de justice européenne ou l'art de créer une usage à gaz', *Blog Libération* (7 April 2015).

[7] Cf. Debré, 'Les prétentions inouïes de la Cour de justice européenne', *Le Monde* (11 January 1979).

law or constitutional law in particular.[8] Hjalte Rasmussen captured that very well when he said that, given the symbiotic relationship between the Court and its scholarship,[9] criticisms were bound to circulate as an 'oral tradition'.[10]

Since the 1990s, both the Court and the context in which it operates have, however, changed dramatically. The CJEU is certainly not 'tucked away in the fairy-tale Grand Duchy of Luxembourg' any longer. To illustrate this, it suffices to track the multifaceted controversy over the cases *Viking* and *Laval* among law professors, politicians, unionists, and think tank members of all blends in order to ascertain the fact that the Court has entered a political age.[11] This is probably no surprise given the fact that the Court has intervened on literally all the salient political issues of EU politics over the past two decades, ranging from refugees to posted workers, discrimination, secularism, the eurozone crisis, and the actions of populist governments in Poland or Hungary. Given the historical role of 'independent' institutions (the Court of Justice, Commission, and Central Bank) in embodying and leading the 'European project',[12] it should be no surprise that the politicization of EU affairs has *not* hit only the institutions that claim to be 'political' (the Council, the Parliament, and to a certain extent the Commission), but has affected *all* EU institutions, including the CJEU and the European Central Bank (ECB). While there have not been, to my knowledge, demonstrations on the Plateau de Kirchberg the way there are in front of the Eurotower in Frankfurt, the CJEU has now become a controversial political object, subject to continuous scrutiny and surveillance.

The problem is that our analytical equipment has not changed alongside this politicization process. When it comes to describing 'the political' in the Court, the toolbox on which scholars of law or of politics rely remains strikingly poor. This is the case whether we simply ascribe to the Court strictly 'political' standpoints, labelling its case law as 'neoliberal', 'federalist', or any other label directly drawn from partisan politics (as if judges were acting *as* ideologues or politicians), or because we rely on normative categories such as 'judicial activism' or *gouvernement des juges* which immediately locate the discussion on the ground of 'un-judge like' and dysfunctional behaviours.[13] It is probably this shared frustration

[8] On this, see in particular J. Bailleux, *Penser l'Europe par le droit* (2015).

[9] Vauchez, 'Transnational Communities of Lawyers before International Courts', in K. Alter and C. Romano (eds), *Handbook of International Adjudication* (2013); Bailleux, 'Comment l'Europe vint au droit. Le premier congrès international d'études de la CECA (Milan-Stresa 1957)', 60 *Revue française de science politique* (2010) 295.

[10] H. Rasmussen, *On Law and Policy in the European Court of Justice* (1986).

[11] J. Arnholz, 'A "Legal Revolution" in the European Field of Posting? Narratives of Uncertainty, Politics and Extraordinary Events' (2014) (PhD thesis on file at University of Copenhagen).

[12] A. Vauchez, *Democratizing Europe* (2016).

[13] Drawing from the 'names and known judicial orientations and philosophies' of the four elected presidents, Hjalte Rasmussen has argued that a 'federalist coup' occurred during the October 2004 election as three of them were of strict federalist creed, thereby maintaining a strong hold on the

and difficulty in seizing the 'political role' of the CJEU that has motivated an unprecedented series of *interdisciplinary* conferences that have followed one another over the past decade, with the aim of enriching not only the analytical toolbox of EU law scholarship but also its methodologies and empirical material.[14] Here is not the place to engage in a full inventory of these undertakings. Suffice it to say that these conferences and related books have all brought EU law into closer contact with new disciplinary developments outside the field of law strictly speaking: political theory and normative theories of justice in the case of the edited volume *Europe's Justice Deficit* (Dimitri Kochenov, Grainne de Búrca, Andrew Williams);[15] sociology and field-theory for *Lawyering Europe. European Law as a Transnational Social Field* (Bruno de Witte, Antoine Vauchez),[16] which attempted to map out the interactions and structural dynamics of the field of EU law actors; critical legal studies and history in the edited volume by Fernanda Nicola and Billy Davies, whose case-oriented approach has allowed for thicker description;[17] and last but not least, socio-legal studies and 'law-in-context' approaches in the edited volumes directed by Bruno de Witte and Mark Dawson,[18] by Michal Bobek,[19] or, more recently in France, under the guidance of Laure Clement-Wilz.[20] Beyond their differences, all this scholarship explores ways to enrich our understanding of EU law and the CJEU by changing the focus to (conceptual, professional, legal) practices whether *at the* Court or *outside* the Court. The common assumption that cuts across the diverse set of research traditions is that 'the political' in EU law and case law has to be examined *at the level of* legal practices through a variety of possible qualitative and quantitative methodologies (discourse analysis, collective biographies of lawyers and judges, case-centred approaches, etc.).

Drawing from these insights, the remainder of this chapter elaborates a possible methodological and analytical strategy to grasp 'the political' without indulging in ontological conceptions of the former. The first part attempts to shape a new research agenda by reconceptualizing the notion of 'the political' by

Court: Rasmussen, 'Present and Future European Judicial Problems after Enlargement and the Post-2005 Ideological Revolt', 44(6) *Common Market Law Review* (2007) 1661; see also J.-P. Colin, *Le gouvernement des juges dans les Communautés européennes* (1966).

[14] See also the research programme led by Loïc Azoulai on the 'forms of life' of EU law: *Forms of Life and Legal Integration in Europe* (Folie), available at https://www.sciencespo.fr/folie/index.html (accessed 3 April 2020).

[15] D. Kochenov, G. de Búrca, and A. Williams (eds), *Europe's Justice Deficit* (2015).

[16] B. de Witte and A. Vauchez (eds), *Lawyering Europe: European Law as a Transnational Social Field* (2014).

[17] B. Davies and F. Nicola (eds), *EU Law Stories: Contextual and Critical Histories of EU Jurisprudence* (2017).

[18] B. de Witte and M. Dawson (eds), *Judicial Activism* (2013).

[19] M. Bobek (ed.), *Selecting Europe's Judges: A Critical Review of the Appointment Procedures to the European Courts* (2015).

[20] L. Clement-Wilz, *Le rôle politique de la Cour de justice de l'Union européenne* (2018).

questioning 'authorship' in judicial decision-making. The second part suggests the adoption of a process-oriented approach that embeds 'the political' in EU law in a processual narrative of cases from their emergence up to their legal, administrative, or political effects 'on the ground'.

2. A Processual Approach to the Making of EU Case Law

There is no doubt that EU law scholarship has some responsibility for this state of affairs, having long thought of the Court's case law as a 'constitutional law without politics'. As famously stated by Martin Shapiro many years ago in an incisive argument, EU lawyers have regarded 'the written constitution as a legal truth; the case law as the inevitable working out of the correct implications of the constitutional text; and the constitutional court as the disembodied voice of right reason and constitutional teleology'.[21] It would be wrong, however, to exonerate political scientists from their responsibility. In their efforts to identify the *real* driver beyond the case law *outside* the law and the legal field itself, they have left the Court and its 'political role' in a curious dead angle. As noted elsewhere,[22] there has been a striking convergence of legal positivism and political science rationalism that has resulted in the Court being viewed in an anthropomorphic manner, as if it were one unitary actor granted with intentions and acting in a strategic manner. While many EU law professors were trying to assess the underlying inner logic of the Court's case law, political scientists were considering its strategies in pursuing pre-existing interests (prestige, independence, power, etc.) in the face of a variety of constraints and interlocutors. In the end, both parts viewed the Court as one reified and self-standing collective pursuing abstract goals and/or institutional interests.

Lacking a more suitable analytical framework, watchers are often left to infer, if not just guess, possible 'political motivations' of the Court taken from hearsay, anecdotes, or past experience. The fact is, in Luxembourg as in any other court, lawyers continuously produce a sort of '*folk* sociology' of courts. Lawyers, be they judges, clerks, or litigants, like any other actors, develop forms of reflexiveness on their own practices, building a practical knowledge of the rules of the legal game, a capacity to situate themselves in their professional field, and an ability to read not just the law but also the social context and political underpinnings of legal action. Like all their peers in national courts, EU lawyers pleading at the Court will attempt to figure out what is in the '*ventre des juges*' (as former Advocate

[21] Shapiro, 'Comparative Law and Comparative Politics', 53 *Southern California Law Review* (1979–80) 537, at 540.

[22] Vauchez, 'Introduction', in B. de Witte and A. Vauchez (eds), *Lawyering Europe. European Law as a Transnational Social Field* (2014).

General Philippe Léger would have it)—a sort of EU version of the 'breakfast theory of jurisprudence'[23] that tries to identify the circumstantial causes/determinations and the hidden political intentions/agenda that lie behind the law. However, such definition of 'the political' remains excessively narrow, as it draws from a distinction between judges 'who have' and judges 'who do not have' an agenda, or between judges 'who are' and judges 'who are not' political or ideological. Empirically speaking, the risk is that the research is driven entirely towards smoking guns and 'judicial coups'. (Which judge cast or pushed for the decisive ballot? What was the turning point?) But by doing this, one would entirely miss the layer of 'the political' that lies outside the classic ideological categories; in particular, its more diffuse and ordinary forms embedded in routine judicial practices. More often than not, courts do politics *sans en avoir l'air*, namely under forms that are specific to the legal world.[24] In legal fields, particularly when it comes to continental law, the argument that appears to be the least political is often the most likely to gather support; demonstrating continuity (and not rupture) with the 'original principles' and the 'founding treaties' is often the safest legal strategy.[25] Conversely, when a judge uses categories directly drawn from the world of partisan politics, it is immediately thought of as a gaffe.[26] In other words, rather than studying the 'political role' of the Court merely by using the categories mobilized to analyse the Council or the Parliament, we need a more refined analytical framework which is able to grasp 'the political' in the law.

A. Who is the Author of EU Case Law?

One of the most challenging epistemological obstacles as we engage in this journey might in fact lie in our understanding of what 'judging' means. More often than not, our conception of 'judgment' follows very closely that of legal theory itself. In a sort of tautology, the judicial decision is equated to what is decided during the *délibéré*. This 'decisionist' bias sees judicial decision-making as a unique and circumscribed moment of decision (*judicial fiat*) whereby a group of free-floating and sovereign minds make a decision on a case. With that analytical framework in mind, it certainly proves hard indeed to see 'the political' as

[23] King, 'A Breakfast Theory of Jurisprudence', 14 *Dicta* (1936–37) 143.

[24] Vauchez, 'Introduction' (n. 22) 1.

[25] W. McIntosh and C. Kates, *Judicial Entrepreneurship: The Role of Judges in the Marketplace of Ideas* (1997).

[26] One can recall the declarations coming from a judge of the tribunal of first instance (now director at the Legal service of the Council) in the French-speaking review *Concurrence* portraying CJEU law clerks as 'true ayatollahs of free competition'. This opinion is thought to have cost him the *Microsoft* case, of which he had charge up until then: Legal, 'Le contentieux communautaire de la concurrence', 2 *Concurrences* (2005) 1.

anything else than a conscious and calculated plan coming from a segment of, if not all, the court.

While it may be critical in terms of institutional imputability and accountability of the case law, the equivalency put between 'judging' and '*délibéré*' is analytically problematic. As American sociologist Howard Becker has it about musicians and their related 'art worlds',[27] judges never operate in a vacuum: rather, they are part and parcel of an wider 'social and professional world' made of support (and competing) groups, and broader networks of cooperation that may compete with each other but still share a number of conventions regarding the scope, value objects, and inner social hierarchies of their activity. In this framework, the 'judicial decision' is the outcome of the cooperative and competitive activity of a variety of groups that does not stop, nor start, at the doors of the CJEU. What Bruno Latour indicates about the French *Conseil d'Etat* is certainly equally valid for the CJEU:

> when the first appeal arrives at the Palais Royal, it has already undergone a long history which for the most part escapes the ethnographer as well as the *conseillers d'État*, but whose traces can be recognized at first sight from the type of letter-headed paper, from the presence and name of some famous and expensive lawyers' firm, from the manner of writing, and from the greater or less display of legal knowledge, texts and decrees and leaders' words taken from Molière.[28]

In other words, authorship in judgment should be reconsidered. Not to deny the role of judges, but as a way to embed them in larger social processes.

Judges do not engage in the act of judging *in abstracto*. They do not write their judgment on a 'blank page'.[29] Their intervention is neither the starting point nor the endpoint of the process. By many standards, the *délibéré* is just one moment in the build-up of a case—one that is certainly critical but which does not contain or condense all 'the political-ness' of a judgment. Not only are the cases brought to sitting judges survivors of a long process of selection (which is certainly not neutral socially and politically) but also their 'career' is bound to continue afterwards, as their legal scope and social effects on the ground are still on trial, and often remain so for a long time and in a variety of arenas. Therefore, rather than artificially isolating the judges and the *délibéré* from the rest, we suggest re-examining our understanding of the professional and temporal boundaries of judicial decision-making in order to better apprehend how and where 'the political' in EU case law is progressively framed. Instead of limiting the lifeline of a case

[27] H. Becker, *Art Worlds* (1982).

[28] B. Latour, *The Making of Law: An Ethnography of the Conseil d'Etat* (2010) 73.

[29] McAuliffe, 'Behind the Scenes of the Court of Justice', in B. Davies and F. Nicola (eds), *EU Law Stories: Contextual and Critical Histories of EU Jurisprudence* (2017) 35, at 47.

to a 'sudden' appearance before the judges (epiphany), we should adopt a processual understanding of judging. By 'processual', we mean an approach which tracks EU law cases from the specific conditions of their emergence (generation) to their later stages on legal, administrative, and political grounds (effectuation).

This micro-analysis of EU case law is not about bringing life to what is otherwise a dry narrative of abstract principles unfolding from the Rome Treaty onwards. Following the cases from generation to effectuation proves heuristic for our understanding of 'the political' in the case law. By following the 'career' of single dossiers within the Court, from the opening of the case to the judgment and from the judgment to implementation, we are able to identify the social and professional formation of EU case law (its relevant primary publics, value objects, inner social hierarchies, etc.). To a large extent, this trajectory is a complex and collective process of voicing as well as silencing, writing and ignoring, selecting and forgetting, in which a variety of actors and organizations, legal or non-legal, take part, thus co-producing EU law. With this analytical *parti pris*, the Court is no longer a self-standing institution operating in an empty social territory; rather, it is embedded in a dense web of (local, national, and European) actors and fields in which the scope and importance of EU case law is debated. By tracking and putting together the trajectories of these cases, we are able to identify the position of EU (case) law in Europe's social space: 'from where' in Europe's social space (professions, social groups, sectors, etc.) EU law cases emerge; as well as 'on where' in Europe's social space they may actually have a structuring effect. Thereby, we are also in a position to be able to map out not only EU law's hubs, holes, unexplored territories, dead ends, but also its points of tensions or *clair-obscurs*. This eventually allows 'the Court' to be viewed from the point of view of its transformative capacity as one decisive point in the fabric of EU case law.

B. Where is 'the Political' in EU Case Law?

This broad analytical framework for judicial authorship calls for a new understanding of 'the political' in EU case law. Instead of the usual ontological definitions of EU case law, we suggest adopting a working definition of 'the political' as lying in its connections to (and disconnections from) Europe's variegated set of social and professional groups (farmers, migrants, students, mobile workers, etc.) and institutions. To put it differently, EU case law considered as a whole does contain a (changing yet rather stable) portrait of that 'Europe' with which EU law is associated (as much as a portrait of that 'Europe' from which it is distant). This framing of 'the political' is both extensive and narrow. Extensive, as it does not limit the 'politics of EU case law' to the Court but extends it more broadly to all forms of administrative, doctrinal, political, and judicial usages of EU law—a move consistent with our process-oriented approach. Narrow, as it does not aim at assessing the political 'intentions' that may or may not lie 'behind' the law but rather focuses on the connections that are made (or not made) through the case law with a specific set of social and professional interests that can be positioned in the 'European society'.

There are, however, different levels through which EU case law displays a specific definition of 'the political'. The first level, identified hereafter as 'paradigmatic', focuses on EU law's broad 'institutional programme' or rationale, as it has solidified around the CJEU; namely, the political role and the social functions that the Court has built for itself and for EU law in the framework of the European project while at the same time defining the 'logic', 'spirit', and 'general economy' of the treaties.[30] In this regard, the Court appears as the 'judicial arm' of a broad political project built around the 'constitutional platform' of the four economic freedoms and fair competition. The second level, labelled hereafter as 'methodological', refers to the set of instruments and keywords that EU lawyers have shaped to generate EU case law. In this regard, EU case law has historically navigated between two poles: on the one hand, a form of 'methodological Europeanism', to paraphrase Ulrich Beck's famous expression, which takes the autonomy of EU law as a sort of starting point beyond discussion;[31] and, on the other hand, an inclination for comparatism as the best methodology to produce authentically *European* case law.[32] While the entrenchment of the 'autonomy' paradigm at the core of the Court's principles can easily be assessed in politically salient decisions such as the one on the relationship between EU law and the European Convention on Human Rights (ECHR) (Avis 2/13[33]) or the one between EU law and international law (*Kadi*[34]) that have triggered a widespread criticism of the Court's 'legal solipsism',[35] this does not preclude EU lawyers and the CJEU from trying to enrol national constituencies through a 'respect' paid to 'national constitutional identities' or the importance given to 'sensitive national interests'.[36] The third and last level on 'the political' in EU law, hereafter identified as 'substantive', lies in its attempt to define

[30] This is what Pierre Pescatore labelled EU law's 'grand dessein d'unification' (great unificatory project) that lay at the core of the Rome treaties: P. Pescatore, *The Law of Integration* (1974, reprinted 2005) 361.

[31] Vauchez, 'Methodological Europeanism at the Cradle: Eur-lex, the *Acquis* and the Making of Europe's Cognitive Equipment', 37(2) *Journal of European Integration* (2015) 193.

[32] See e.g. Rozakis, 'The European Judge as a Comparatist', 80 *Tulane Law Review* (2005) 257; Lenaerts, 'Interlocking Legal Orders in the European Union and Comparative Law', 52 *International & Comparative Law Quarterly* (2003).

[33] CJEU, Opinion of the Court 18 December 2014, Avis 2/13 (EU: C: 2014: 2454).

[34] Joined Cases C-584/10 P, C-593/10 P, and C-595/10 P, *Kadi* (EU:C:2013:518).

[35] See, among other examples, Koskenniemi, 'International law between fragmentation and constitutionalism', Canberra University, 27 November 2006, available at http://www.helsinki.fi/eci/Publications/Koskenniemi/MCanberra-06c.pdf (accessed 3 April 2020).

[36] Azoulai, 'The European Court of Justice and the Duty to Respect Sensitive National Interests', in M. Dawson, B. De Witte, and E. Muir (eds), *Judicial Activism at the European Court of Justice* (2013) 167.

and hierarchize Europe's value objects and social groups. The case of the four freedoms or fair competition (and the related delimitation of its basic principles and exceptions: '*entrave*', '*abus de position dominante*', '*pratiques anti-concurrentielles*', '*aides d'Etat*', etc.) best exemplifies the EU case law's capacity to prioritize specific social and economic issues over others.[37] Such a perspective would also require consideration of the many keywords whose *European* definition as 'autonomous notions' have in large part been shaped by EU case law ('firm', 'worker', '*produit similaire*', '*marché pertinent*', etc.).[38] Sector by sector, EU case law locates the ability and OOOOresponsibility for the 'rational guidance' of EU integration processes in particular institutions, social groups, and value objects.

Such a path towards a renewed understanding of 'the political' in EU case law has therefore led us to question our temporal and professional definition of what 'judging' means. As we have moved towards a process-oriented understanding, we have broadened our working definition of 'the political' in EU case law, pointing at the various types of ways and levels through which the former connects to value objects and social groups. Thereby, we hope the grand talk about the 'political role' of the Court will be substituted with fine-grained inquiries into the (selective) connections and interactions between EU law and 'European society'.

3. EU Case Law—3D

These preliminary reflections have allowed us to identify the *travail politique* of EU lawyering, which happens in this complex and selective process of connection (and dis-connection) between EU case law and Europe's social and professional groups and interests. The study of such linkages requires a fine-grained exploration of the transformative process that turns (or, most often, does not turn) the innumerable flow of social claims and grievances that continuously arise from society into fully fledged EU law complaints deserving to be decided by the Court. Equally, this calls for a detailed inquiry into the process of production and transformation of the Court's decisions into legal, political, and social effects within (and even sometimes outside) the EU. This two-fold process of generation and effectuation of case law has nothing spontaneous or natural about it: while 'EU law' issues could arguably be found in virtually all social complaints and claims, very few happen to be framed in both 'legal' and 'European' terms and make their

[37] Among many other examples, one could also think about all the sector-specific developments made by the ECJ in defining the 'objectives of public service', in erecting 'financial stability' as a superior objective for the EMU, in identifying the 'finalités' of the 'aides d'Etat' within the framework of Europe's competition policy, in containing the 'principes du droit social communautaire revêtant une importante particulière', etc.

[38] On this, see P. Maddalon, *La notion de marché dans la jurisprudence de la Cour de justice* (2007).

way to the Court; similarly, not all CJEU decisions have the same effect/posterity across countries, sectors, and social classes. Thereby, the process-oriented perspective brings us to the social fringes of EU law, where its presence is least obvious, but where its meaning and scope are most discussed and contested. Yet, it is precisely by studying these side-lines of EU law, where its appeal to European publics and causes is at stake, that a political portrait of EU case law may be sketched.

A. Testing the No-Hypothesis

We still know very little about the conditions under which specific claims and grievances are turned into EU law issues, for a variety of reasons. While this classic socio-legal question has long stood beyond the remits of EU law scholarship, it did not fit into the research agenda of CJEU neo-functionalists or neo-institutionalists, who were primarily interested in accounting for the success of Europeanization through 'legal integration', rather than looking at its failures. In a paradigm where 'empowerment through ECJ case law' (of national judges, transnational firms, etc.) was considered as the essential trigger for the dynamics of judicialization of Europe, the reverse narrative—i.e. the 'no-hypothesis'—has never garnered much interest. As EU case law, and in particular ECJ preliminary references, were identified as a success story of progressive 'rise and rise', there was little room left for inquiries into cases in which actors did not identify or take up EU law and rights.[39]

A new generation of studies is now emerging that questions this dead end of legal integration studies. Coming from a variety of academic sites, this new stream of scholarship reflects frustration with the neo-functionalist narrative of EU legal integration that has consolidated as a result of the bias of earlier research. As Jos Hoevenaars indicates: 'not only are we not seeing the failed attempts, or non-attempts, [but we] also fail to consider that preliminary references may not always constitute a "demand" for a ruling, nor an attempt at participation or expecting a net gain from invoking EU law'.[40] As such, this emerging stream of research stands in the continuation with some early socio-legal inquiries into access to the EU judiciary.[41] Instead of assuming an interest in EU law or case law, this new stream of studies gives equal consideration to EU law, failed attempts,

[39] In this tradition of research, see Van Oorschot, 'Non Take-up of Social, Security Benefits in Europe', 1(1) *Journal of European Social Policy* (1991); Warin, 'Le non-recours aux droits', *SociologieS*, 15 November 2012.

[40] J. Hoevenaars, 'A People's Court? A Bottom-Up Approach to Litigation Before the Court of Justice of the European Union' (2018) (PhD thesis on file at Radboud Universiteit Nijmegen).

[41] See in particular Schepel and Blankenburg, 'Mobilizing the European Court of Justice', in G. De Búrca and J. Weiler (eds), *The European Court of Justice* (2002) 9.

and indifference. A handful of statistical inquiries have mapped out the interests and social groups that could access the CJEU data, showing 'the Court' to be an uneven playing field. Takis Tridimas and Gabriela Gari demonstrated a structural advantage for firms and interest groups in their capacity to bring their complaints to the ECJ. Of a total of 340 cases brought before the Court of First Instance over the 2000–2005 period, 87 per cent had been submitted by 'legal persons' (for the most part firms and business interest groups), while only 9 per cent (30 cases) had been brought by individuals.[42]

These statistical studies displayed a different picture of EU case law: not only a never-ending story of integration-through-case law where 'progresses' and 'resistances' alternated, but also a story of 'holes', 'avoidance', and 'spheres of indifference' to EU law. Yet they called for fine-grained qualitative studies on the social and economic conditions that determine this socially selective portrait of EU case law. In a PhD study that mapped out the usages of preliminary rulings tribunal-by-tribunal in France, Germany, and Italy, Tommaso Pavone carried out research investigating the unequal spatial distribution of *recours* (and their causes).[43] By providing an in-depth analysis of the idiosyncrasies of local configurations in terms of legal, judicial, and economic infrastructure, he was able to identify what lies behind the variations in inclination to frame social complaints into issues of EU law. Starting with similar assumptions, Jos Hoevenaars has taken an even more in-depth localized and contextual approach in order to describe the heavily selective process of translating/coding social complaints into EU legal issues.[44] By working on a limited corpus of cases and using a 'magnifying glass' to investigate more closely, he is able to consider how in practice individuals, social interests, NGOs, legal experts, and national judges articulate around (or remain indifferent to) EU law issues.

Under this empirical light, the emergence of an 'interest in EU law' looks like a rather unlikely—if not somewhat irrational—event, for the plaintiffs, the lawyers, and the local judges themselves. Filing a complaint in the terms of EU law most often means taking the risk of slowing down the procedure and introducing an additional element of uncertainty in the midst of already costly/lengthy national procedures. Even the litigants who would likely appear as the most natural candidates for raising 'an interest in EU law' often act as reluctant players who are essentially concerned about the prospect of additional workload in a domain of law that they very rarely master.

[42] In the same vein: while half of complaints filed by individuals before the Court of First Instance are declared inadmissible, only 30% of the legal persons are. Only 10% of individuals succeed but 35% of legal persons succeed: Tridimas and Gari, 'Winners and Losers in Luxembourg: A Statistical Analysis of Judicial Review before the ECJ and the CFI (2001–2005)', 2 *European Law Review* (2010) 131.

[43] Pavone, 'The Origins of Preliminary References to the European Court of Justice: Legal Pioneers, Judicial Practices, and the Mobilization of Specialized Knowledge', Paper presented at LUISS, March 2017.

[44] In his PhD thesis (n. 40), Jos Hoevenaars explores 40 preliminary rulings lodged in the Netherlands between 2008 and 2012.

On the whole, this localized and context-rich approach allows us to demonstrate the probability that a 'social complaint' will end up being framed as an EU law issue. The picture of EU law that emerges from these micro-analyses carried out *at the fringes* of EU law is certainly very different from the one we have when looking at the core domains of EU law (competition, etc.). In these areas, the possibility of EU law issues appearing is rather unlikely. Given the extra time and extra cost involved for both lawyers and plaintiffs, NGOs and academics play a critical part in keeping EU litigation alive, by alerting when new opportunities or risks are seen. In national legal fields where legal actors are weakly socialized, or not exposed at all, to EU law, the fate of EU case law remains heavily dependent on EU legal entrepreneurs (EU lawyers, EU law academics, NGOs) who share a long-term interest and agenda regarding EU law, its cases, and its causes (e.g. asylum law, labour law). As they bring their support structure and legal expertise to bear, most often as *pro bono*, these repeat players are critical in the process of enrolling specific social claims and social groups into the EU judicial arena. In other words, only a complex and highly contingent 'cocktail' of individual entrepreneurship of the plaintiffs, personal commitment of their lawyers, as well as support from a variety of collectives (such as unions or an association of landowners, in particular those capable of financing the costs of the trial), is able to generate European litigation and counterbalance the structurally in-built indifference of national legal fields towards EU law. Thus, by using a microscope instead of macro perspectives and large-n databases, it becomes possible to provide new hypotheses regarding the connections (or absence thereof) between EU case law and European society.

B. The Effectuation of EU Case Law

Surely enough, such process tracing cannot stop at the doors of the CJEU. If one actually pursues this avenue of research, it will be necessary to look at the many hands that manipulate/frame the case before it is even seen by the judges. As we know, judges deliberate on the basis of a *projet de décision* which is presented to the chamber; amendments and rewriting only take place on this terrain. Far from being circumscribed into one 'critical moment' of decision, the production of judicial decision is a long thread to which 150 *référendaires*, the 600 and more lawyer-linguists, and the hundreds of lawyers and EU law scholars contribute.

As may be clear from the discussion earlier, the purpose is not here to go look for the 'femmes and hommes de l'ombre'[45] who really decide 'à la place des juges',

[45] Johansson, 'Les référendaires de la Cour de justice des Communautés européennes: Hommes et femmes de l'ombre', 3 *Revue des affaires européennes* (2008) 563.

as is often seen in the literature on CJEU *référendaires*.[46] Described as the 'legal Rasputins' of Europe, to paraphrase Judge Rehnquist's famous quote on US Supreme Court law clerks, *référendaires* are often granted an ('unduly') decisional role. This perspective, however, overlooks the fact that *référendaires* are equally (if not more) subject to the set of constraining relations and conventions that structure the long internal process of producing judgments in Luxembourg. As the first drafters of the *projets de décision*, they are actually particularly exposed to the weight of organizational routines in Luxembourg and the rigid writing formats and templates. This comes out clearly from the interviews undertaken by Karen McAuliffe with *référendaires*, who seem to feel a continuous pressure to cite previous judgments 'word-for-word' or even 'paragraph-for-paragraph'.[47] As another CJEU law clerk indicates: 'because we are writing in a foreign language, there is a tendency to do a lot of "cutting and pasting" and so the style (in which the CJEU's judgments are written) reproduces itself'. All in all, the judicial decision is not just 'this abstraction built by law' but is best understood as the outcome of a set of routines, practices, and '*micro-procédures*' that weigh on the *dossier* and shape its actual content.[48]

Here, the profound transformation of the Court of Justice during the six decades (and more) of its existence has to be taken into account. There is no denying the fact that 'the Court' that existed in 1952 (a quasi-aristocratic club of gentlemen assisted by half a dozen *référendaires* and sitting in the small Villa Vauban) has very little to do with the complex (and sometimes conflictual) organization of more than 2,000 employees that make up 'the Court' today. This is not the place to engage in a sociological study of the Court's organization (something that is still very much lacking[49]) that would document the centrifugal forces that challenge the capacity of 'the Court' to maintain a consistent jurisprudence: heterogeneity of the process and criteria of nomination across countries; the departure of the first generation of judges and *référendaires* in the 1970s; progressive waves of enlargement leading to a rapid increase in the number of judges and

[46] This is what Hubert Legal seemed to indicate when pointing at the fact that 'une bonne part du pouvoir réel d'élaboration des décisions du Tribunal est entre les mains des référendaires qui sont des collaborateurs des juges et sont de plus en plus jeunes depuis l'élargissement, frais émoulus des collèges européens et sans expérience juridictionnelle, administrative ou diplomatique' [an important part of the tribunal's power of decision-making lies in the hands of law clerks who are collaborators of the judges and who are younger and younger since the expansion, recently graduated from European universities with no prior jurisdictional, administrative or diplomatic experience]: Legal (n. 26). The best reference on the issue remains: Kenney, 'Beyond Principals and Agents. Seeing Courts as Organizations by Comparing Référendaires at the European Court of Justice and Law Clerks at the US Supreme Court', 33 *Comparative Political Studies* (2000) 593.

[47] McAuliffe, 'Hybrid Texts and Uniform Law? The Multilingual Case Law of the Court of Justice of the European Union', 24(1) *International Journal for the Semiotics of Law* (2011) 97.

[48] Latour (n. 28).

[49] See, however, M. C. Reale, 'Il tribunale di primo grado delle Comunità europee: un'analisi sociologico-giuridica' (1998) (PhD thesis on file at the EUI, Florence).

référendaires; the creation of a Court of First Instance, now General Court (1991); and the increasing turnover of *référendaires* who rarely stay more than three years.

More interesting to our purpose here is the reaction to these centrifugal forces and, in particular, the double movement towards rationalization and centralization of the court's judicial activities that has developed. It seems as if, in light of these risks, a rising concern for 'consistency' had emerged within the Court itself, leading to a variety of countermoves aimed at maintaining the *acquis jurisprudentiel* and entrenching it in the routines of the Court's organization and operating standards. Under the guise of 'centralization' (around the Court's presidential office), it is possible to identify old elements (the fact that the composition of the Court's chambers is decided by the President of the Court, or that the President chooses the *rapporteurs* case by case), or new elements seen since the Nice Treaty preparing the EC for enlargement (the institution of the *Grande Chambre* in which the President and Vice-president are the only two permanent members, with the other judges rotating; the creation in 2012 of the office of the Vice-president of the Court, the advisory committee auditioning candidates for CJEU judicial office, etc.).[50] Interesting empirical work by Christopher Krenn shows how, through the centralized allocation of positions as *juge-rapporteurs* at the *Grande Chambre*, a select group of judges has taken the lead in shaping EU case law. Looking closely at the case assignment practice during the years 2003 to 2015, which corresponds to the presidency of Vassilios Skouris, he is able to identify the existence of an 'elite-club' of *rapporteurs*. For example, Lenaerts has been *juge-rapporteur* in 145 cases, 'only two of which have been three-judge chamber decisions', while 'through the course of his ten year career at the ECJ from 2004 to 2014, Cypriot judge George Arestis has drafted the judicial opinion in only 6 Grand Chamber cases (0,6 cases/year)'.[51] Thus, the centralized organization of the CJEU has gone hand-in-hand with the formation of an elite group that has a particularly strong influence on structuring the court's jurisprudence.

Under the cap of 'rationalization', one can see the development of *vademecum* (1976), writing software, databases of cases, and vocational training[52] aimed at streamlining the production of judicial decisions (and their preparatory documents). We can also see the rise of new professional figures within the Court such as the lawyer-linguists and the *lecteurs d'arrêts*, who are in charge of avoiding 'defaults' in the process of fabricating judgments. In the end, the *délibéré* itself is deeply embedded in this thick network of specialists and of instruments that

[50] On all this, see Cohen, 'Judges or Hostages? Sitting at the Court of Justice of the European Union and the European Court of Human Rights', in B. Davies and F. Nicola (eds), *EU Law Stories. Contextual and Critical Histories of EU Jurisprudence* (2017) 58.

[51] C. Krenn, 'Legitimacy in the Making. The Procedural and Organizational Law of the European Court of Justice' (2017) (PhD thesis on file at Goethe University Frankfurt am Main) 203.

[52] Interestingly, Mathilde Cohen refers to the recent creation of vocational training at the ECJ aimed at socializing the new *référendaires* to the customs of the Court, to the 'langue du délibéré' (i.e. French), as well as to the usage of legal and case law databases: Cohen (n. 50).

continuously impinge on the dossier, progressively turning it into a 'decidable' EU law case for CJEU judges. In the absence of an ethnographical work studying the Court that opens up this 'black box' and explores it from close quarters, it remains difficult to move beyond a general working hypothesis. What appears clear, however, is that 'judicial decisions' at the CJEU are best understood as the outcome of a collective framing that goes all the way through from the filing of the case to its actual publication on the Court's website.

This requires the development of parallel investigations into the various social, political, administrative, and legal effects of CJEU decisions once they have been delivered. To be sure, ECJ raw judicial decisions have no intrinsic, immediate, and *erga omnes* effects on social and professional actors. The legal meaning and the political/social effects of a given decision are highly dependent on the ramifications of EU law and how that law is relayed among Member States. This starts within the Court itself, as early studies of the changing media attention given to CJEU decisions point to the role of the CJEU press unit in highlighting or ignoring cases. While case salience (here measured through media coverage) is very rare,[53] a CJEU press release strongly contributes to bringing a case out of anonymity.[54] This also leads to a consideration of the work of aggregation and solidification of CJEU case law that is continuously happening within the 'Court's world', at the core of its support groups and networks of cooperation.[55] More generally, however, this raises the question of how national social, political, economic, and bureaucratic actors take up, ignore, and compromise with the Court's decisions and make selective use of them in their daily practices. This is not the place to delve more deeply into what remains at this stage a research agenda. What is important here is to have identified the 'political role' of the Court at the intersection between input and output, between the socially selective structure of a request coming from civil society 'parties' (the narrowing down of social complaints into EU law claims) and the generation of an effective answer (from raw judicial decisions to effective 'jurisprudence').

4. Conclusion

After decades during which political scientists have accumulated large-n databases in order to identify the (intergovernmental or supranational) trends of the

[53] If we consider Julian Dederke's data, only 13.5% of court rulings (608 out of 4,357 court cases between 1997 and 2016) have been reported in a newspaper.

[54] Dederke, 'Media Attention Against all Odds or Politicization as Usual. Introducing Case Salience Data for CJEU Cases', Paper presented at iCourts, September 2018 (on file with the author).

[55] For a more complete argument on this, see Vauchez, 'EU Law Classics in the Making: Methodological Notes on *Grands arrêts* at the European Court of Justice', in B. Davies and F. Nicola (eds), *EU Law Stories. Contextual and Critical Histories of EU Jurisprudence* (2017) 21. See also Sadl and Madsen, 'A "Selfie" from Luxembourg: The Court of Justice and the Fabrication of the Pre-Accession Case-Law Dossiers', 22 *The Columbia Journal of European Law* (2016) 327.

Court, often failing to provide cumulative results, research interest is moving towards 'thick description' and methodologies that provide localized and fine-grained observation of EU law in action.[56] As we have attempted to exemplify here, this proves very promising. Not only because the local and contextual *détour* is the best antidote to teleological narratives of the 'rise and rise' of the Court; but also because it allows us to describe precisely *how* social interests, legal actors, and the CJEU are connected (or not) to one another. By articulating micro, meso, and macro levels of analysis, one escapes ontological discussions about the nature of the Court ('neoliberal', 'political', 'federal', etc.). Instead, the process-oriented approach allows a research strategy to measure empirically the connections (and absence thereof) between the Court and European society to be devised. While there is no denying the fact that the scope of EU legislation and case law is becoming ever greater, it would be misleading to consider that the CJEU concerns and affects all EU citizens and social groups equally, even though it is keen on appearing to be the 'court of the people'.[57]

[56] C. Geertz, 'Thick Description: Toward an Interpretive Theory of Culture', in *The Interpretation of Cultures: Selected Essays* (1973) 3. In a different sense, nevertheless see also Orford, 'In Praise of Description', 25(3) *Leiden Journal of International Law* (2012) 609.

[57] Schepel and Wesseling, 'The Legal Community: Judges, Lawyers, Officials and Clerks in the Writing of Europe', 3 *European Law Journal* (1997) 165.

3
Waiting for the Barbarians
Inside the Archives of the European Court of Justice

Fernanda G. Nicola

> All creatures come into the world bringing with them the memory of justice. 'But we live in a world of laws,' I said to my poor prisoner, 'a world of the second best. There is nothing we can do about that. We are fallen creatures. All we can do is uphold the laws, all of us, without allowing the memory of justice to fade.'
>
> J. M. Coetzee, *Waiting for the Barbarians*

1. Introduction

This chapter offers some methodological insights to those who wish to embark on a study of the archival history of the European Court of Justice (ECJ). The Court opened its archives after years of intense advocacy by researchers and, in particular, legal historians and sociologists against the scepticism of the administrative committee at the Court in charge of its historical records. After an assessment of the Court's archives in 2010 by French experts, with the encouragement of Dieter Schlenker—the director of the Historical Archives of the EU (HAEU) at the European University Institute (EUI) in Florence—in 2014, under the Skouris presidency[1], the Court decided to open the archives to the public.[2] In December 2015, the HAEU hosted the official inauguration of the historical archives of the ECJ, which created public access for its historical records going back to 1952. President Koen Lenaerts used this occasion to address the competing interests in balancing transparency and secrecy, including the fundamental protection of data privacy, stating that the Court's historical archives 'can only contribute to

[1] *The Court of Justice of the European Union under the Presidency of Vassilios Skouris (2003–2015)*, available at https://curia.europa.eu/jcms/upload/docs/application/pdf/2015-9611/actes-5Fdu-5Fcolloque-5F2015.pdf (accessed 23 September 2020).

[2] Decision concerning the deposit of the historical archives of the ECJ at the HAEU (EUI:2015:C 406:02).

Fernanda G. Nicola, *Waiting for the Barbarians: Inside the Archives of the European Court of Justice*. In: *New Legal Approaches to Studying the Court of Justice*. First edition. Edited by Claire Kilpatrick and Joanne Scott, Oxford University Press (2020). © Fernanda G. Nicola. DOI: 10.1093/oso/9780198871477.003.0004

society when they can be publicly accessed'.[3] In a similar vein, Mr Schlenker added '[s]tudents will be able to touch the legal history of Europe and find out how this law has been made step by step'.[4]

Well preserved in Villa Salviati on the hills of Florence, the HAEU holds the historical records of many of the EU institutions and even some of the personal archives of prominent civil servants, including some insightful oral histories of well-known European lawyers, scholars, and politicians. The HAEU is in a stunning location, and its administrative staff, mostly archivists fluent in many languages, do an exceptional job archiving and creating electronic records that are available to scholars throughout the world. Every two or three years the ECJ sends its historical files to the HAEU where they are digitalized before being stored in a secure cloud archive. If a researcher makes a request to the HAEU to consult the historical file of an ECJ judgment or *dossiers de procédure* the file goes back to the ECJ to be redacted before being sent to the researcher. This is done on a case-by-case basis. Consulting the historical files allows researchers to achieve a better understanding of the negotiation and moulding of EU law through adversarial processes before the Court and its interlocutors. This is in itself an exciting prospect for all social scientists interested in the history of the integration through law project.[5]

There is much at stake in such promise. The richness of archival material deposited in the HAEU will improve our understanding of the multilingual and transnational context of the Luxembourg court.[6] In looking inside the ECJ archives, lawyers will become more aware of their research methods and how to reconcile the evolution of history with law.

Rather than focusing on the role of cases in bringing about a necessary evolution in EU law, lawyers can learn from the open-endedness of the historical context and analyse how social, political, and economic circumstances influenced the actors involved in each case. The lawyers who begin this transformative voyage by looking inside the ECJ archives will experience the culture of the Court through the rich life of its *dossiers de procédure* that collect any written instructions by the President to the judges, the oral proceedings, and the briefs of the lawyers and all the other intervening parties in the litigation. The *dossiers de procédure* also prominently show the exchanges between the Registrar of the Court with the Member States, the Commission, and the Council, which are in continuous

[3] See *Opening of the historical archives of the European Court of Justice* (18 December 2015), available at https://www.eui.eu/Research/HistoricalArchivesOfEU/News/2015/12-17-Official-2Dopening-2Dof-2Dthe-2DEuropean-2DCourt-2Dof-2DJustices-2Dpapers (accessed 23 September 2020).

[4] Ibid.

[5] See Byberg, 'The History of the Integration through Law Project: Creating the Academic Expression of a Constitutional Legal Vision for Europe', 18 *German Law Journal* (2017) 1531.

[6] See McCauliffe, 'Behind the Scenes at the Court of Justice: Drafting EU Law Stories', in F. Nicola and B. Davies (eds), *EU Law Stories: Contextual and Critical Histories of European Jurisprudence* (2017) 35.

dialogue throughout a case. In opening a *dossier de procédure*, the researcher can trace the entire procedure of a judgment from its very beginnings, as it originated from a dispute in a Member State, to its development in Luxembourg through a back and forth between domestic and European legal actors. In the exchanges articulated among lawyers, judges, and civil servants at the Court, the legal procedures that mark the relatively autonomous discourse of EU law become palpable.[7] This judicial practice highlights the virtues and the shortcomings of domestic legal concepts deployed in solving legal disputes, and it shows the abundance of sources behind the case law including legal scholarship, newspaper articles, and international treaties relevant to the judicial deliberation.[8]

To those who wish to undertake such important research, the relevance, as well as the difficulty, of collaboration between lawyers and historians is not a novelty. In describing the encounter between lawyers and historians, Ben Palmer points to basic commonalities and differences.[9] Lawyers are used to researching and writing under strict deadlines, often mandated by the needs of their clients rather than purely research constraints, whereas the ability to find a private or public archive dictates the legal historian's timeline. Lawyers have conceptual and mental frameworks based on categories often narrated through rhetorical fictions that account for the evolution of legal doctrines.[10] Historians' central use of documents, gathered in the archives and woven through time and context, helps them to explain the internal or external evolution of law. Even though lawyers use legal categorization as a starting point rather than archival documentation, both lawyers and historians operate through legal narratives based on legal documents and, in part, driven by their own personal agenda. This process inevitably taints the type of legal history they will narrate by depicting a particular viewpoint in the legal struggle, similar to what the historians of *histoire croisée* have called a 'self-reflective process'.[11] In engaging with the 'hermeneutic of suspicion',[12] legal historians, just like lawyers, will have to grapple with the fact that law remains

[7] See F. Nicola and B. Davies, *EU Law Stories: Contextual and Critical Histories of European Jurisprudence* (2017) 11.

[8] See Schütze, '"Re-reading" *Dassonville*: meaning and understanding in the history of European law', 24 *European Law Journal* (2018) 376.

[9] See Palmer, 'The Historian and the Lawyer', 32 *American Bar Association Journal* (1946) 530, explaining that: 'Lawyers and historians face common problems: The analysis of documents and of evidence, the choice and arrangement of materials to make a convincing case. The lawyer's purpose is frankly partisan; the historian's, professedly impartial. But the layman, whether juror or reader of history, may be skeptical or unconvinced.'

[10] See A. Amsterdam and J. Bruner, *Minding the Law* (2000).

[11] See Werner and Zimmermann, 'Beyond Comparison: Histoire Croisée and the Challenge of Reflexivity', 45 *History & Theory* (2006) 30, explaining how this method includes 'selecting the object, meaning the categories of analysis and the relationships between researcher and object that can be generative of meaning'.

[12] See Kennedy, 'The Hermeutic of Suspicion in Contemporary American Legal Thought', 25 *Law Critique* (2014) 91.

indeterminate and that every actor in their story will attempt to exploit any 'wiggle room' available.

2. From Comparative Law to Legal History

Comparative lawyers engage in diachronic comparisons that use historical justifications to explain gaps, conflicts, and ambiguities in legal rules. For instance, the category of 'legal traditions' has widely influenced the Anglo-American study of comparative law.[13] In Mary Ann Glendon's work, legal traditions are a malleable category understood by comparative lawyers through their dynamic and pluralistic dimension.[14] In the words of John Henry Merryman, legal traditions point to 'a set of deeply rooted, historically conditioned attitudes about the nature of law, the role of law in the society and in the polity'.[15] From Harold Berman to James Gordley, scholars have relied on legal histories to map the secular and the religious boundaries of the Western legal tradition;[16] for example, how the medieval roots of European contract law led to the will theory in modern contract law.[17]

According to Michele Graziadei, legal history has freed comparative lawyers from the strict traditional boundaries by proving a critical understanding of their own legal system. As such, comparative legal methodology has led to the 're-orientation of legal historiography', focusing not only on legislative, but also judicial innovation in Italian scholarship.[18] In the same vein, legal historians have embraced research across legal traditions to achieve three different goals through a comparative approach. First, they explore the construction or fabrication of legal traditions; second, they aim to cast new light on those extra-legal sources critical to a legal system; and, finally, they avoid insularity through comparisons and cosmopolitan influences.[19]

Even though lawyers, especially those interested in comparative law, take legal history as a constitutive element of their discipline,[20] Mathias Reimann and Alain Lavasseur explained that comparativists tend to be mere and modest consumers

[13] See P. Glenn, *Legal Traditions of the World: Sustainable Diversity in Law* (2010).

[14] See M. A. Glendon, P. Carozza, and C. Picker, *Comparative Legal Traditions* (2007).

[15] See J. H. Merryman, *The Civil Law Tradition* (1994) 2.

[16] H. J. Berman, *Law and Revolution* (1983).

[17] See J. Gordley, *The Philosophical Origins of Modern Contract Doctrine* (1991).

[18] See Graziadei, 'Comparative Law, Legal History, and the Holistic Approach to Legal Cultures', 7 *Zeitschrift für Europäisches Privatrecht* (1999) 531.

[19] See A. Musson and C. Stebbings (eds), *Making Legal History: Approaches and Methodologies* (2012) 6.

[20] See Markesinis, 'Judicial Style and Judicial Reasoning in England', 59 *Cambridge Law Journal* (2000) 272. As Markesinis put it: 'The comparative lawyer must also have a different, double look: backwards and forwards . . . legal history in my view goes hand in hand with comparative law. For the past often explains what may otherwise be obscure in the present.'

of legal history.[21] This modest consumption is not only due to disciplinary and methodological challenges for lawyers, but also due to the difficulty of 'doing' comparative legal history.[22] Making legal history in a transnational or comparative setting requires not only a deep understanding of the evolution of at least two different legal systems, but also the careful research of sources through archival materials and new historiography in multiple languages.

For lawyers, re-conceptualization and re-categorizing is central to showing synchronic legal evolution especially across different legal systems in a new light.[23] The research of primary sources and archival materials is of relatively limited importance for mainstream comparative lawyers addressing how legal elites fostered legal transplants, for instance.[24] Their normative claims are crucial to their legal research; a lawyer footnotes her legal research to show her reliance on an epistemic community, while also recognizing the authority of other scholars. Rather than focusing on reconstructing the realities beyond her claims through original documents, what matters is the reconstruction of the discursive or adversarial context and the interpretative claims made by legal elites. This approach leads lawyers to spend less time with original sources or historical facts and encourages them to pay greater attention to categorizing, narrating stories, and persuading through legal rhetoric.[25]

For some historians, this normative exercise is something that can undermine the objectivity of the historical research, and even though the debate between history and social sciences goes back to the insights of Max Weber,[26] the research of the 'truth' still animates their quests. However, intellectual historians, who take a more normative position in selecting the multiplicity of possible 'intercrossings' among historical dimensions,[27] still have to ensure that their legal sources cover all of the bases so their narrative does not blend into mere personal preference or advocacy.[28] Historical data can be interpreted to lead in many different directions—it can display multiple narratives and it can be contradictory—but the meticulous work of the legal historian allows her to maintain the connection with the truth while deciding how to narrate it through her archival discoveries. Despite these efforts, the agents of historical reconstructions remain historically situated so that logical operations in the production of knowledge are

[21] See Levasseur and Reimann, 'Comparative Law and Legal History in the United States', 46 *American Journal of Comparative Law* (1998) 309.

[22] See Sir John Baker, *Reflections on 'Doing' Legal History* (2012).

[23] See Sacco, 'Legal Formant: A Dynamic Approach to Comparative Law', 39 *American Journal of Comparative Law* (1991) 1.

[24] See A. Watson, *Legal Transplants* (1970).

[25] See A. Amsterdam and J. Bruner, *Minding the Law* (2000).

[26] See M. Weber, *The Protestant Ethic and the Spirit of Capitalism* (1930).

[27] See Werner and Zimmermann (n. 11) 39.

[28] See S. Moyn, *Not Enough: Human Rights in an Unequal World* (2018).

continuously in tension with the 'historicity of both object and the approach produced by such knowledge'.[29]

Alfred Brophy has described the turn to history in law as 'applied legal history' or a self-conscious engagement of historians with the present.[30] In this vein, legal history has served to expose past injustices or to show alternative and often progressive intellectual legal traditions frequently obscured by the mainstream ideology.[31] In other cases, similar to the findings of European historians and sociologists, applied legal history served to challenge or destabilize the notion that the Treaty of Rome had provided an accepted and irreversible constitutionalization of the Community legal order. In reality, a constitutional practice casts new light on transnational resistances and the negotiations of EU law by professional networks of jurists, lawyers, and civil servants.[32] In many cases, the motivation behind this applied legal history is prompted by the desire to find an explanation, and possibly a solution, for a contemporary crisis; however, what is more valuable is learning how desirable legal change often came about through the mobilization of lawyers as well as civil society.[33]

3. The Significance of Opening the Court's Archives

Morten Rasmussen has given a passionate account of why being unable to gain access to the archives of the ECJ was a setback for legal historians who were committed to a better understanding of judicial deliberations. In limiting such access, a multiplicity of actors participating in the written or oral decision-making process in Luxembourg were rendered invisible:

> To make things worse the accessibility to public sources is currently restricted to the court judgment and the position of the Advocates General, whereas positions of the parties of the case and national governments are not made publicly available. Also the early practise of producing minutes of the oral presentation of the case seems to have been abandoned. Only a time-consuming visit to national or European archives can provide further documentation on the court cases of the ECJ.[34]

[29] Werner and Zimmermann (n. 11) 50.

[30] See Brophy, 'Introducing Applied Legal History', 31 *Law & History Review* (2013) 233.

[31] See L. Kalman, *The Strange Career of Legal Liberalism* (1996); S. Carle, *Defining the Struggle: National Racial Justice Organizing, 1880–1915* (2013).

[32] See A. Vauchez, *The Force of a Weak Field: Law and Lawyers in the Government of the European Union* (2008) 128.

[33] See T. Brown-Nagin, *The Courage to Dissent: Atlanta and the Long History of the Civil Rights Movement* (2011).

[34] Rasmussen, 'Law Meets History: Interpreting the Van Gend en Loos judgment', in F. Nicola and B. Davies (eds), *EU Law Stories: Contextual and Critical Histories of European Jurisprudence* (2017) 103.

In collaborating with the new legal historians,[35] I learned that European legal history of the early 1950s and 1960s clearly showed how EC law was riveted by political, financial, and rule of law crises. While today EU law has lost some of its appeal to US law students for different geopolitical and disciplinary reasons,[36] this discipline is also regaining momentum as an anti-model for democratic and constitutional integration due to its immigration policies and the spread of populism and illiberal democracies within the Union.[37] These changes go hand in hand with an increase in economic inequalities, xenophobia, and unemployment rates, especially in European peripheral regions.[38]

In the midst of these crises, European legal historians have contributed to a new historiography that has challenged the notion of an accepted and necessary constitutionalization of EU law.[39] Instead, they have shown that this was a contested constitutional practice spearheaded by some judges in Luxembourg while opposed by others.[40] Beyond the utopian ideal of the constitutionalization of European law, sociologists have shown that there were key personalities in the legal services of the Commission, such as Michel Gaudet, influenced by a US law professor, Eric Stein,[41] who together were the legal entrepreneurs advocating a federalist vision while actively fostering the creation of legal and professional European elites.[42] With the change of personnel at the ECJ in 1967, a Court composed of more integrationist and activist judges also triggered greater

[35] See Rasmussen, 'Constructing and Deconstructing European "Constitutional" European Law: Some Reflections on How to Study the History of European Law', in H. Koch *et al.* (eds), *Europe: The New Legal Realism* (2010) 639; B. Davies, *Resisting the European Court of Justice: West Germany's Confrontation with European Law 1949–1979* (2012); 14 *Journal of European Integration History* (Special Issue) (2008); 21 *Contemporary European History* (Special Issue) (2012); and 28 *American University International Law Review* (Special Issue) (2013).

[36] See Caruso, 'European Union Law in US Legal Academia', 11 *Tulane Journal of International and Comparative Law* (2011).

[37] See Scheppele and Pech, 'Illiberalism Within: Rule of Law Backsliding in the EU', 19 *Cambridge Yearbook of European Legal Studies* (2017) 3; Scheppele, 'Autocratic Legalism', 85 *University of Chicago Law Review* (2018) 545;W. Sadurski, *Poland's Constitutional Breakdown* (2019); Koncewicz, 'Understanding the Politics of Resentment: of the Principles, Institutions, Counter-Strategies, Normative Change, and the Habits of Heart', 26 *Indiana Journal of Global Legal Studies* (2019) 501.

[38] See Nicola, 'Another View of the Cathedral: What Does the Rule of Law Crisis Tell Us about Democratizing the EU?', 25 *Maastricht Journal of European and Comparative Law* (2018) 133.

[39] See Rasmussen, 'Revolutionizing European Law: A History of the *Van Gend en Loos* Judgment', 12 *International Journal of Constitutional Law* (2014) 136.

[40] See Rasmussen, 'Rewriting the History of European Public Law', 28 *American University International Law Review* (2013) 1187, at 1219.

[41] See Boerger, 'At the Cradle of Legal Scholarship on the European Union: The Life and Early Work of Eric Stein', 62 *American Journal of Comparative Law* (2014) 859.

[42] See A. Vauchez, *Brokering Europe: Euro-lawyers and the Making of a Transitional Polity* (2015); A. Vauchez and B. de Witte (eds), *Lawyering Europe: European Law as a Transnational Social Field* (2013).

national resistance at the Member State level in the 1970s.[43] While some social scientists have focused on the internal and doctrinal developments of law or legal institutions by tracing legal ideas back to some well-known activist judges,[44] others have paid more attention to how external factors have influenced legal change by assessing the reaction of civil society, national judges, and diplomats through media coverage in the Member States.[45]

Despite the early claim that the European Community was a constitutional supranational legal order, as stated by the ECJ in its famous *Les Verts* case,[46] the new legal historians have critically assessed the constitutionalization of the EC Treaty that happened much later.[47] Thus, when rewriting the legal history of the constitutionalization of Treaties, lawyers should pay renewed attention to the changing milieu and viewpoints, rather than just focusing on what the Court's rulings say without connecting this to a broader historical context.[48] In addressing the extra-legal methods used by lawyers, Justice Benjamin N. Cardozo explained how judges have to reconcile their logical and philosophical method with history, tradition, and sociology because 'history, in illuminating the past, illuminates the present, illuminates the future'.[49] Although researchers can be left feeling some scepticism, while being aware that the legal history might not add more legitimacy to EU law they should be prepared to cope with history, which, as Robert Gordon puts it, 'refuses to conform to our prejudices, jolts us out of accepted assumptions, and allows us to imagine a wide array of possible futures'.[50]

Through these new historical and sociological approaches to the European constitutional practice and role of legal elites in shaping EU law,[51] this literature has opened up new methodological avenues to approach the archival documents of the ECJ. These new approaches and methodologies in researching EU law make lawyers turn their attention from what historians have called 'what the law

[43] See Davies and Rasmussen, 'From International Law to a European Rechtgemenischaft: Towards a New History of European Law, 1950–1979', in J. Laursen (ed.), *Institutions and Dynamics of the European Community, 1973–1983* (2014) 97.

[44] See V. Fritz, *Juges et avocats généraux de la Cour de Justice de l'Union européenne (1952–1972)* (2018); V. Klostermann, *Une approche biographique de l'histoire d'une révolution juridique* (2018).

[45] See Davies (n. 35).

[46] Boerger and Rasmussen, 'Transforming European Law: The Establishment of the Constitutional Discourse from 1950 to 1993', 10 *European Constitutional Law Review* (2014) 199.

[47] See Boerger and Davies, 'Imagining the Course of European Law? *Parti Ecologiste "Les Verts" v. Parliament* as a Constitutional Milestone', in F. Nicola and B. Davies (eds), *EU Law Stories: Contextual and Critical Histories of European Jurisprudence* (2017).

[48] See Davies, 'Why EU Legal History Matters', 28 *American University International Law Review* (2013) 1337, at 1343 explaining that: 'Just because the ECJ says it has constitutionalized and federalized the Treaties does not make it so. Indeed the question as to whether the ECJ has managed to promote the federalization of Europe or whether this has been a high-profile failed attempt remains the impetus for most of the historical research being undertaken.'

[49] B. N. Cardozo, *The Nature of the Judicial Process* (1921).

[50] See R. Gordon, *Taming the Past: Essays on Law in History and History in Law* (2017) 360.

[51] See B. De Witte and A. Vauchez, *Negotiating Europe* (2013).

is' to 'how the law works', which means taking a closer look at 'legal outcomes', or distributive consequences, as well as 'how the law is perceived and received' differently according to each context.[52] Thanks to this new methodological turn, the archives of the ECJ represent a rich source of material that scholars, now well equipped with quantitative and qualitative research skills as well as critical legal history tools, should start exploring.

4. The ECJ Archival Challenge

Since July 2014, the ECJ has had an agreement to deposit documents in the HAEU. It was a memorable moment when, on 9 December 2015, in the presence of the President and the Registrar of the ECJ, the HAEU hosted the official opening of its archives in Florence. Immediately afterwards, the new legal historians funded by the Danish government organized a conference in conjunction with this event entitled *Towards a New History of European Public Law*. It became clear that historians had been waiting for years to unearth documents pertaining to European institutions in private, state, and European archives, with the goal of re-opening a debate around different interpretations of the role and nature of European institutions and European law. While there was a lot of promise and novelty in the research that the new legal historians and sociologists had undertaken since the early 2000s,[53] one shortcoming of their work was that it included very few pioneering female lawyers in the quest for a more textured and contextualized history of EC law featuring social networks and political turmoil.[54] It was therefore a fundamental step for lawyers to chart, together with legal historians and sociologists, what happened in the first decades of the ECJ's life and to look inside its archives to find out more about the judgments as well as the lawyers involved in each case.

Just like some of its Anglo-American counterparts, the HAEU aims to use new technology to catalogue and distribute files electronically with special scans, since each *dossier* is leather bound and needs extreme care in handling. This means that there is no paper access to the ECJ archives unless attending a conference or formal presentations given by HAEU archivists, where a couple of original decisions may be circulated to show the original signatures of the judges or the form of the *dossiers de procédure* of the cases. Before 1980, these were readily accessible only if someone else had already made a request to 'open' them so that they were 'ready' for the public.

[52] See Musson and Stebbings (n. 19) 5.

[53] Cohen, 'Ten Majestic Figures in Long Amaranth Robes: The Formation of the Court of Justice of the European Communities', 60 *Revue française de Science politique* (2010) 227.

[54] Kenney, 'The Judges of the Court of Justice of the European Communities', 5 *Columbia Journal of European Law* (1998) 101.

Otherwise, if the researcher was the first to request the opening of a *dossier*, it meant a delay of several months due to the time-consuming process of scanning all the documents and following the procedure established by the ECJ to redact the documents *ex post*. To open its archives more speedily, in contrast to what other EU institutions have done, the Court has sent its original files to the HAEU. Once the *dossiers de procédure* are digitalized, the Court redacts them, making sure that both its deliberations and the preliminary report in which the reporting judge makes the very first assessment of the case are redacted and not accessible for public consultation.

The Court's symbolic gesture of opening its archives was in line with the values of the Union and the provisions of open governance contained in the Treaty; however, the redaction of the *dossiers de procédure* contains no explanation as to what parts of the files were blacked out and why.[55] By censuring entire sections of the *dossiers ex post*, the Court has reduced the possibility of understanding the full nature of its cases while retaining the power to decide what it will or will not make open to the public. In becoming legal archivists, researchers will have to pay renewed attention to the private archives of jurists in their memoirs,[56] as well as to the archives accessible in the Member States to complement the ECJ archives.

Today, in the Court's archives there are two types of documents that are of interest to researchers: the *dossiers de procédure* open to the public up to the early 1980s due to the 30-year rule, and the ECJ *administrative archives*. Both types of documents could help prompt very important findings on the practice, acceptance, and resistance to the Court's jurisprudence, even though some of the constraints in accessing *dossiers de procédure* limit what researchers are able to reconstruct in their archival quest.

Unfortunately, the administrative archives are not available yet because they are still in the process of digitalization by the HAEU, after which the ECJ will approve the content. This collection includes the decisions and regulations that concern the Court, as well as information on the composition of its members. There is an abundance of information concerning the President of the Court, its cabinet, and the organization of the Court, including the exchanges between the various services inside the ECJ. Additionally, there are documents and reports of the Court's meetings with official delegations from other courts, bar associations, and civil servants from other international organizations. These materials could provide an important insider's view to understanding the hierarchies and

[55] See Art. 15 TFEU: 'In order to promote good governance and ensure the participation of civil society, the Union institutions, bodies, offices and agencies shall conduct their work as openly as possible.'

[56] See Becherucci, 'Gli Archivi dei Giuristi', 2 *Le Carte e la Storia* (2018).

functions of the Court's bureaucracy, as well as the judicial diplomacy and transnational networks created by its judges and staff outside Luxembourg.[57]

For these and other reasons, archival research might not live up to the promise lawyers were hoping for at the beginning of their quest. However, this only partially explains why researchers have not yet seriously raided the ECJ archives. In practice, what limits researchers on their archival search is that the Court is only opening its documents to the public subject to two major EU law constraints.[58] The first constraint is that the documents related to judicial proceedings have a 30-year wait period, calculated from the date the proceedings ended,[59] even though a recent Decision has created more flexibility on this period.[60] A second constraint arises from the fact that the Court's Statute protects the secrecy of its deliberations, so these are not publicly accessible; according to the President of the Court, this point is very much central to the Court's own identity.[61] When the secret deliberations are at stake, whether in their preliminary or final versions, the Court retains the power to 'blacken' or 'redact' the *dossiers de procédure* because 'under no circumstance shall access be given to documents relating to the secrecy of deliberation'.[62]

Finally, the Court is also bound to follow EU law when archival access could encroach upon the protection of individual and data privacy or commercial secrets.[63] Once the HAEU has digitalized the documents, the Court can redact and control the archival materials open to the public through administrative steps, including tracking procedures that list all those who have access to its archives, and there are delays due to the enormous amount of work necessary to prepare the sanitized electronic documents.[64]

However, the Court maintains discretion on whether to create more access to its archives without violating EU law in at least two instances. First, some important documents are not made available by the Court for public consultation, such as the French translations of all the documents used by the judges, since

[57] See Tatham, 'Off the Bench but Not off Duty: The Judicial Diplomacy of the Court of Justice', 22 *European Foreign Affairs Review* (2017) 303.

[58] Regulation 45/2001 of the European Parliament and of the Council of 18 December 2000, OJ 2001 L 8/1.

[59] See Art. 2, Decision of the Court of Justice of the European Union of 10 June 2014, OJ 2015 C 406/2, explaining that all original documents listed in the catalogue should become historical archives according to the classification plan of the catalogue that will be amended based on the decisions taken by the Administrative Committee.

[60] Ibid. Arts 2, 3.

[61] Ibid. Art. 4 (detailed rules on the opening to the public of the historical archives).

[62] Ibid. Art. 4(2).

[63] See *Historical Archives*, Court of Justice of the European Union, available at https://curia.europa.eu/jcms/jcms/P_184874/ (accessed 23 September 2020).

[64] See Council Regulation (EU) 2015/496 of 17 March 2015 amending Regulation (EEC, Euratom) No. 354/83 as regards the deposit of the historical archives of the institutions at the European University Institute in Florence, OJ 2015 L 79/1, para. 11: 'The institutions and EUI should, where possible, make the historical archives available to the public in digitised and digital form, so as to facilitate their consultation on the internet.'

French still remains the language of deliberation of the court. Even if the French translations are not technically part of the *dossiers de procédure*, they are crucial to the judge's interpretation of laws and these could shed light on the linguistic ability and sensibility needed to work successfully in a multilingual environment. Even if the Court might be fearful that the French translation of a hearing will reveal some mistake in the language used by the interpreter, this is nevertheless a historical document that should be accessible—especially 30 or even 50 years after the judgment. Finally, with the opening of cases that took place in the 1980s, more Greek, Spanish, and Portuguese cases will be available for consultation and the lack of the French translation will make the archives less accessible to researchers.

Equally relevant are the comparative or research notes and studies that judges use to decide which legal rule should prevail in each case and how this is similar or different in the Member States' legal systems. These comparative notes, prepared by the Research and Documentation department of the Court, are not prepared for each case decided. However, this department has established that these notes in the historic *dossiers* were part of the deliberation, because they were central to the reasoning of the judges, so these have also been blanked. This is a very stretched interpretation by a department of the ECJ of what should be considered 'a secret deliberation', which has prevented researchers from reading such comparative notes in order to shed light on the 'settled practice' of using comparative law in a unique transnational and multilingual decision-making setting.[65] Very recently, the Research and Documentation department has selectively opened some of its research notes and studies to the public with a sampling that goes back only to 2016, but shows a more positive attitude towards openness.[66] Opening the ECJ archives remains a work in progress and advocacy by researchers will be key to obtaining greater access.

5. The Life of a Case: The *Dossiers de Procédure* of Case C-6/64, *Costa v. ENEL*

The life cycle of a judgment becomes visible through the *dossier de procédure* that contains the various phases of the case before the Luxembourg Court. The *dossier* gathers the entire case brief, including the documents accessible to judges in the original language and the different briefs of the parties. This may result in a lengthy file, such as the file for *Costa v. ENEL*, decided on 15 July 1964—amounting to

[65] Lenaerts and Gutman, 'The Comparative Law Method and the European Court of Justice: Echoes Across the Atlantic', 64 *American Journal of Comparative Law* (2017) 841.

[66] See CJEU Judicial Network of the EU, Notes and Studies, available at https://curia.europa.eu/jcms/jcms/p1_2170124 (accessed 23 September 2020).

over 500 pages and hard to scroll electronically. The written procedures at the beginning of each case change depending on whether the case is a preliminary reference coming from a national court or results from an infringement procedure brought by the Commission against a Member State. Either way, the written procedure tends to be the first and longest part of the *dossier de procédure*, followed by the Instructions of the Court to the Member States or, if necessary, the Council or the Preparatory Inquiry by the Commission.

In the *Costa* file, following the written procedure there is the preliminary report that the judge submits as the very first summary of the case and a transcript of the public hearing that took place on 22 June 1964. Inevitably, the actors, including the lawyers, the judges, and the other civil servants involved in the life of the case, become much more real because the Registrar of the Court is continuously involved in maintaining the written records for the parties. These include domestic lawyers and foreign ministries of the Member States. The role of the President of the Court—in *Costa*, the well-known Robert Lecourt—emerges not only in the deliberation, but also through formal written requests for Advocate General Lagrange or the reporting judge to take on their respective tasks for the case at hand.

The Court in *Costa v. ENEL*, once again reinstated the doctrine of primacy in EU law, explaining in the most 'straightforward'[67] way the primacy doctrine, by which EU law overrides conflicting national laws as 'internal' primacy.[68] Just one year after the decision of *Van Gend en Loos* (*VGL*) in 1963 that established the direct effect of EU law, *Costa* is associated with *VGL* for its creation of a new legal order whereby Member States agreed to limit their sovereignty and Community law bestowed rights directly upon an individual. Yet in *VGL* the monistic Dutch legal order did not raise the question of a potential conflict between a domestic law and Community law, as happened with the Italian dualist legal regime. When the Milanese lawyer Flaminio Nicolino Costa, a lawyer, consumer, and shareholder of ENEL, refused to pay his electricity bill to the nationalized Italian energy company, the Giudice Conciliatore Vittorio Emanuele Fabbri, in an order of 16 January 1964, stayed the proceeding and referred the case to both the ECJ and the Italian Constitutional Court (ICC).[69] In holding that Mr Costa had never entered into a contract with ENEL, the order of the small claims tribunal of Milan asked the ECJ to assess whether the Italian law was in conflict with several provisions of the Rome Treaty and asked the ICC to assess its compatibility with Italian constitutional law. The boldness of this referral was striking in the aftermath of a prior failed attempt in 1963 by Flaminio Costa to bring the same

[67] See D. Chalmers and G. Monti, *European Union Law: Cases and Materials* (1998) 208.

[68] See De Witte, 'Direct Effect, Primacy and the Nature of the Legal Order', in G. De Búrca and P. Craig (eds), *The Evolution of EU Law* (2011) 329.

[69] See *Costa v. ENEL dossier*, Flaminio Costa's brief, 15 November 1963 (referring to Case 1907/63 from the small claims tribunal in Milan).

claim before the small claims tribunal in Milan, which had referred the case to the ICC while refusing to do the same regarding the ECJ.[70]

As it emerges from the *Costa dossier*, the ECJ was composed of President Andreas Donner and six judges: Charles-Leon Hammes, Rino Rossi, Alberto Trabucchi, Louis Delvaux, Walter Strauss and, lastly, the reporting judge (who was also the architect of the *VGL* victory), Judge Robert Lecourt.[71] Advocate General Maurice Lagrange replaced Karl Roemer through a procedural rule of the Court (Article 10 §1-2). By common agreement of the two Advocates General, President Donner approved this crucial replacement just a few days before the oral argument started in Luxembourg on 11 June 1964. On 25 June 1964, the opinion was delivered in French by Advocate General Lagrange, who was much more supportive of the European federalist vision than his German counterpart.[72]

While the entire *Costa dossier* is over 500 pages, mostly in the language of the case (Italian), the language of the secret deliberation we know must have been French, as were Advocate General Lagrange's conclusions and the report of the hearing by Judge Lecourt. The written observations begin with the order by the *Giudice Conciliatore* of Milan to suspend the case and remand preliminary questions to the ECJ and the Italian Constitutional Court. Subsequently, there are the files of each party that the tribunal in Milan transferred to Luxembourg. Here, however, a 60-page gap of redacted files simply states that 'the original files are not available to public consultation'. This redacted part of the *Costa dossier* is most probably the national file, which technically was not supposed to be archived by the ECJ in the first place. However, because this file is missing in the Italian national archives, the Court has finally allowed for *in loco* consultation without the possibility of making copies of the original *Costa dossier*. After making a preliminary request to consult the *Costa dossier* only on paper, the researcher must physically attend the HAEU. When I was given permission to consult the *Costa dossier* in paper form, I found some very important insights on the Italian political economy in the complete file. This was highly relevant to understanding the political economy considerations of the ENEL lawyers, who favoured the nationalization of electricity in Italy in order to create more equality between the production and distribution of energy in the North and South, and consequently creating economies of scale.

The *Costa dossier* contains the extensive brief, over 65 pages, on behalf of Mr Costa by the Italian professor and lawyer Gian Galeazzo Stendardi, who had

[70] See B. Nascinbene (ed.), *Costa-Enel: Corte Costituzionale e Corte di Giustizia a confronto, cinquant'anni dopo* (2015).

[71] See Phelan, 'The Revolutionary Doctrines of European Law and the Legal Philosophy of Robert Lecourt', 28 *European Journal of International Law* (2017) 935, at 954.

[72] See Lagrange, 'The Court of Justice as a Factor of European Integration, 15 *American Journal of Comparative Law* (1966) 709.

previously written about the relationship between the Italian and the Community legal order, arguing in favour of the primacy of Community law over Member State laws in the area of competence of Community law.[73] The depth and substance of Stendardi's brief makes him an effective 'Eurolawyer', able to address the incompatibility of Italian law 1243/63 nationalizing the production and distribution of electricity with the goals and specific anticompetitive provisions in the EEC Treaty.[74] Early on, Stendardi introduces his liberalizing rhetoric against the law nationalizing electrical production in Italy and stresses that this will exclude other Member States from such activity, while creating a new monopoly implicating discriminatory treatment and favourable tax advantages for ENEL at the expense of other European electrical companies.[75]

According to Stendardi, the underlying goal of the law was to destroy the free market economy and apply 'Marxist and Leninist principles', in sharp contrast with the goals of the internal market.[76] Professor Stendardi's intervention about the need to liberalize the Italian economy relies on the local courts to make sure to not push for unnecessary liberalization unless their 'judgments are more likely to be solicited at the right time and to be perceived as responsive to community needs'.[77] This methodological approach of focusing on the argumentative style and the local knowledge of the domestic court shows how the Stendardi brief was an important breakthrough.[78] However, this emerges from the archives together with the equally important briefs of the opponents deposited by the Italian government, in particular the brief by the ENEL lawyer Professor Massimo Severo Giannini, a towering figure in Italian administrative law and former student of the scholar Santi Romano.[79]

Another prominent jurist, Riccardo Monaco, a professor of international law in Rome and judge in the Consiglio di Stato, as well as a fervent opponent of the 'supranational' interpretation of the ECSC Treaty,[80] represented the Italian government and joined the Court as a judge just a few months later after the *Costa* judgment (from 1964 to 1976). The position of the Italian government presented by Monaco and Luciano Tracanna is rather slim, focusing on the procedural aspects addressing the inability of the Italian judge to both suspend the application of Italian law and to refer a case to Luxembourg outside the competence of the ECJ. Finally, they argued that the control of the compatibility of the Italian legislation within the Treaty falls under the scrutiny of the European Commission rather

[73] See G. G. Stendardi, *Il rapporto fra ordinamenti giuridici italiano e delle Comunita' europee* (1958).

[74] Vauchez, *Brokering Europe* (n. 42).

[75] Brief for Gian Galeazzo Stendardi, *Costa v. ENEL*, Case 6/64, (1963) 34.

[76] Ibid. 35–36.

[77] See Pavone, 'From Marx to Market: Lawyers, European Law, and the Contentious Transformation of the Port of Genoa', 53 *Law & Society Review* (2019) 851.

[78] See Arena, 'From an Unpaid Electricity Bill to the Primacy of EU Law: Gian Galeazzo Stendardi and the Making of *Costa v. ENEL*', 30 *European Journal of International Law* (2019) 1017.

[79] See S. Romano, *L'Ordinamento Giuridico* (1918).

[80] See Boerger and Rasmussen (n. 46).

than the Court.[81] In substance, they highlighted that the Italian law entailed a fundamental socio-economic intervention under article 43 of the Italian Constitution, which empowered the Italian government to reform public and essential services such as the distribution and production of electricity.[82]

As to the anticompetitive nature of the Italian nationalization, also at the core of Stendardi's brief, Monaco and Tracanna cited the brief of the ENEL lawyers. In his brief, Professor Giannini offered an in-depth analysis of the consequences and necessity of state control over electricity production to secure energy self-sufficiency as well as the political stability of the country. The brief of Giuseppe Marchesini, who was the Italian lawyer trained in the legal system and language from which the case had originated and chosen by the Legal Services of the Commission to argue a central case for European law, followed the same line.

Even though the Commission was not a party in the case at stake, the Legal Service, led by Michel Gaudet, was nevertheless very influential in shaping legal doctrines before the Court.[83] As it emerges in the *Costa dossier*, the significant role of Marchesini, speaking for the Commission rather than for the Italian government or one of the parties involved in the trial, created an important bridge between the Italian legal context and Community legal order. In his brief, Marchesini referred to the troubling ruling of the Italian Constitutional Court on 24 February 1964, that had dismissed, just a month earlier, the conflict presented by the *Giudice Conciliatore* of Milan and granted precedence to an Italian statute in conflict with Community law.[84]

In his key brief shaping the future of primacy for EU law, Marchesini contended that the Commission could not stay silent if the Italian ruling implied that the Treaty of Rome would not have superior authority over Italian ordinary law. Here, we find exactly the same functional reasons used by the ECJ in *VGL*, in that this would create negative consequences not only for a Member State and its population, but it would have repercussions on all Member States and in the entire Community legal system.[85] Such a notion takes full life in Will Phelan's article tracing the intellectual origins of Judge Robert Lecourt's judicial and scholarly work.[86]

Right before Advocate General Lagrange's opinion and the well-known ECJ ruling, the Court had expunged two files, each over 50 pages long, from the

[81] Costa *dossier*, Riccardo Monaco & Luciano Tracanna's brief, Memoria 20 May 1964, 8.

[82] Ibid. 8–9.

[83] Rasmussen, 'Establishing a Constitutional Practice of European Law: The History of the Legal Service of the European Executive, 1952–1965', 375 *Contemporary European History* (2012) 21; A. Vauchez, *L'Union par le droit: L'invention d'un programme institutionnel pour l'Europe* (2013); Bailleux, 'Michel Gaudet, a Law Entrepreneur: The Role of the Legal Service of the European Executives in the Invention of EC Law and the Birth of the Common Market Law Review', 50 *Common Market Law Review* (2013) 359; J. Bailleux, *Penser l'Europe par le droit* (2014).

[84] *Costa dossier*, Memoria of the EEC Commission by Agent Giuseppe Marchesini, 5.

[85] Ibid. 5.

[86] Phelan (n. 71) 954.

dossier de procédure. One can only assume that these are the files pertaining to the deliberations, possibly the French translations of some of the documents, and, finally, the research notes prepared by the ECJ experts on comparative matters.

6. Looking Inside: Tracing the UK Resistance to Europeanization

The UK, under Prime Minister Harold Wilson, twice applied for membership of the European Economic Community (EEC), in 1961 and 1967. Both applications failed due to French President Charles de Gaulle's veto. Eventually, in 1973, Prime Minister and Conservative Party leader Edward Heath brought the UK into the EEC with the strong support of the Confederation of British Industry. However, since the early 1960s the possibility that the UK would join the ECC had created both legal and political concerns. The fear of a clash between the different legal cultures of a common law country such as the UK and the six founding Members of the Community was a source of concern for two main reasons. First, there was the fear that Community law would displace the Westminster-style parliamentary sovereignty based on a constant dialogue between courts and parliament rather than a higher law constitutional regime. Second, common law lawyers retained both stylistic and legal reasoning differences in judicial law-making when compared to civil law lawyers, including the binding use of precedents, *stare decisis*, the wide use of facts, an open engagement with policy considerations, and a long commitment to plain meaning interpretation of statutes.[87]

This Section shows how the opening of three *dossiers de procédure* in early cases involving the UK litigating before the ECJ highlights the legal resistance to reception of European law by the UK.[88] These dossiers include the first infringement procedure against the UK (*Commission v. United Kingdom*), the first preliminary reference from the UK to the ECJ (*Van Duyn*), and an equal pay case that is a preliminary reference from Belgium in which the UK government intervenes as a Member State (*Defrenne II*). In all these cases, the *dossiers* show how British lawyers and politicians alike were learning to present their arguments in Luxembourg and that they needed to transform their factual arguments regarding their scepticism about European harmonization or the crushing costs of the new European legal order into more or less successful legal arguments before the ECJ.

[87] See McCrudden, 'Using Comparative Reasoning in Human Rights Adjudication: The Court of Justice of the European Union and the European Court of Human Rights Compared', 15 *Cambridge Yearbook of European Legal Studies* (2013) 64.

[88] See Nicola, 'The Luxembourg Style With or Without the UK', 40 *Fordham International Law Journal* (2017) 1505.

A. Commission v. United Kingdom (1979)

The legal fiction of maintaining traditional parliamentary sovereignty in statutes while opening the British legal system to Community law was central for the purpose of the UK's accession to the EEC in 1973. The early legal resistance of the UK government, controlled by the Labour party, against Brussels was to consider that European regulations were not always binding law in the UK. The first infringement procedure was initiated by the Commission against the UK in 1978. The UK government, in support of labour union interests, expressly denounced a transport safety regulation adopted by the previous government that burdened lorry drivers with unnecessary and expensive safety features. In the *dossier de procédure* from the exchanges between the Commission and the UK's permanent representative, it emerges that both industry and unions were opposed to the implementation of Council Regulation 1463/70 on the introduction of recording equipment to road transport.

Although the UK government argued that there were no detrimental effects of such non-implementation on other Member States, the Commission set out in its reasoned opinion the fact that the UK was in violation of the Treaty and needed therefore to implement the regulation.[89] In response, the UK representative explained that to introduce this regulation would create 'serious industrial dislocation in many sectors of the economy', create 'unacceptable wage demands without offsetting gains in productivity', and, finally, fuel 'the continuing and deep-seated resistance from many parts of the industry'.[90]

In the *dossier*, there are several newspaper articles set out in annexes, including one featuring Labour Secretary of State for Transport William Rodgers, who openly stated that Community harmonization provisions were not binding on the UK since these were not laws adopted by Parliament.[91] Not surprisingly, the ECJ judgment reiterated the prohibition on a Member State applying Community law in an incomplete or selective manner, thereby effectively annulling the aspects of Community legislation it opposed or deemed contrary to national interests.[92] The Court further noted that even implementation difficulties or the distributive economic implication of the regulation could not preclude a Member State from fulfilling its obligation.[93]

The Court fuelled the UK resistance against the harmonization of a measure that was supported neither by the industry, nor by the labour unions, by holding

[89] See Letter by UK Office of the Permanent Representative to Emile Noel, Secretary General of the Commission (10 January 1978) 3.

[90] See Letter by UK Office of the Permanent Representative to Emile Noel, Secretary General of the Commission (14 April 1978) 2.

[91] See Case C-128/78, *Commission v. United Kingdom* (EU:C:1979:32) (or '*Tachographs*'), *Dossier de Procédure* (1979).

[92] Ibid. 11–12. [93] Ibid. 12.

that a unilateral Member State's failure in the duty of cooperation undermined the Community legal order.[94] However, in light of the media and political reactions included in the *dossier de procédure*, the ECJ decision appears much less severe when taking into account the serious challenges launched by the British politicians to the Community legal order.

B. Van Duyn (1974)

Van Duyn is a key case in the evolution of the direct effect doctrine of EU directives but it was also the first preliminary reference from the UK to the ECJ in 1974.[95] Once again, a case decided under the Presidency of Robert Lecourt, who held this position from 1967 until 1978, became a landmark decision during the Court's foundational period.[96] As legal historians showed, the Lecourt Court more often than not followed the legal arguments articulated by the Commission's legal service.[97] The plaintiff—Ms Van Duyn, a Dutch national and a practicing Scientologist—arrived at Gatwick Airport in England on 9 May 1973, with the intention of accepting an offer of employment as a secretary of the Church of Scientology of California established at Saint Hill Manor, East Grinstead College in Sussex, England. On the same day, however, Ms Van Duyn, after being interviewed by the immigration officer about the scope of her travel and her previous affiliation with the Church of Scientology, had to return to the Netherlands. When questioned by Mr Parselle, the British lawyer of Ms Van Duyn, the Treasury solicitor first questioned the direct applicability of Directive 1612/68 and then justified the behaviour of the UK immigration officer who handed the plaintiff a document which stated that her request for leave to enter the UK to take employment with the Church of Scientology had been denied because of public policy considerations. In relying on the policy announced in 1968 by the Minister of Health in the House of Commons, it was 'undesirable to give anyone leave to enter the United Kingdom on the business of or in the employment of that organization'.[98]

The Treasury solicitor asserted that even though Article 48 of the Treaty establishing the European Economic Community conferred the right of free movement of workers, the UK relied on its public policy exception, arguing that the activities of the Church of Scientology stood contrary to British public

[94] Ibid. 13. [95] Case C-41/74, *Van Duyn v. Home Office* (EU:C:1974:133).

[96] See W. Phelan, *Great Judgments of the European Court of Justice. Rethinking the Landmark Decisions of the Foundational Period* (2019).

[97] See Boerger and Rasmussen (n. 46).

[98] High Court of Justice, Chancery Division *Yvonne Van Duyn v. Home Office*, 1 March 1974, p. 1353.

policy.[99] Thus, even if Council Directive 64/221 was directly applicable there was a legitimate basis for refusal of leave of entry according to its Article 3(1) stating that 'measures taken on grounds of public policy or public security shall be based exclusively on the personal conduct of the person concerned'.[100] Because the implementing directive offered little guidance as to what falls under the concept of public policy, the national governments were given the option to determine such concept.[101] The Treasury solicitor alleged that there must be some element of discrimination by a state in favour of its own nationals so far as entry into its borders was concerned. For example, a Member State would be justified in refusing to admit a:

> . . . drug addict who is a national of another State even though it would be obliged to admit a drug addict who was one of its own nationals.[102]

This argument, based on distrust of foreigners taking jobs in the UK in what seemed more like a cult than a religious organization, was deeply rooted in stereotypes, which were publicly shared by the Ministry of Health's policy referring to Scientology as 'the world's largest mental health institution' and 'a pseudo-philosophical cult'.[103] The UK argument, interpreting the public policy exception broadly, was based on the argument that the UK government maintained full discretion on immigration policies so that domestic officials could refuse leave to enter the country due to the fact that the Secretary of State considered it 'undesirable' to have someone who was associated with Scientology, even merely by working for them, coming into Britain.[104]

The plaintiff's solicitor, Mr Steven Bird, in his brief to the ECJ asserted that Article 48 of the Treaty of Rome, subject to limitations on the grounds of public policy, allowed the plaintiff, due to the direct effect of the Treaty, to accept offers

[99] Transcript of the shorthand Notes of Marten, Meredith & Co., Case C-41/74, *Van Duyn v. Home Office* (1974), at 11.

[100] Council Directive 64/221.

[101] Ibid., explaining that: 'It would be of little practical use to compile a list of diseases and disabilities which might endanger public health, public policy, or public security, and it would be difficult to make such a list exhaustive. Whereas, it is sufficient to classify such diseases and disabilities in groups.'

[102] Statement of facts submitted by Treasury Solicitor of Mathew Parker Street on Behalf of the United Kingdom, Case C-41/74, *Van Duyn v. Home Office* (1974), at 11.

[103] *Scientology Written Answer 1*, 25 July 1968, available at https://api.parliament.uk/historic-hansard/written-answers/1968/jul/25/scientology (accessed 23 September 2020), explaining that: 'The government [is] satisfied having reviewed all the available evidence that scientology is socially harmful. It alienates members of families from each other and attributes squalid and disgraceful motives to all who oppose it; its authoritarian principles and practice are a potential menace to the personality and well-being of those so deluded as to become its followers; above all its methods can be a serious dangers. There is evidence that children are now being indoctrinated.'

[104] Transcript of the shorthand Notes of Marten, Meredith & Co., Case C-41/74, *Van Duyn v. Home Office* (1974), at 1–2.

of employment and move freely within the territory of the Member States for this purpose.[105] In addition, Article 3 of Directive 64/221 provided that measures taken on the grounds of public policy shall be based exclusively on 'the personal conduct of the individual concerned'.[106] The prohibition from entering the UK was not based exclusively or at all on the plaintiff's personal conduct, but on a general government policy not to admit into the UK Scientology workers and students who were foreign nationals.[107]

Mr Bird reasoned that Ms Van Duyn was 'blameless' in seeking to enter the UK in order to work 'for an organization in whose employment the nationals of the Member States are perfectly free to engage. It assumes that the Member State adopts a double standard; one for its own nationals and one for nationals of other Member States'.[108] To put it bluntly, the argument was that the Member State can chose to either ban everyone associated with Scientology, including UK citizens, or to allow both foreigners and British citizens to work for the same organization.

Thus, the main contention between the parties was about the meaning to be attributed to 'personal conduct' introduced by the Treaty in Article 48(3) and Article 3 of Directive 64/221. While the UK government and Advocate General Henri Mayras characterized the facts according to the public policy exception, saying that the mere association of Ms Van Duyn with Scientology was considered 'socially harmful', the Commission took a radically different path, following Mr Bird's anti-discrimination narrative. The Commission's legal services brief authored by Anthony McClellan first carefully reconstructs the judicial precedents and the teleological interpretation of the ECJ noting that:

> No legal restrictions are placed upon the practice of Scientology in the United Kingdom nor upon British nationals (with certain immaterial exceptions) wishing to become members of or take employment with the said Church of Scientology of California.[109]

Mr McClellan follows the anti-discrimination narrative put forward by the plaintiff's brief, arguing that the case was not about the distinction in entry for nationals of one Member State versus another for certain illegal activities, but rather that UK nationals were allowed to be employed by the Church of Scientology whereas foreign nationals were prohibited from the same opportunity. This opened the door to a clear anti-discrimination violation based on nationality of the free movement of workers in Article 48 of the Rome Treaty and its implementing directives.

[105] Plaintiff's Statement of Claim, Case C-41/74, *Van Duyn v. Home Office* (1974), at para. 5.

[106] Ibid. para. 5. [107] Ibid. para. 8.

[108] Written Observations by Yvonne Van Duyn the Plaintiff in the main action before the Court of Justice of the European Communities, Case C-41/74, *Van Duyn v. Home Office* (1974), at 13.

[109] Commission's Submission, Case C-41/74, *Van Duyn v. Home Office* (1974), at 3.

When turning to the public policy exception, Mr McClellan highlighted that it was essential to 'achieve the fundamental principle of the fundamental freedom of movement of workers'[110] to put nationals of Member States on an 'equal footing' with foreign nationals.[111] He noted that public policy must be 'restrictively interpreted'[112] since only 'personal conduct' was at the basis for invoking public policy as a concept of Community law and therefore its content should be interpreted in the context of EC law while the 'national criteria are only relevant in its application'.[113]

Finally, Mr McClellan suggested possible disastrous consequences of Member States setting their own interpretations of public order such as 'the principle of freedom of movement being emptied of all meaning'.[114] The Commission went on to say that '[p]ersonal conduct which is acceptable when exercised by a national of one Member State cannot, in that State, be unacceptable, under Community law, when exercised by a national of another Member State'.[115]

It goes without saying that the Court, under the guidance of reporting judge Max Sørensen, the first Danish judge at the ECJ, followed the Commission in upholding the direct effect of directives as well as the powerful non-discrimination rhetoric for the free movement of workers of the Community. Under the Presidency of Lecourt the teleological interpretation elevated individual rights while reasserting equality among Member States in a way that suppressed local resistances and required a narrow interpretation of the public policy exception.[116] This interpretation not only strengthened the rights of individuals protected by direct effect but also prevented Member States from unilaterally undermining EC law and its uniform interpretation.[117]

C. Defrenne II

The *dossier de procedure* of *Defrenne II* brings to life the case of Gabrielle Defrenne, the flight attendant who sued the Belgian airline company Sabena for forcing her, but not her male counterparts, to retire at the age of 40.[118] This discriminatory treatment clearly violated Article 119 EEC, which mandates that women should receive equal pay for equal work. The first document of the *Defrenne II dossier* in its written observations includes an International Labour Organization (ILO) Report from its 60th session in 1975 on the equality of remuneration with numerous annexes of social statistics. This long document shows the relevance of the ILO Convention no. 100 and its recommendation no.

[110] Ibid. 13. [111] Ibid. 13. [112] Ibid. 13. [113] Ibid. 13–14. [114] Ibid. 14.
[115] Ibid. 14. [116] See Phelan (n. 71).
[117] Case C-41/74, *Van Duyn v. Home Office*, judgment (1974), at 1350.
[118] Case C-43/75, *Defrenne II* (EU:C:1976:56).

90 on equal pay, which takes up much space in the *dossier*, together with information showing the relevance of the social and economic context for the Member States. There are also written observations by the UK and the Irish governments that emerge extensively in the opinion of Advocate General Alberto Trabucchi and in the report of the hearing by the reporting judge, Pierre Pescatore.

In examining the scope of Article 119 EEC, Advocate General Trabucchi not only refers to the ILO Convention, but also the broader goal, according to the *traveaux preparatoires* of the Rome Treaty,[119] of eliminating social dumping because of the possibility of employing women at lower cost than men and thus preventing the distortion of competition in the internal market.[120] In answering the objections of the UK and Irish governments that the non-discrimination provision was only applicable against the Member States and not private parties, Trabucchi highlights that this would go against the principles of Community law elaborated by at least 20 years of ECJ jurisprudence.[121] The Advocate General explains that if the provision did not have direct effect towards public, private employers, and collective bargaining organizations, the realization of the fundamental objective of the Treaties would be severely undermined.[122]

The arguments put forward by the UK and Irish governments, as they appear in their rebuttals, stressed that there would be very high direct costs in implementing the equal pay provisions in the private sector, especially if these were to apply retroactively. Even though both the UK and Ireland maintained that the direct applicability was going to burden private industry and increase inflation, each government produced an estimated increase of labour costs of only 3 per cent for the UK and 5 per cent for Ireland.

Advocate General Trabucchi dismissed the economic arguments about the distributive consequences of the direct effect of equal pay for equal work in the private sector, as external to the legal argument. He instead cited an ECJ ruling dismissing this financial implication raised by Germany.[123] The brief by Marie-Thérèse Cuvelliez, who was one of the two legendary Eurolawyers in *Defrenne* and was co-counsel with Eliane Vogel-Polsky for the plaintiff, rejected the economic argument made by the UK and Ireland. Using the Commission's report on the employment of women in Ireland, the UK, and Denmark, she showed how Denmark had implemented the principle of equal pay for equal work without endangering its economy.[124]

President Robert Lecourt, with Pescatore as rapporteur and Judges O'Keeffe, Donner, Martens de Wilmars, Sørensen and Kutscher for the Court, upheld the direct effect of Article 119 against private employers. However, the Court's

[119] See Miettinen and Kettune, 'Travaux to the EU Treaties: Preparatory Work as a Source of EU Law', 17 *Cambridge Yearbook of European Legal Studies* (2015) 145.

[120] See Opinion of AG Trabucchi in *Defrenne II*, at 5.

[121] Ibid. 12.

[122] Ibid. 14.

[123] Ibid. 21.

[124] Seconde Memoire pour Mademoiselle Defrenne par Marie-Thérèse Cuvelliez.

compromise on the distributive consequences highlighted by the Irish and UK governments was to establish the retroactivity of the equal pay principle from the date of the judgment, 1976 rather than 1962.[125] We cannot tell from the *dossiers* what made the ECJ depart from Advocate General Trabucchi's position and give more weight than expected to the distributive arguments put forward by the UK and Irish governments. On this outcome, Eliane Vogel-Polsky, whose client had been unfavourably impacted by the decision, commented: 'C'est en réalité un arrêt totalement politique, pris sous la pression très forte de la Grande-Bretagne. Mais je suis restée amère',[126] denouncing a totally political ruling made under pressure from the UK, which left her resentful.

What emerges from the *Defrenne dossier* is the influence of the brief of the intervening Member States, the UK and Irish governments, in the ECJ ruling. Clearly, the Court was reluctant to increase the resentment of two newly acceded governments so that what appeared to be a victory for Community law was also a great loss for Gabrielle Defrenne.

7. Who are the Barbarians?

> The Empire does not require that its servants love each other, merely that they perform their duty.
>
> J. M. Coetzee, Waiting for the Barbarians

All European institutions have and manage their own archives that are relevant to their own institutional practice and witness their life cycle. These archives also follow the 30-year rule, after which the institutions should open their files for consultation to the public. in Regulation 2015/86 the Council established the deposit of the EU's historical archives in the single location of the EUI in Florence with the purpose of making documents available for public consultation on-site after the expiry period of 30 years.[127] The Regulation also makes clear that the HAEU are not the exclusive archives for the documentation of EU institutions; each may maintain their own historical archives in addition and each remains responsible for opening them to the public.[128] However, the Council Regulation creates an exception for two institutions that, due to the 'specific nature of the activities of the [ECJ] and the European Central Bank (ECB) justifies their

[125] *Defrenne II*, paras 72–74; see also Sharpston, 'The Shock Troops Arrive in Force: Horizontal Direct Effect of a Treaty Provision and Temporal Limitation of Judgments Join the Armoury of EC law', in M. Poiares Maduro and L. Azoulai (eds), *The Past and Future of EU Law: The Classics of EU Law Revisited on the 50th Anniversary of the Rome Treaty* (2010) 251.

[126] E. Gubin, *Éliane Vogel-Polsky: Une Femme de Conviction* (2007).

[127] See Council Regulation 2015/496 of 17 March 2015, OJ 2015 L 79/1.

[128] Ibid. para. 9 of the Preamble.

exclusion from the obligation set out in this Regulation to deposit their historical archives at the EUI. The ECJ and the ECB may deposit their historical archives at the EUI on a voluntary basis'.[129] The Court has taken this voluntary commitment very seriously, as evidenced by its decision to move its archives to the EUI in Florence, beginning in 2014. However, through the Regulation and its subsequent Decision, the ECJ maintains broad discretion over access to its documents and places upon itself the huge bureaucratic burden of regulating what type of documents will be released to the public.

A. Overcoming the Redactions in the Dossiers de Procédure

The procedure for accessing the ECJ archives appears on the website of the HAEU.[130] It requires a written request by email to the HAEU archivists, who will coordinate with the staff of the Court of Justice in Luxembourg to process the request. Once the request has been accepted by the HAEU, the archivists who have possession of the paper documents create the electronic files. Next, the Court will redact the file according to its procedure, taking into consideration the hard law on the protection of individual and data privacy, commercial and trade secrets or *secrets d'affaires*, and of course the secret deliberations of the judges, which cannot be revealed according to the Statute of the Court. After several months, the HAEU archivists will send the *dossier de procédure* redacted by the Court back to the researchers.

Despite the 30-year rule, the Court justifies redacting the *dossiers de procédure* to protect its secret deliberations. This is in conformity with one of the Court's most important rules, found in Article 35 of its Statute, by which '[t]he deliberations of the [ECJ] shall be and shall remain secret'.[131] In the same vein, the oaths before the Court by the judges and the Registrar all reflect a central practice 'to perform his duties impartially and conscientiously and to preserve the secrecy of the deliberations of the [ECJ]'.[132] The secret deliberation remains part of the core identity of the ECJ, which takes pride in its collegial decision-making process. Certainly, during the deliberative process judges can change their minds while maintaining their anonymity so that their views are not traceable directly back to them, thus preventing their reappointment as a form of retaliation by a Member States after their five-year term.[133] When judges reach an agreement during their secret deliberations,

[129] Ibid. para. 10 of the Preamble.

[130] See Cour de justice de l'Union européenne, CLEU, available at https://archives.eui.eu/en/fonds/230050?item=CJUE (accessed 23 September 2020).

[131] See Statute of the Court of Justice of the EU, available at https://curia.europa.eu/jcms/upload/docs/application/pdf/2016-9608/tra-2Ddoc-2Den-2Ddiv-2Dc-2D0000-2D2016-2D201606984-2D05-5F00.pdf (accessed 23 September 2020).

[132] See Arts 2 and 10 of the Statute of the Court of Justice.

[133] See Dunoff and Pollack, 'The Judicial Trilemma', 111 *American Journal of International Law* (2017) 225.

these become part of the judgments. However, due to the nature of the compromise behind the deliberation, the decisions remain vague and legal arguments might remain opaque to an external audience. In this respect, scholars have asked for more transparency in the reasoning of the Court because the judgment is often hard to reconcile with a clear adversarial process and clear legal reasoning on the part of the judges. Not surprisingly, many European judges publish in scholarly journals and engage in conversations with the scholarly community to clarify the interpretation and the evolution of the Court's jurisprudence.[134]

The fact that judge's deliberations should remain secret due to the potential for judges to change their minds after hearing the arguments and explanations is a powerful notion that gives further freedom to judges to change their minds through a deliberative process. In fact, the deliberation is something that even US Supreme Court justices will not reveal because they want to maintain the freedom to discuss, deliberate, and ultimately, change their views. This is one of the most precious moments of judicial deliberation that have shaped some of the hard cases in the history of the US Supreme Court. For example, in *Casey*,[135] Justice O'Connor sided with the liberal justices not to overturn the well-known abortion case *Roe v. Wade*. In amplifying the rule of law,[136] Justice Roberts in *NFIB v. Sebelius* wrote what appeared to be an incoherent opinion because, in changing his mind, what was supposed to be a dissent ended up becoming the majority opinion upholding a portion of the Affordable Care Act.[137]

The secrecy of the deliberation is clearly present in the *dossiers de procédure* when, after the oral procedure by the reporting judge and before the opinion of the Advocate General, there are large redactions accompanied by the text: 'the original files are not available for public consultation'. These might be referring to the secret deliberation even though the researcher is given no explanation as to what part of the *dossier de procédure* was expunged. If we think more like historians rather than lawyers, one should ask whether the secret deliberations should be accessible perhaps after 40 or even 50 years from now.

Should the deliberations be destroyed, or should they be preserved to show what type of deliberations our ancestors were capable of so that the next generation will make sense of the compromises that informed the creation of fundamental EU Law doctrines?[138] Even in *Van Gend en Loos*, Paolo Gori, the former *référendaire* of Alberto Trabucchi, has openly explained the positions of

[134] See Lenaerts, 'La vie après l'avis: Exploring the principle of mutual (yet not blind) trust', 54 *Common Market Law Review* (2017) 805.

[135] See *Planned Parenthood of Southeastern Pa. v. Casey*, 505 U.S. 833 (1992).

[136] See Minow, 'Affordable Convergence: "Reasonable Interpretation" and the Affordable Care Act', 126 *Harvard Law Review* (2011) 117.

[137] See *NFIB v. Sebelius*, 567 US 519 (2012).

[138] Phelan (n. 71) 942: in this respect, the question posed by Will Phelan finds some answers in the richness of actors and positions emerging from the dossiers: 'The more challenging question, then, is why the European states, the national courts, firms, private lawyers and legal academia came to accept

the judges in that case.[139] In this sense the underlying commitment of archivists is to preserve historic documents and memories of human beings who we can see coming 'alive again' when walking in the corridors of the Villa Salviati archives.[140]

Finally, if the redacted parts of the *dossiers de procédure* actually do contain the secret deliberation, or any other part that the Court has redacted because of individual and data privacy as well as trade secrets,[141] it would be simple to say so. Certainly, this explanation might create more delays for the archives in making the redacted documents accessible to the public, but it would be very helpful to understand the flow of a case. For instance, in the *Costa dossier*, the file pertaining to ENEL industrial policy and the Italian government briefs in support of the nationalization and distribution of electric energy were missing. Similarly, in *Defrenne II*, the brief from the Belgian Sabena airline (liquidated in 2001) is not available in the *dossier de procédure*. Even though I can speculate that in both cases, the missing parts pertain to the national files, the HAEU should at least refer to what the Court has redacted in the *dossiers de procédure*.

B. The Archivist's Double Bind and the Missing Information in the Archives

The archivists at the HAEU in Florence are caught in a double bind because they receive two conflicting messages that put them in an awkward position. On the one hand, archivists want to give more access to researchers and scholars, whom they wish to attract to their premises or online as their primary consumers. On the other hand, archivists have to abide by the access requirements and procedures of consultation created by the ECJ that trusts them with some of the documents revealing the inner soul of one of the EU's most powerful institutions.

The goal of Council Regulation 2015/496 was to promote public access to the historical archives of the EU institutions to increase transparency and stimulate research on these institutions. Because of the prestige of the EUI, the regulation expressly mentions the advantages of centralizing the EU archives in one

these new doctrines when the compatibility of these with their own self-interests appears to be rather more ambiguous.'

[139] See Gori, 'Souvenikrs d'un survivant', in *50th Anniversary of the Judgement in Van Gend en Loos 1963–2013* (2013) 29.

[140] I am appropriating here an image resulting from a conversation with Dieter Schlenker at Villa Salviati in the spring of 2017.

[141] See Council Regulation 2015/449 para. 12 of the Preamble, explaining that: 'Personal data contained in the historical archives of the Union deposited at the EUI should be processed in accordance with Regulation (EC) No 45/2001 of the European Parliament and of the Council of 18 December 2000 on the protection of individuals with regard to the processing of personal data by the Community institutions and bodies and on the free movement of such data.'

location.[142] The archivists in Florence work tirelessly to create more visibility for the HAEU to promote research concerning European integration. With respect to the ECJ archives, archivists are also the link between the researchers and the Court. While they are responsive and open to attracting the highest number of scholars who are devoting their time to archival research, they are also responsible for giving the researchers only the information approved by the Court.

I was thrilled at first to scroll through the *dossier de procédure* of *Van Gend en Loos*, but when I realized that I had completely underestimated the relevance of the language to the procedure, I had to go back to the many secondary sources. The majority of the documents were in Dutch and, due to my linguistic ignorance, I had to give up my commitment to a close reading of the briefs and documents produced for the hearing. Even though the ECJ is by far one of the exemplary multilingual and transnational courts, it seems unlikely that the non-Dutch judges and the Advocate General would not have access to a French translation of the Dutch files to prepare for the oral procedure. Because the language of the deliberation is French, there must have been translations in French. We also know that the memorandum that Alberto Trabucchi prepared to convince the majority of judges who were against the direct effect of a Treaty provision was actually in French.[143] Unfortunately, not only are the notes of the judges that could reveal their position in the deliberation not in the *dossiers*, but also the French translations they have used to inform their reasoning are missing from the *dossiers de procédure*.

To obtain these translations, we asked the HAEU archivists to access the French translations kept in the official records. After several weeks of consultation with the ECJ, the HAEU archivists denied our request because the French translations, which are included in the ECJ archives, were not part of the official historical record and therefore were not public.[144] Simply because these translations were not, according to the Court, officially part of the historical record, but rather internal working documents for the judges, they were not publicly accessible. But by not including the French translations, the Court took a discretionary decision not mandated by EU law. Therefore, if the translations do exist and the

[142] See Council Regulation 2015/496 of 17 March 2015, OJ 2015 L 79/1 explaining in para. 7 of the Preamble that: 'The purpose of the deposit of the historical archives of the institutions at the EUI is to provide access to these archives from a single location, to promote their consultation and to stimulate research into the history of European integration and the European institutions. The EUI is a renowned centre of academic research and learning with a focus on Europe and European integration. It has almost 30 years of experience in managing the historical archives of the Union, provides state-of-the-art repository and research facilities built expressly for the preservation and consultation of those archives, and has an international reputation as the centre for those archives.'

[143] See Rasmussen, 'Revolutionizing European Law: A History of the Van Gend en Loos judgment', 12 *International Journal of Constitutional Law* (2014) 136.

[144] Email correspondence with HAEU 'la position de la Cour de Justice par rapport à la question soulevée est la suivante: les traductions en français des mémoires ne font pas partie des Archives historiques et ne sont donc pas communicables'.

Court is committed to more transparency, these should be included in the *dossiers de procédure* and open for study by the researchers.

Another similar point of friction are the comparative notes prepared by the Court's researchers for the judges. These show the relevance of the comparative law method of the Court since its founding as 'a settled practice'.[145] The comparative method not only informs the Court, but it provides an opportunity to fill the gaps in interpretation and compatibility review. The comparative notes of the Court are only a positivist assessment of the state of the different legal systems in the EU, and the judges know well that they cannot display their preferences for one single legal tradition over another in their decisions. Because of the unique functioning of this transnational and multilingual Court, the comparative notes are not only valuable to understanding what type of legal knowledge judges rely on, but are also relevant to chart the dialogue between the Court and the national courts, as well as the dynamic relationship between the EEC and its Member States.[146]

The decision to not give access to the comparative notes is again a discretionary decision of the Court that might be the result of an excessively broad interpretation of how to protect the secrecy of its deliberations. By not revealing these notes, the Court is imposing on researchers the burden of reconstructing them, rather than learning from the work of one of the most innovative transnational courts with a multinational research team. This discretionary exclusion from the *dossiers de procédure* of the French translations and the comparative notes, seriously limits the research possibilities in the field. As researchers committed to achieving a better understanding of the fabric of EU law, we must keep advocating for better access to these documents.

8. Conclusion: The Archival Quest inside and beyond the Court

At the end of my own voyage inside the ECJ archives, I humbly realized that working on archival documents is harder than expected and that often the promise of finding the 'white truffles in an unexplored forest' can remain unfulfilled. This is because each research project on the ECJ requires building on new research methodologies that historians, sociologists, and more recently, lawyers have started to implement in their own work. From the very outset of the project, researchers must choose among the different methodological tools and understand what kind of access might be granted to the different types of archival materials we are dealing with.[147]

[145] Lenaerts and Gutman (n. 65) 841. [146] Ibid.
[147] See M. R. Madsen, F. G. Nicola, and A. Vauchez, *Researching EU Law: New Approaches and Methodologies* (2020).

There is obviously a lot of value in unearthing European legal history through the archives to better chart the acceptance and resistance to EU law and its institutions as well as the ideological and professional alliances created by the transnational professional networks of Eurolawyers, judges, scholars, and civil servants inside or outside the EU. However, this enterprise is a communal, rather than an individual, one, in which researchers ought to be open to explore new methodological avenues by looking a variety of disciplinary tools.

In this process, researchers should share both their methodological and archival findings and continue pushing for more transparency in the ECJ historical archives. For this reason scholars should continue to ask the Court to release more documents to the public, thus allowing better access in terms of language and legal reasoning. This constant back and forth between the Court and the scholarly community is important in order to make judicial decisions available to a greater audience. It is through this continuous engagement between the Court, its researchers, and civil society that EU law acquires meaning, especially in a complex multilingual and transnational context. From this perspective, the Court should continue to open its archives and preserve its secret deliberations to allow researchers to cast more light on its crucial role in European integration.

Finally, the ECJ archives are only one of many nodes of historical records available, including those of other EU institutions, especially the Commission and the European Parliament and the national archives of the Member States. Additionally, exploring the private collections of judges, Advocates General or *référendaires* can be revelatory of judicial reasoning or networks shaping an era. These private archives belonging to scholars, lawyers, and national judges who have played a central role in EU law from a peripheral local context can be even more revealing when seeking to trace the origins of legal ideas and the extra-legal influences in the early days of the ECJ.[148]

[148] See Becherucci (n. 56) 5.

4

The Relevance of the Network Approach to European Case Law

Reflection and Evidence

*Urška Šadl and Fabien Tarissan**

1. Introduction

The main question which this chapter seeks to answer is how network analysis is (or could become) relevant to studying the case law of the Court of Justice of the European Union (the Court)? To respond to this question of the relevance of network analysis as a viable methodology in legal empirical research, we begin by addressing two of the most commonly raised objections: first, that the approach is quantitative in nature, hence incompatible with qualitative legal methods, and, second, that what it can measure does not reveal the 'true' character of jurisprudence. While such critique is pertinent and merits further discussion, it fails to appreciate the full potential of the approach. To demonstrate this potential, we present three case studies: first, we show how to obtain detailed information about the law from the citation network; second, we demonstrate how to assess the legal relevance of cases by looking at case citations; and, third, we illustrate how to infer the doctrinal influence of selected landmark cases. All examples use various citation network tools to map the structure of the case law, and our method includes a mode for studying the legal discourse of the Court which we use to focus, frame, and guide the legal analysis. This clearly shows that network analysis can support, refute, and contest legal arguments on empirical grounds without compromising their evaluative (prescriptive) core.

* We thank the editors of this volume, the participants of the Workshop with the authors (Florence, February 2018), and our research assistants, Lucia Lopez Zurita and Martin Lolle Christensen. Our friend, Ioannis Panagis, has been a constant source of inspiration, ideas, and data.

Urška Šadl and Fabien Tarissan, *The Relevance of the Network Approach to European Case Law: Reflection and Evidence.* In: *New Legal Approaches to Studying the Court of Justice.* First edition. Edited by Claire Kilpatrick and Joanne Scott, Oxford University Press (2020). © Urška Šadl and Fabien Tarissan. DOI: 10.1093/oso/9780198871477.003.0005

2. The Legal Method and the Lure of Networks

The network approach[1] to anything is structural. This means that it prioritizes structures and the relations that exist between units rather than the individual units[2] while taking an interest in the patterning of these relations. It asks: how do patterns emerge and endure, and what consequences do they have?[3] For instance, the structural approach will seek to explain individual behaviour via the prism of connections linking an individual with her social environment.[4]

Durkheim's study of suicide[5] was an early examination of the influence of social structure and interpersonal relations on individual behaviour. Similarly, Granovetter investigated how large-scale social structures (at the macro level) influenced individual behaviour (at the micro level) in finding a job. His finding that individuals found jobs through loose connections rather than through closed groups of strong connections is an early and original social-scientific application of the network methodology—and its structural approach—which established the strength of weak ties.[6] These relations and their strength became visible only once they were mapped.

If we approach the case law or the jurisprudence of courts from the network perspective, we approach it as a set of relations that form a structure. As in social networks, the enduring patterns of interpersonal relations constrain the behaviour of the individual; the relations between cases define an individual case. Mapping renders the properties of relations and the effect of the constraints visible.

Over the past decade, a rapidly growing body of literature has emerged using network analysis to study law and courts. Yet there has been little to no reflection on how to translate the network approach into a *legal study* of case law and courts.[7] This chapter aims to embark upon some of this long overdue reflection. More concretely, we will address the question of what new legal insights the network approach can offer when integrated into classical legal studies.

[1] A network is a structure composed of nodes, such as judgments, and links between those nodes, such as citations of judgments.

[2] L. C. Freeman, *The Development of Social Network Analysis: A Study in the Sociology of Science* (2004) 2.

[3] B. Wellman and S. D. Berkowitz, *Social Structures: A Network Approach* (1988) 5; For a more recent mapping of the existing literature see Borgatti *et al.*, 'Network Analysis in the Social Sciences', 323 *Science* (2009) 892.

[4] Wellman and Berkowitz (n. 3); Wellman, 'Network Analysis: Some Basic Principles', 1 *Sociological Theory* (1983) 155; Marin and Wellman, 'Social Network Analysis: An Introduction', in J. Scott and P. J. Carrington (eds), *The SAGE Handbook of Social Network Analysis* (2011).

[5] E. Durkheim, *Suicide: A Study in Sociology* (2005).

[6] Granovetter, 'The Strength of Weak Ties', 78 *American Journal of Sociology* (1973) 1360.

[7] For an exception, see the editorial in the *GLJ* introducing its 'Special Section: Network Analysis and Comparative Law Methods', Petersen and Towfigh (eds), with its focus on the value of comparative law and citation networks, 18 *German Law Journal* (2017) 6.

We understand the classical legal approach to be the process of constructing valid legal arguments based on the reading and the interpretation of legal sources with formally binding or non-binding authority, such as statutes, case law, and scholarly literature. The process of analysis (the legal method) involves the use of different methods of interpretation, as well as conceptualizations such as the value of precedent. The purpose of the analysis is to understand and present the problem—which can be either theoretical or practical—as a legal problem and to offer a legal solution or a range of possible legal solutions. There is no universal legal approach because there is no single understanding of 'the law'. The examination of legal material will hinge on a *theory* of law, typically involving an allegiance to categories such as legal-positivist, realist, critical, or contextual. These allegiances will shape the understanding of the problem, rearrange the hierarchy of legal sources, and influence the methods of interpretation as well as the proposed solution. Arguably, however, regardless of which theory of law an analyst employs, the analysis will almost certainly rely on a selective study of legal doctrine, and on a reading of jurisprudence and legislation, while adhering to the criteria of valid argumentation: legal correctness (logical deduction), coherence, consistency, and judicial consequences.[8] There will usually be no account of the process by which legal material was selected. Nor is it customary to provide an explicit consideration of the relevance or representativeness of such material. When analysing case law, a legal scholar will approach cases individually and investigate them as distinct units that form a chain of justification, legal development, reasoning, argumentation, and so forth. Since such perspectives are primarily attuned to the legal concepts which courts elaborate over time, they are most often historical and linear.

The network perspective shifts the analytical focus away from case attributes and prioritizes case-to-case relations. The cases become nodes (the dots) and the relations become links (lines or arrows). Together they form a network. This does not mean that individual cases lose their attributes. Rather, the latter are defined and analysed based on these interactions. The approach traces the patterns systematically and comprehensively, often involving large numbers of cases and a capacity to consider all links between the cases. The selection of nodes that form a network is justified via pre-established criteria of relevance. Our intent is to explore this approach using a legal lens, while responding to the most commonly raised objections to its application. First, though, we must understand the context in which such objections are raised. Here, we ask: what is the appeal of networks in the brave new world of artificial intelligence and 'all things computational', and how does this determine their use?

[8] N. MacCormick, *Rhetoric and the Rule of Law: A Theory of Legal Reasoning* (2005); N. MacCormick, *Legal Reasoning and Legal Theory* (1994).

Network analysis is often characterized as 'mere methodology'—a packaging option that some network scholars endorse[9] and others evade.[10] In fact, network analysis has leveraged fast-developing technology and computing power to deliver new and intriguing methods (quantitative, objective), as well as more transparent, systematic, comprehensive, reproducible, and falsifiable studies.[11] Social scientists have turned to legal network analysis, asking the most vexing questions about the law and judicial behaviour. They have been able to base their inquiries on complete and readily available datasets, on free and official data sources, and on algorithms and explicit connections, rather than speculative relations. They have studied judicial activism,[12] the rise of *stare decisis*, the depreciation of precedents in the United States Supreme Court (USSC),[13] citation strategies of international courts as well as their authority,[14] the (strategic) behaviour of individual judges,[15] the nature and working of precedents,[16] the politics of case citations,[17] the predictability of judicial outcomes, the social capital of legal scholars and practitioners,[18] and the structure of jurisprudence.[19] Often, this has involved complex statistical modelling, hypothesis testing, and mandatory use of computer software.[20]

[9] Scott speaks of 'theoretically informed methods' in J. Scott, *Social Network Analysis* (2017) 8.

[10] Borgatti *et al.* (n. 3) 893.

[11] See Frankenreiter, 'The Politics of Citations at the ECJ: Policy Preferences of E.U. Member State Governments and the Citation Behavior of Judges at the European Court of Justice', 14 *Journal of Empirical Legal Studies* (2017) 813; Fowler and Jeon, 'The Authority of Supreme Court Precedent', 30 *Social Networks* (2008) 16; Derlén and Lindholm, 'Goodbye *van Gend en Loos*, Hello *Bosman*? Using Network Analysis to Measure the Importance of Individual CJEU Judgments', 20 *European Law Journal* (2014) 667; Ruhl, Katz, and Bommarito, 'Harnessing Legal Complexity', 355 *Science* (2017) 1377.

[12] Fowler and Jeon (n. 11) 30. The idea is that a court disrespectful of precedent (an activist court) will cite fewer precedents than a court which is less activist (the latter court will prefer to embed a decision in previous case law).

[13] Black and Spriggs, 'The Citation and Depreciation of U.S. Supreme Court Precedent', 10 *Journal of Empirical Legal Studies* (2013) 325.

[14] Lupu and Voeten, 'Precedent in International Courts: A Network Analysis of Case Citations by the European Court of Human Rights', 42 *British Journal of Political Science* (2012) 413; For a study of strategic litigation and the creation of precedents in the WTO, see Pelc, 'The Politics of Precedent in International Law: A Social Network Application', 108 *American Political Science Review* (2014) 547.

[15] Lupu and Fowler, 'Strategic Citations to Precedent on the US Supreme Court', 42 *Journal of Legal Studies* (2013) 151.

[16] Fowler and Jeon (n. 11) 30; Derlén and Lindholm, 'Is It Good Law? Network Analysis and the CJEU's Internal Market Jurisprudence', 20 *Journal of International Economic Law* (2017) 257.

[17] Frankenreiter (n. 11).

[18] Puig, 'Social Capital in the Arbitration Market', 25 *European Journal of International Law* (2014) 387.

[19] Fowler *et al.*, 'Network Analysis and the Law: Measuring the Legal Importance of Precedents at the U.S. Supreme Court', 15 *Political Analysis* (2007) 324.

[20] Bommarito *et al.*, 'Distance Measures for Dynamic Citation Networks', 389 *Physica A: Statistical Mechanics and its Applications* (2010) 4201; Koniaris, Anagnostopoulos, and Vassiliou, 'Network Analysis in the Legal Domain: A Complex Model for European Union Legal Sources', 6 *Journal of Complex Networks* (2018) 243; Smith, 'The Web of Law', University of San Diego Law and Economics Research Paper Series (2005), available at https://digital.sandiego.edu/lwps_econ/art8 (accessed 22 September 2020). Note that there are numerous studies using approaches which are only tangential to law, though they seem to be taking the law as their focal point. Many studies harness the technology to

While science and society have embraced the capacities of the network approach with few reservations,[21] legal scholars have remained cautious about including it in their legal research methodology.[22] Their objections fall within two categories. First, network analysis relies on quantitative methods, and hence fails to capture the law's internal aspects. This is deemed to render it incompatible with legal analysis.[23] Second, the network metrics (what the network analysis measures) do not reveal the actual properties of jurisprudence.

To flesh out the first objection, legal rules are normative claims (claims about what should happen in a certain situation) and not empirical observations. The question of whether x has a valid claim against y must be resolved 'within' the law, by looking at the concrete claim and whether this claim follows from a distinct rule which is valid. The conditions for rule validity are not the same as the conditions for its effectiveness. In the second objection, we encounter the eternal question about the reasons that citations are found within a judgment.[24] Simply by mapping citations one cannot distinguish the type of citation: does the Court cite a case because it considers it a binding precedent, a *de facto* applicable precedent, a relevant analogy, an irrelevant analogy, or an example of practice which is no longer in place? Is the Court citing the case to overrule it or to distinguish it from previous cases? Alternatively, does the Court mention the case because the national court or the European Commission raised the question of its relevance in the question submitted in the preliminary reference procedure? In addition, such objections to the quantitative nature of the network approach stress the fact that there are important differences between civil and common law courts. Even if the network metrics may offer valuable insights into the working of the latter, they cannot reveal much (if anything) in the case of the former, which do not have an established practice of precedent and precedent citation.[25]

map relations between legal practitioners (e.g. representation before the US Supreme Court) but often without further considerations such as interpretation of obtained findings. While these studies are interesting, we do not include them in this literature review.

[21] See Whalen, 'Legal Networks: The Promises and Challenges of Legal Network Analysis', *Michigan State Law Review* (2016) 539 for a general discussion on the popularity of the network perspective.

[22] See for instance discussion in M. A. Jacob, *Precedents and Case-Based Reasoning in the European Court of Justice: Unfinished Business* (2014) 2–6.

[23] Ibid.; Klabbers, 'Whatever Happened to Gramsci: Some Reflections on New Legal Realism International Law and Its Methodology', 28 *Leiden Journal of International Law* (2015) 469.

[24] For further discussion, see Pauwelyn and Elsig, 'The Politics of Treaty Interpretation', in J. L. Dunoff and M. A. Pollack (eds), *Interdisciplinary Perspectives on International Law and International Relations: The State of the Art* (2012) 445; Alschner and Charlotin, 'The Growing Complexity of the International Court of Justice's Self-Citation Network', 29 *European Journal of International Law* (2018) 83.

[25] Šadl and Olsen, 'Can Quantitative Methods Complement Doctrinal Legal Studies? Using Citation Network and Corpus Linguistic Analysis to Understand International Courts', 30 *Leiden Journal of International Law* (2017) 327, at 334.

Finally—and importantly—network analysis produces a static image of the law, even though it is constantly evolving.[26]

In this chapter, we contend that the network approach can support legal research methodologically, and we demonstrate how legal research can absorb and benefit from network methods. We proceed in three steps. First, we draw on the history of the approach and its broad presence in social sciences to support our claim that the network approach is not essentially quantitative. This requires distinguishing the main ideas of the approach from the current application of network analysis in research on law and courts. While the latter is predominantly quantitative, the former is not. Second, we provide evidence that it is possible to re-imagine and re-calibrate the network approach to study the law as a system of norms without doing violence to its own inner rationality and methods. Arguably, this must happen at the stage of research design and must encompass the process of selecting the materials to be included in the network, the use of several complementary measures of case centrality, and by employing a more detailed but comprehensive study of legal language. Third, we deal with the practical limitations of the network approach, highlighting its potential as a complement *to*, rather than a methodological replacement *of*, the legal methodology.

The ensuing discussion is organized into three sections. Section 3 will consider and address two objections to network analysis. Section 4 will outline three methods of citation network analysis and explore how they can be used to answer legal questions. This will draw on our previous and current work related to the case law of the Court.[27] First, we will present how complementary metrics of case importance highlight different properties of individual cases and different network properties. Second, we will present insights from the study of landmark cases from a long-term and dynamic perspective. Third, we will outline a method which relies on text similarity to highlight the legal content of individual cases. We conclude with a general discussion of the relevance of the network approach in Section 5.

3. Two Objections

This section deals with two reservations to the network approach: namely, that the citation network approach is quantitative (Section 3.A) and that it cannot measure the law (Section 3.B). As a framework for this discussion, we briefly outline legal thinking that draws on the idea of webs amid efforts to envisage and scrutinize the relevance of citations to legal authority in judicial opinions. We also highlight research that demonstrates the validity of the citation network approach.

[26] See S. Müller-Mall, *Legal Spaces: Towards a Topological Thinking of Law* (2013).

[27] Ibid. 82.

Arguments for a comprehensive study of citations are not new to legal thinking and neither are network metaphors. Two examples of the former are Merryman's precursory studies of citations of authority in judicial opinions.[28] Merryman argues that citations of authority in legal writing deserve discussion because they can reveal the nature of authority or the function of precedent.[29] Regarding the latter, the most prominent metaphors include Dworkin's reference to Maitland's seamless web, Finnis' duty to obey 'the law' which presents itself as a seamless web, and Raz's critique of Finnis, which asserts that the web is not seamless and that the 'goodness' of the law must be constantly evaluated.[30] Yet what we experience here remains a metaphor—a parable that enables thinking but leaves intact the prevailing methods already embraced.[31] The network approach with its distinct methodology is more tangible than metaphors and much more stringent in terms of data collection, research design, and the interpretation of findings.

To date, research relying on citation networks has clearly demonstrated the face validity of the approach and contributed to the advance of research agendas which (wishfully) take the content of judicial opinions as a starting point for analysis.[32] It has also shown that real world networks such as legislative networks, the World Wide Web, and scientific citation networks share fundamental similarities with case law citation networks. The evolution of law mimics the evolution of other network phenomena and can be studied in the same way.[33] Nonetheless, most research in this vein is concerned with phenomena that are related to law but contribute little to answering legal questions.[34] In the following sub-sections, we situate the discussion in a more exacting legal setting.

[28] Merryman, 'The Authority of Authority', 6 *Stanford Law Review* (1954) 613; Merryman, 'Toward a Theory of Citations: An Empirical Study of the Citation Practice of the California Supreme Court in 1950, 1960, and 1970', 50 *Southern California Law Review* (1977) 381.

[29] 'Presumably a citation means something to the person citing, and presumably he anticipates that it will have some meaning to a reader. What these meanings are, and how they can be rationalized with a realistic view of the judicial process as the conscious or unconscious weighing of personal and social values by the judge, deserve some discussion.' Merryman, 'The Authority of Authority' (n. 28) 613.

[30] Finnis, 'The Authority of Law in the Predicament of Contemporary Social Theory', 1 *Notre Dame Journal of Law, Ethics & Public Policy* (1984) 115, at 120; J. Raz, *Ethics in the Public Domain: Essays in the Morality of Law and Politics* (1994) 350 *et seq.*

[31] Examples include Maitland's hesitation to 'tear the seamless web of history', Dworkin's interpretivism (constructive interpretation) designed to preserve the web and show it in its best light, Finnis' holism, and Alexy's coherence criteria. Coherence is most often used as a method and a benchmark for criticism in legal analysis. See Maitland, 'Prologue to a History of English Law', 14 *Law Quarterly Review* (1898) 13; R. Dworkin, *Law's Empire* (1986); J. Finnis, *Natural Law and Natural Rights* (2nd ed., 2011); R. Alexy, *A Theory of Legal Argumentation: The Theory of Rational Discourse as Theory of Legal Justification* (2010). See also MacCormick's justificatory triad of consistency, coherence, consequences: MacCormick, *Legal Reasoning and Legal Theory* (n. 8).

[32] Fowler and Jeon (n. 11) 16 *et seq.* [33] Ibid. 344. [34] See examples in Section 3.A.

A. Network Analysis is Quantitative

In this section we argue that when legal scholars object to the network approach because it is quantitative, they elide the broader applications created for the method by political-scientific research, thereby failing to do justice to its character and techniques. First, though, we make some preliminary observations about the law and legal scholarship, which shed light on the context of this *problématique*.

Legal scholarship is normative, meaning that it treats law as a system of *valid* norms.[35] This means that the law consists of statements about what one ought to do. This conception of law as normative requires a normative approach and largely excludes descriptive or empirical approaches. A conclusion about what one ought to do (i.e. what the law requires in the concrete case) cannot follow from a statement of facts—from what is.[36] An important implication for doctrinal legal scholarship is that *if* non-legal factors can be integrated into legal analysis, they will be at best tangential to it.[37] They will provide the context of judicial decisions, will be considered relevant and to an extent explanatory, but they can never be translated into a distinct methodology or be seen as a determining factor of legal outcomes.[38] This methodological stance adopted by legal scholarship is sometimes said to be uninterested in the dynamics of social and political change driven by courts.[39]

Underpinning the quantitative objection is the idea of legal methodology as qualitative and interpretative. It feeds into a much broader methodological—if not ideological—disagreement between legal scholarship and political science,[40] or the opposition between qualitative and quantitative approaches to the study of

[35] H. Kelsen, *Pure Theory of Law* (1967). Continental positivism is especially disposed to treat law as a coherent system of norms, and judicial decisions as their instantiations. One might question whether non-positivists, and especially critical legal scholars, would endorse such a definition. However, as Kelsen claimed, 'even an anarchist, if he were a professor of law, could describe positive law as a system of valid norms, without having to approve of this law', ibid. 218, fn. 82. Similarly, Hart convincingly argued that legal realists had to rely on the law as a system to launch their critique. H. L. A. Hart, *The Concept of Law* (2012) 136–147.

[36] The approach presupposes that there is a sharp division between 'is' statements and 'ought' statements, which is attributed to Hume.

[37] An ought statement (what the law requires) can only be derived from another (higher) valid ought statement. This established the hierarchy of norms.

[38] Cf. Hart (n. 35) 154. Hart argues that the rule sceptic is welcome only at the fringe but we should make sure that this 'does not blind us to the fact that what makes possible these striking developments by courts of the most fundamental rules is, in great measure, the prestige gathered by courts from their unquestionably rule-governed operations over the vast, central areas of the law'.

[39] For a concise summary of the misunderstanding between law and political science, see de Búrca, 'Rethinking Law in Neofunctionalist Theory', 12 *Journal of European Public Policy* (2005) 310, at 314.

[40] On the interplay in international courts between international law and international relations, see Aalberts and Venzke, 'Moving Beyond Interdisciplinary Turf Wars: Towards an Understanding of International Law as Practice', in J. d'Aspremont *et al.* (eds), *International Law as a Profession* (2017) 287.

the same phenomenon.[41] True, the distinction between disciplines does not map perfectly into the distinction between doctrinal (legal) and quantitative (political science) methodology. It is nonetheless useful in illustrating the quantitative objection, especially because the network approach has so far mostly been used as a supplement to hypothesis testing and statistical modelling.

Hypothetically speaking, a study of the political preferences of judges can predict with a 72 per cent probability that a judge will behave in a certain way. For instance, that she will vote in favour of a conservative position outlined in a given case, or that she will vote to strike down one set of state measures and vote in favour of upholding others.[42] Suffice to say, however, from a legal point of view a hypothesis such as this unduly discounts the role of law. Because it concentrates on the vote and the outcome of the case, it dispenses with legal argumentation, which is central. The fundamental premise of the study of probability is that non-legal factors rather than statutes and case law (legal sources) determine case outcomes. To legal scholars it should be interesting, even if in a negative way, that the study refuses to take the courts' own stated reasons at face value: if judges disagree about the outcome (which they explicitly do in cases where there is a dissenting minority), law cannot explain the disagreement or the vote.

Less hypothetically, a study applying citation network analysis to the case law of the Court will map case citations and show that European judges are more likely to cite judgments authored by judges appointed by Member State governments with similar preferences regarding European integration.[43] It will present evidence that judges cite more cases when they overrule existing precedents,[44] or that international courts cite more cases when they rule against the interest of national governments.[45] It will provide concrete evidence that the political preferences of Member State governments are reflected in the behaviour of European judges.[46] The findings should be—in principle—thought provoking because they highlight the non-legal context of individual decisions of the Court. They could inspire research on questions of general interest to law, like judicial independence and institutional structure when thinking about and evaluating the reform of procedural arrangements.[47] They could potentially

[41] Clearly, this is a simplistic view. For a more comprehensive account, see Knight, 'Are Empiricists Asking the Right Questions about Judicial Decisionmaking?', 58 *Duke Law Journal* (2009) 1531.

[42] See e.g. S. A. Lindquist and F. B. Cross, *Measuring Judicial Activism* (2009); Katz, Bommarito, and Blackman, 'A General Approach for Predicting the Behavior of the Supreme Court of the United States', 12 *PLoS ONE* (2017) e0174698.

[43] Frankenreiter (n. 11) 839.

[44] Fowler and Jeon (n. 11) 29.

[45] Lupu and Voeten (n. 14) 438.

[46] Larsson and Naurin, 'Judicial Independence and Political Uncertainty: How the Risk of Override Affects the Court of Justice of the EU', 70 *International Organization* (2016) 377.

[47] Cf. Alemanno and Pech, 'Thinking Justice Outside the Docket: A Critical Assessment of the Reform of the EU's Court System', 54 *Common Market Law Review* (2017) 129; Dumbrovsky, Petkova, and Van Der Sluis, 'Judicial Appointments: The Article 255 TFEU Advisory Panel and Selection Procedures in the Member States', 51 *Common Market Law Review* (2014) 455; Alemanno and Stefan,

spark further empirical investigation and evaluation (even if from a strictly legal doctrinal point of view they appear somewhat unsubstantiated). They would merit further engagement even if we declare that, from the legal point of view, the important element is not how many cases a court cites, but which prior cases it overturns and which state practices it deems to be in violation of international treaties and under what circumstances. At present, however, it appears that empirical legal accounts of judicial decision-making irritate rather than stimulate legal research agendas.[48] It is this general sense of irritation with the buzzwords 'quantitative' and 'empirical' that underscores reservations about the network approach.

The argument that largely neutralizes the mindset of 'quantitative objection' presented earlier concerns the roots of the approach and its present application by social scientists. The history of social network analysis suggests that the network perspective was not conceived with quantitative methodology, statistical modelling, and hypothesis testing in mind. In fact, the pioneering work comes from sociology, anthropology, and social psychology—all largely disciplines that rely on interviews, questionnaires, and participant observation that can involve any degree of quantification (including none).[49] The first *sociogram*,[50] a visualization of interactions between girls and boys in a classroom and their preferences for each other, was presented in 1933 by Jakob Moreno, who was a pioneer of group psychotherapy.[51] The representation provided a concrete and appealing image of a social system and generated a structure that could be analysed qualitatively *or* quantitatively.[52]

Today, anthropologists continue to embark on small-scale studies of kinship relations, friendship, and gift giving among people; social psychologists focus on affections; political scientists carry out large projects concerning power relations among people, organizations, or nations; while economists investigate trade and organizational ties among firms using big data. Research history—and present research trajectories—show that investigations of social ties among actors do not have to involve hypothesis testing: the approach can remain exploratory and limited to the ties that can be mapped without computer software.[53] The central

'Openness at the Court of Justice of the European Union: Toppling a Taboo', 51 *Common Market Law Review* (2014) 97.

[48] For a lively debate in international law on the New Legal Realism advocating the empirical study of law, see Klabbers (n. 23), as well as the articles in the special issue.

[49] S. Wasserman and K. Faust, *Social Network Analysis: Methods and Applications*, vol. 8 (1994) 10.

[50] Sociogram refers to a graphical representation of group structure.

[51] The story was picked up by *The New York Times*. Moreno, 'Emotions Mapped by New Geography; Charts Seek to Portray the Psychological Currents of Human Relationships', *The New York Times* (3 April 1933), available at https://www.nytimes.com/1933/04/03/archives/emotions-mapped-by-new-geography-charts-seek-to-portray-the.html (accessed 25 October 2018).

[52] S. Leinhardt, *Social Networks: A Developing Paradigm* (2013) xiv.

[53] W. De Nooy, A. Mrvar, and V. Batagelj, *Exploratory Social Network Analysis with Pajek* (2018).

objective of the network approach is to map relations and reveal patterns that are not plainly visible.[54] Expressed differently, it is an approach that seeks to detect and interpret patterns of ties among units of analysis. In social networks these units are actors; in academic citation networks they are academic works; and in legal citation networks they are usually the citations of legal sources. The findings obtained via network methods must be interpreted and interpretation can include hypothesis testing; yet a network approach does not require it.

The quantification of network methodology has certainly become interwoven with the momentum of technological advances.[55] At the present time, researchers use elaborate computer software[56] to visualize and examine large networks, explore social structures, and test theories about structured social relationships and hypotheses about their structural properties.[57] Yet continuity is also in evidence—researchers still work to visualize the relationships among schoolboys and schoolgirls in classrooms worldwide without the use of advanced technology. On a core level, such applications are all interested in social detail, which means they are not primarily quantitative.[58]

Hence, while the best-known and most widespread application of network approaches to case law may currently create an impression that network analysis works best when paired with statistical modelling,[59] the method's history and application in other fields suggests otherwise. Network analysis provides a separate methodology, which can be built into a range of research agendas and integrated into mixed methods, qualitative or quantitative.[60]

B. Network Metrics Do Not Measure the Law

The second objection to the network approach spans several related concerns about its potential to capture the content of law in judicial decisions. All converge

[54] Scott (n. 9) 7. [55] Scott, 'Computational Social Network Analysis', in Scott (n. 9).

[56] Huisman and van Duijn, 'Software for Social Network Analysis', in P. J. Carrington, J. Scott, and S. Wasserman (eds), *Models and Methods in Social Network Analysis* (2005) 270. For a more recent but less detailed overview, see Huisman and van Duijn, 'A Reader's Guide to SNA Software', in J. Scott and P. J. Carrington (eds), *Social Network Analysis* (1st ed., 2011) 578.

[57] Wasserman and Faust (n. 49) 17.

[58] Wolfe, 'The Rise of Network Thinking in Anthropology', 1 *Social Networks* (1978) 53; Mitchell, 'Social Networks', 3 *Annual Review of Anthropology* (1974) 279; Knox, Savage, and Harvey, 'Social Networks and the Study of Relations: Networks as Method, Metaphor and Form', 35 *Economy and Society* (2006) 113; McPherson, Smith-Lovin, and Cook, 'Birds of a Feather: Homophily in Social Networks', 27 *Annual Review of Sociology* (2001) 415.

[59] To that effect, see Frankenreiter, 'Network Analysis and the Use of Precedent in the Case Law of the CJEU—A Reply to Derlén and Lindholm', 18 *German Law Journal* (2017) 687. This speaks to criticism that the network approach is not paired with theory and hypothesis testing.

[60] Pairing NA with legal methodology: Panagis and Šadl, 'The Force of EU Case Law: A Multi-Dimensional Study of Case Citations', 279 *Frontiers in Artificial Intelligence and Applications* (2015) 71. Alschner and Charlotin (n. 24).

into one main point of resistance, which can be labelled the 'legal relevance' claim. Much simplified, the legal relevance claim asserts that network measures (metrics) do not measure the law and, *ad absurdum*, that the law cannot be measured. To address this criticism, it might be helpful to sketch an outline of citation network analysis—presenting its basic concepts and assumptions—and then note the tools at its disposal.

Citation network analysis is the sub-field of network analysis that is closest to legal research. Citation networks have distinct properties[61] and the mapping of citations has a distinct research aim. Citation analysis is geared towards tracing the diffusion of ideas, knowledge, and scholarly influence. It is applied to evaluate scholarly contributions, and research (evaluative citation analysis).[62] Moreover, it is widely used in bibliographical research for information retrieval.[63] The field was pioneered by de Solla Price[64] but received much more attention after the advent of research studying the internet and online social networks.[65] The construction of case law citation networks can be traced back to FLEXICON[66] and KONTERM,[67] where those systems also included links to past cases. It has been adopted in Eurlex, the legal portal of the European Union.[68]

Citation network analysis has two key characteristics: first, it typically takes the macro perspective, which invariably entails large datasets, algorithms, and computer software. Second, citation network analysis generally assumes that a citation represents the citing author's use of the cited work. It thus infers influence of the cited work on the citing work. By implication citations are 'tokens of recognition' and a measure of academic impact. This inference sits uncomfortably with legal practice where citations have at least two *separate* roles: they are both communication devices, and an indication of the legal bearing of the cited case on the citing case. Doctrinal law is interested in the latter and analyses how much legal bearing (relevance) the cited cases had on the citing case. The spectrum of possible legal influence of the cited case on the citing case is wide and manifold. In

[61] See e.g. Nooy, Mrvar, and Batagelj (n. 53); Tarissan and Nollez-Goldbach, 'Analysing the First Case of the International Criminal Court from a Network-Science Perspective', 4 *Journal of Complex Networks* (2016) 616. Citation networks are acyclic, hence metrics used in social networks (typically cyclic) do not always work.

[62] Garfield, 'Citation Analysis as a Tool in Journal Evaluation', 178 *Science* (1972) 471; Borgman and Furner, 'Scholarly Communication and Bibliometrics', 36 *Annual Review of Information Science and Technology* (2002) 2; E. Garfield, I. H. Sher, and R. J. Torpie, *The Use of Citation Data in Writing the History of Science* (1964). See also de Solla Price, 'Networks of Scientific Papers', 149 *Science* (1965) 510.

[63] For an overview, see Zhao and Strotmann, 'Evolution of Research Activities and Intellectual Influences in Information Science 1996–2005: Introducing Author Bibliographic-coupling Analysis', 59 *Journal of the American Society for Information Science and Technology* (2008) 2070.

[64] de Solla Price (n. 62).

[65] See for instance Nooy, Mrvar, and Batagelj (n. 53).

[66] D. Gelbart and J. Smith, *Flexicon: An Evaluation of a Statistical Ranking Model Adapted to Intelligent Legal Text Management* (Proceedings of the 4th ICAIL 1993).

[67] E. Schweighofer and D. Scheithauer, *The Automatic Generation of Hypertext Links in Legal Documents* (1996).

[68] http://eur-lex.europa.eu/homepage.html (accessed 25 October 2018).

comparison, the spectrum considered by the network approach is reductionist. We will return to this point later.

Network metrics also raise some noteworthy issues. One of the key concepts of the network approach is the concept of centrality or importance in a network.[69] Several measures of centrality have been developed. Some are simple, like citation counts (in degree, out degree[70]), others are more advanced.[71] The simplest is in-degree centrality. It counts citations to identify the most frequently cited cases. This measure is clearly biased towards older cases that have had more time to accumulate citations, and hence it may not support convincing arguments about their landmark status. Such standing can be supported by more complex measures (mathematically speaking)[72] which apart from the number of citations also account for their importance (hub and authority scores, Page Rank[73]). This method successfully eliminates the bias of time: the importance of a case is based on the quantity (the number) as well as the quality of citations (their importance). By analogy, the importance of a given scientific paper is proportionate to the importance of papers that cite it, or the importance of the journal in which it is cited (i.e. the number of citations the citing paper itself receives). But what, if anything, can any of these metrics say about the legally pertinent reason for citation?

If we begin by discussing some further metric complications, we can proceed towards a fuller answer. From the point of view of the legal discipline, the concept of centrality seems simplistic. Yet in network science, the concept is—like central concepts in any discipline—contested.[74] There is no unanimity about defining centrality or its conceptual foundations, and there is very little agreement on the proper procedure for its measurement.[75] All measures of centrality are continuously evaluated, probed, tested, and contested. The mathematics underpinning measures of centrality is not blind to the problems of social (or legal) reality being mapped and analysed and not averse to feedback.

Alas, citation network analysis—at least as implemented by the first generation of legal citation studies—typically treats all citations as equally important and does not discriminate between different types of references. From the citation network perspective, it is not pertinent whether a judge presiding in case B cites

[69] Borgatti, 'Centrality and Network Flow', 27 *Social Networks* (2005) 55.

[70] Number of incoming citations and number of outgoing citations.

[71] Including degree centrality, closeness, betweenness, eigenvector centrality, information centrality, flow betweenness, the rush index, the influence measures; see Borgatti (n. 69); or Scott (n. 9).

[72] Kleinberg, 'Authoritative Sources in a Hyperlinked Environment', 46 *Journal of the ACM* (1999) 604. See also Fowler and Jeon (n. 11).

[73] For hubs and authorities see Kleinberg (n. 72). For Page-Rank see Brin and Page, 'The Anatomy of a Large-scale Hypertextual Web Search Engine', 30 *Computer networks and ISDN systems* (1998) 107. For academic citations see Garfield (n. 62).

[74] Freeman, 'Centrality in Social Networks Conceptual Clarification', 1 *Social Networks* (1978) 215, at 217.

[75] Ibid.

case A as persuasive authority that compels the outcome of case B (as well as case C, which she cites but discards as irrelevant to case B). The citation metric will naturally 'capture' a link between A, B, and C without further information regarding its content. It will omit the content that is crucial for any evaluation of what is valid law and which cases are the truly important reference points in a court's repository.

This problem affects the fundamentals of legal analysis: citation network methods displace cited cases as argumentative sources, installing case citation as the means of building networks and gaining insight into 'the big picture'. In literature relying on citation networks to study jurisprudence and courts, precedent citations are typically conceptualized as *latent judgments*. They are defined as the assessments of judges as to which past decisions were central to the development of the law and which provided justifying *reasons* for deciding present (i.e. the citing) cases on the basis of previous relevant cases.[76] Concretely, studies assume that 'citation behavior of the Court provides information about which precedents serve important roles in the development of . . . law',[77] as well as that 'a judgment's value as a source of law is limited if it has never been cited by the Court of Justice [footnote omitted]'.[78] Clearly, this assumption is problematic.

Studies using the network approach have yet to offer persuasive arguments to address these pertinent challenges. At times, criticism is not taken seriously. Again, one senses irritation rather than imagination. One objection, raised by legal scholars and practitioners alike, is that the Court often reproduces an argument without citing the case in which it first appeared. This objection is often simply shrugged off by pointing out that legal qualitative case analysis and quantitative analysis using the network approach identify the same cases as central to the network, meaning that the overlap between qualitative and quantitative methods of identifying important precedents is significant. Judgments identified as important by citation network analysis are more or less the same judgments cited and discussed by legal scholars.[79] The criticism that the approach works for common law courts with an established citation practice but does not work with civil law courts that do not refer to past cases as precedents is again rejected as a misreading. The latter courts will simply have fewer links between the cases than the common law courts, but the relationship between more cited (important) and

[76] Judges in international courts do not always draft opinions themselves but leave all or most of the drafting to legal secretaries, who may be constrained by writing manuals, protocols on linguistic formulations, and strict citation guidelines. For the US Supreme Court, see Cross *et al.*, 'Citations in the US Supreme Court: An Empirical Study of Their Use and Significance', 2010 (2) *University of Illinois Law Review* (2010) 489; Fowler and Jeon (n. 11).

[77] Fowler and Jeon (n. 11) 17.

[78] Lindholm and Derlén, 'The Court of Justice and the Ankara Agreement: Exploring the Empirical Approach', *Europarättslig Tidskrift* (2012) 462, at 474.

[79] This was convincingly demonstrated by M. Derlén and J. Lindholm: Derlén and Lindholm (n. 11).

less cited (important) cases will remain stable and the network structures will look very similar.[80] However, our point here is different: an advance in the understanding of courts and jurisprudence depends on whether one can re-imagine the network approach. In what follows we present three modifications, which should be read as variations on the theme of the problem of legal relevance. All are interconnected and aim to approach the law by relating the properties of the networks and the network measures with characteristic judicial language and the typical discourse of the Court. The novelty of these methods is in finding and capitalizing on existing concepts, patterns, practices, measures, and connections.

Section 4.A presents our first case study. We delve into the leading cases in EU law to argue that different metrics highlight different properties of the landmark cases and hence identify different properties of the network structure and the structure of the law. This shows that the leading cases are a separate category, which the approach can accurately identify. Thus, the 'importance' of a case is not entirely separate from its 'centrality'.

4. The Network Approach Re-Imagined

A. What Citation Metrics Can Tell Us About Case Law (and Vice Versa)

i. Research Design

Courts typically cite older cases less frequently than recent cases. Literature attributes this to the fact that the precedential value of cases diminishes over time: older cases are less likely to contain principles and reasoning that would be relevant for the resolution of contemporary problems and issues.[81] Yet our previous research shows that certain groups of cases in the EU legal order remain continuously cited.[82] A few even begin to attract relatively more citations as they age. Why do certain cases in EU law resist the passage of time?

One explanation of the continuous or increasing centrality scores of individual cases would suggest that these cases carry important legal information and continue to provide legal (practical) solutions for novel situations. By contrast, cases with diminishing centrality scores become legally irrelevant with the passage of time. The methodological interest behind the *problématique* is to test

[80] Šadl and Olsen (n. 25) 348. [81] Black and Spriggs (n. 13).

[82] Tarissan, Panagis, and Šadl, 'Selecting the Cases that Defined Europe: Complementary Metrics for a Network Analysis', 2016 IEEE/ACM International Conference on Advances in Social Networks Analysis and Mining (ASONAM) (2016).

whether citation patterns indeed reflect the legal importance of cases and probe which network metrics, if any, can capture this.

We focused on a list of 50 landmark cases, which the Court identified as important case law prior to the accession of 10 new Member States to the European Union in 2004.[83] These 50 cases are part of the Court's jurisprudence, which includes 5,599 judgments and opinions of the Court, issued from 1954 to March 2002, and 13,609 case citations between the judgments. The information was freely available online from official sources (Curia and Eurlex).[84]

Our hypothesis was that importance in legal terms was much broader than case centrality in citation network terms, and that the Court compiled a group of landmark cases based on various criteria, including their historical significance, symbolic status, and, not least, because they could still provide practical solutions to emerging legal problems. Only the latter would potentially (with the caveats outlined in the previous section) be reflected in the citation count. We also hypothesized that not every important landmark was equal: some judgments have a wide-ranging significance for the whole legal order, while others have a narrower scope of application. Finally, a consideration that played into the research design was that some judgments reached back to the time where the Court's practice was to repeat the arguments fashioned in previous judgments without referring to those judgments by name or any other unique identifier.

The research design also tried to reflect the administrative aspect of the Court's work. Namely, when the Court decides a case, the Research and Documentation Directorate, supervised by reporting judges, in individual cases assigns it one or more classifications, depending on the legal questions considered in the case.[85] Each case is also accompanied by keywords, which give an indication of the legal content of the case. The objective is to facilitate the work of the Court as well as research. The classifications are fed into several databases, including Eurlex. They contain several subject matters and are available on the official website where they are stored as bibliographical information.

[83] See selection on http://curia.europa.eu/ (accessed 25 September 2020).

[84] Apart from the judgments and the decisions, the Eurlex database contains information on every judgment (the so-called metadata). This includes information on the full title of the case, the date of decision, the application date, the CELEX number, the subject matter of the case and keywords, the type of procedure (e.g. action for annulment), the reporting judge, the sitting judges (the composition of the Court), the interveners, and the Advocate General. In addition, the Court provides a section called 'Linked documents' next to each judgment. This section contains all references that the judgment has made to legal sources, including the judgments of the Court. The data can be (and has so far been) directly used to build a case-to-case network of citations to precedent. The same data cannot, however, be used to build a paragraph-to-paragraph network, simply because the website seldom provides detailed information on the cited paragraphs. This information can only be obtained directly from the text of the judgments.

[85] For more detailed information on the role of the Research and Documentation Directorate, see Research and Documentation Directorate, CURIA, available at https://curia.europa.eu/jcms/jcms/Jo2_11968/direction-de-la-recherche-et-documentation (accessed 22 September 2020).

In the first step, we wanted to group the cases according to the pre-established criteria. We used the primary classification that designated the content of the case most generally, in order to avoid too many thematic sub-groups. We corrected for the primary classification only if the subsequent keywords provided a close description of the content of the case and they *all* fell under the second most general classification, indicating that the primary classification was not the most general or misleading. For instance, the famous *Defrenne* case[86] has a single subject matter, 'social policy', which corresponds to its actual content—and thus we did not alter the classification. *Van Gend en Loos*[87] is assigned two subject matters: customs union and free movement of goods. We kept the classification free movement of goods because it was the most general and because the substance of the case concerned the free movement of goods. The well-known *Simmenthal case*[88] is assigned three subject matters: agriculture and fisheries; veterinary legislation; and beef and veal. Its secondary classification is: the Community legal order/Community law and national law/Direct effect, primacy and uniform application of the Community law. The only keyword assigned to the case on the website is 'Discarding by the national court of a law contrary to Community law'. This is the aspect of case (primacy) that literature has discussed most voluminously. Hence, we re-assigned the subject matter of the case to the secondary classification, i.e. the Community (EU) legal order. To obtain cohesive sub-groups in which legal relevance could be assessed without patent errors, we carried out a similar process for all cases in the network and in the database.

As an alternative to the Court's classification, we also categorized the landmark cases based on close reading—and on existing leading textbooks—using the Notes relating to the decision[89] for guidance. The cases are systematized based on four criteria. First, their practical and symbolic importance. For instance, according to this criterion cases that literature considers as fundamental fall into the category of cases with mainly symbolic importance while others, discussed for their relevance for solving concrete problems, fall into the category of cases that had primarily practical importance. The symbolic significance or importance of a case relates to its legal standing but transcends the legal issues that the case solved. For instance, while *Costa v. ENEL*[90] resolved the problem of primacy of conflicting legal sources, it also became equivalent to the fundamental characteristic of the European legal order and became associated with the processes of constitutionalization and autonomization (emancipation) of the European legal

[86] Case C-43/75, *Defrenne* (EU:C:1976:56).
[87] Case C-26/62, *Van Gend en Loos* (EU:C:1963:1).
[88] Case C-106/77, *Simmenthal* (EU:C:1978:49).
[89] A bibliography published alongside every text of the judgment on Eurlex.
[90] Case C-6/64, *Costa v. ENEL* (EU:C:1964:66).

order from international law.[91] The same is true for *Francovich*,[92] which established the principle of state liability and thereby solved a practical problem related to the non-implementation of directives which did not have direct effect. By contrast, *Van Duyn*[93] is an example of a case with primarily practical importance, where the Court extended direct effect to directives without proclaiming any new principles. This symbolic move was accomplished in *Van Gend* by proclaiming the principle, and, subsequently, in *Francovich* by the doctrinal leap of constructing a new principle on its basis.

Second, we placed cases in two categories based on the Court's law-making initiative: establishment of new judge-made principles and interpretation of Treaty Articles. These categories distinguish between outcomes that were not strictly based on the Treaty Articles[94] but were judge made, such as direct effect, or the principle of state liability, and cases which were more firmly grounded in the interpretation of Treaty Articles, such as *Beer Purity*.[95] This criterion is not clear cut at the margins, but the classification process follows the discussion in scholarly literature, where certain cases as a rule appear associated with judicial law-making, or judicial policy-making. As we only had to apply the four detailed categorizations to 50 cases which were very well known and widely commented upon, this was not an impossible task.

The third classification relates to juridical consequences and effects. Cases were grouped into two categories according to whether the Court had limited or mitigated the consequences of its rulings in practice (yes/no). The classification process was based primarily on a reading of the texts of the judgments. Again, the forms of such mitigation are diverse but *grosso modo* include deference to the national court;[96] limiting the temporal effect of the judgment; or finding a reason to decouple the abstract legal principle from the terms of its application in the concrete case (the remedy). The latter means that while, generally speaking, the Court will proclaim the principle of state liability for national highest courts, it

[91] Stein, 'Toward Supremacy of Treaty-Constitution by Judicial Fiat: On the Margin of the Costa Case', 63 *Michigan Law Review* (1965) 491; Spiermann, 'The Other Side of the Story: An Unpopular Essay on the Making of the European Community Legal Order', 10 *European Journal of International Law* (1999) 763.

[92] Case C-479/93, *Francovich* (EU:C:1995:372).

[93] Case C-41/74, *Van Duyn* (EU:C:1974:133).

[94] For instance, the Treaty does not mention primacy or a constitutional charter, so cases in which the Court derives conclusions based on these concepts, fall within the judge made category. The cases which are based on the interpretation of specific Treaty articles, even if that interpretation is purposive, will typically fall within the category Interpretation of Treaty articles.

[95] Case C-178/84, *Commission v. Germany (Beer Purity)* (EU:C:1987:126).

[96] In the preliminary reference procedure, the national court will always take the final decision in the main proceedings. Deference to the national courts can range from complete deference to minimal deference. For instance, a completely deferential court will not perform the proportionality test or decide that the decision hinges on a particular aspect of the national law, which the national court should interpret. A minimally deferential court will provide the national court with clear and detailed guidelines or a complete solution of the case while insisting that the national court has the freedom to apply these guidelines.

will not hold the principle valid in the concrete case in which the referring court raised the question.

Fourth, we divided the historic case law according to the age of the judgments into old cases, decided between 1954 and 1979, and new cases, decided between 1980 and 2001. The rationale of this classification is directly related to the Court's decision-making, and the argument that the Court changed its practice of citing past cases in the late 1970s. In addition, the categorization considers the bias of specific network metrics, discussed in Section 3.B. For instance, the network metric of in-degree, which counts the number of citations, favours older cases. Relative in-degree, which calculates the importance of cases by dividing the actual citations with the number of possible citations, favours newer cases or the so-called rising stars.

Fifth, and last, we grouped cases according to the primary object of protection. According to this criterion, the cases fell into four categories: those that were mainly aimed at the protection of the individual (referred to further as category A); those that protected the authority of the legal order (category B); those that intended to secure the functioning of the internal market (category C); and the cases that established the general principles of EU law (category D). These four categories were established after a close reading of all cases that scrutinized their commonalities and differences. Scholarly opinion played an important role, as did a reading of the judgments. For instance, judgments in which the Court stressed the proper functioning of the market and where this seemed—after preliminary analysis—one of the key arguments justifying the outcome of the cases were placed into category C. This was also the case where other considerations, such as the authority of the legal order, were present in the text of the judgment.

ii. Findings and Interpretation

The findings show that all metrics highlight a distinct profile of cases included in the list of landmark cases when compared to a group of randomly selected cases from the dataset. The computed metrics for landmark cases are on average a few orders of magnitude higher than the metrics of a non-landmark case (meaning a case not included on the list). Cases of doctrinal importance obtain high authority scores almost 30 years after they were decided.

That said, different metrics highlight different properties of the landmark cases and hence identify different properties of the network structure. The findings are displayed in Table 4.1. The rows in Table 4.1 show the metrics that we used to detect the cases which the Court selected as landmark cases (i.e. to approximate the Court's own selection by using the network approach). The Table's first column from the right lists the categories together with how many cases were categorized and in which sub-category. For instance, the category of age included 12 old cases (decided before 1980) and 37 new cases (decided from 1980 to 2001). The number and percentage pairings in Table 4.1 display the findings—providing

Table 4.1 Detecting landmark cases using different measures

Category		In-degree	Authority	Relative in-degree	Longevity
Total		17	8	10	7
Age	old (13)	7 (41%)	4 (50%)	2 (20%)	**7 (100%)**
	new (37)	10 (59%)	4 (50%)	**8 (80%)**	0 (0%)
Importance	practical (41)	**15 (88%)**	**8 (100%)**	**10 (100%)**	4 (57%)
	symbolic (9)	2 (12%)	0 (0%)	0 (0%)	3 (43%)
Mitigate	no (30)	9 (53%)	2 (25%)	6 (60%)	5 (71%)
	yes (20)	8 (47%)	6 (75%)	4 (40%)	2 (29%)
Principle	no (20)	6 (35%)	4 (50%)	6 (60%)	3 (43%)
	yes (30)	11 (65%)	4 (50%)	4 (40%)	4 (57%)
Protection	A (16)	**7 (41%)**	2 (25%)	3 (30%)	**3 (43%)**
	B (11)	4 (24%)	1 (12%)	0 (0%)	2 (29%)
	C (15)	4 (24%)	**4 (50%)**	**6 (60%)**	2 (29%)
	D (8)	2 (12%)	1 (12%)	1 (10%)	0 (0%)

Note: The table shows the detection of landmark cases using different measures of case centrality/importance/number of landmark cases in the list of the 50 most important cases according to the network analysis. Absolute values in the table stand for the number of common cases between the list made by the Court and the one identified by network analysis (row entitled 'Total' in the table). To understand the impact of each metric better, we also provide the distribution of the common cases according to the additional classification presented in Section 4.A.i. The percentage stands for the proportion of common cases in each category. For example, if we look at the category 'Age', based on the in-degree held in common with the 50 landmark cases, 41% of the top 50 cases belong to the category 'Old' whereas the rest (59%) belong to the category 'New'.

an indication of how many landmark cases on the Court's list of landmark cases were detected by different network metrics. In other words, the pairings show the extent to which the selection of the Court matched the 'objective' importance according to the network metrics.

The results were less than encouraging. In-degree (the number of times a case was cited by another case in the network, in absolute numbers) detected 17 landmark cases, relative in-degree[97] 10 and so on (second row in Table 4.1). As expected, in-degree (citation count) was biased towards old cases. Relative in-degree and average longevity[98] provided a contrasting view. Relative in-degree focused on recent cases while average longevity focused on old cases. Authority scores[99] detected cases with practical importance but did not capture cases with so-called symbolic importance. For instance, the authority scores correctly identified all cases that were classified as having practical importance. By

[97] In-degree divided by the number of cases decided later in time (the case cited by all cases which could cite it in the future).

[98] The average citation age over all citations of a case between the first and the most recent citation.

[99] Hub score measures how many authoritative cases a case cites. Authority score measures how many good hubs cite a case.

contrast, it did not detect cases that were of symbolic importance to the European legal order (fourth row in the third column).

While the information might be valuable in subsequent legal analysis, it is a fact that the cases identified by network analysis did not always match the cases which the Court identified as the most important. Multiple scenarios may have produced this mismatch. First, the Court may not have explicitly referred to those cases even if it considered them important or relevant. Second, the Court may not have solely relied on the strictly legal doctrinal aspect of cases. Third, a case that the Court identified as important might have had an impact on only one legal domain in its case law, or was crucial in a specific point in time. By this logic, a case which was important in a narrow domain is not important in the global network of cases comprising several domains and sub-domains of various sizes.

iii. Research Redesign: Approximating Legal Reality

The limitation of the analysis presented previously is that it aggregated all information contained in the dataset and placed all topics addressed by the Court at the same level. To provide a more nuanced picture of which cases are important in different domains of EU law, we relied on the subject matter of the case, as specified earlier. We divided the network into sub-networks according to the subject matter. The sub-networks were composed only of cases falling within the same subject area, sharing the legal context of the landmark cases (for instance, it comprised only the cases that fell within the subject matter 'competition'). As demonstrated in Table 4.2, the accuracy improved greatly. For instance, in detecting authoritative cases, the sub-networks produced results that were 10 times more accurate (in the sense that they matched the Court's selection more closely) compared to the same metrics performed on the complete networks (the bottom row in Table 4.2).

The example shows that different metrics are complementary, for both the static (structural) and the evolutionary (temporal) network properties. Average longevity detects cases with protracted relevance based on purely legal criteria, whereas relative in-degree spots the rising stars. This is expected because the metric favours newer judgments. In-degree also performs well. It is not surprising

Table 4.2 Detecting landmark cases in complete networks and sub-networks

Network	In-degree			Authority			Relative in-degree			Longevity		
	top 5	top 10	top 50	top 5	top 10	top 50	top 5	top 10	top 50	top 5	top 10	top 50
Complete	4	5	17	1	1	8	1	1	10	1	3	7
Sub-network	11	**14**	26	8	**10**	19	10	**12**	26	5	**14**	20
Ratio	2.75	**2.8**	1.5	8	**10**	2.4	10	**12**	2.6	5	**4.67**	2.9

that some of the important cases are well cited; however, the less cited cases sink according to this metric. From the evolutionary point of view, it becomes clear that authority scores, obtained by studying citations, to a large extent reflect the landmark status of the cases, supported by the doctrine and the Court's interpretation of its case law. On the other hand, relative in-degree, even though it favours the more recent cases, shows that cases with authoritative profiles retain their high ranks over time.

iv. A Short Reflection

The results obtained on the classifications used in this study are compelling. If one focuses for instance on the importance of the landmark cases, it is remarkable that most network metrics (if not all) capture landmark cases that have or had a practical importance (they solved concrete legal issues). In contrast, it leaves undetected the cases that had a more symbolic character (they did not solve concrete problems but defined the nature of the legal system and its fundamental features). This, though, is alleviated by the fact that practical cases make up more than 80 per cent of listed cases. Such a finding is interesting because it provides empirical evidence that the motivation of the Court when selecting the landmark cases was to consider cases that are not widely used and cited but important on a principled level.

On the level of methodology, this finding has multiple implications. First, that citation networks can contribute to legal research with a clearly defined purpose. Second, the finding exposes the limits of citation networks. Namely, it is impossible to mimic legal logic completely. Third, it clearly demonstrates that the network approach requires a clear research question, which can guide the selection of empirical material and help researchers to choose among numerous tools and techniques. Fourth, it exposes the need for legal doctrinal input even at the initial stage of research design. Lines of legal logic as well as institutional practices are not always plainly evident to non-experts. Hence, it is the responsibility of research design to make such matters explicit. The most valuable input will come from lawyers and from a symbiotic relationship between the approaches.

B. Legal Relevance as a Dynamic in CJEU Case Law Structure

The following modification of network methodology is an extension of the study of landmark cases presented in Section 4.A and builds on the insights obtained from that study. Instead of looking at the structure of the network, it focuses on its growth. The main aim is to test whether the network approach can provide a picture of the evolving network, which would provide a legally relevant insight into the evolution of the law—capturing its inherently dynamic nature.

The analysis conducted on the sub-set of landmark cases selected by the Court supported the conclusion that the Court adopted a historic perspective. Translated into the network approach, this means that the coefficients capturing the importance of a case might have been high at some point in the past but were low in 2002. This explains why the importance of the case remained undetected by the static analysis. Hence, we tried to attune the network approach further to the legal reality of the Court with a temporal analysis. Tangibly speaking, we focused on how different metrics evolved over time. We mimicked the growth of the network and computed the values of the coefficients at each time step and for each case.

This perspective allowed us to examine two questions. First, is there a specific profile in the evolution of the properties for the selected landmark cases that distinguishes them from non-landmark cases? Second, does the evolutionary historical perspective provide an explanation for the presence of landmark cases undetected in the previous analysis?

i. The Long-Term Perspective on Case Relevance as a Mode of Continuous Authority

How and when do particular cases gain and maintain authority in the networks? We hypothesized that cases became important during a particular moment in time and remained important until they were supplanted by subsequent cases. To illustrate this point, we focused on the landmark cases that were selected by the Court and fell into the category of free movement of goods according to their assigned subject matter. This category is interesting for two reasons: first, it is the category which contains the most landmark cases (i.e. 10) self-selected by the Court. This reveals an emphasis that the Court must have placed on the internal market in the process of selection. Second, in this category the Court's selection coincides to a large degree with the network metrics, meaning that the so-called objective-quantitative and subjective-qualitative points of view converge.

Figure 4.1 presents the evolution of the authority score (a) and the relative in-degree (b) as a function of time for the landmark decisions related to free movement of goods. Taking into account the authority scores, one can see that *Dassonville*[100] (61974CJ0008, light blue line) is the most prominent case in the group with a unique citation pattern, followed by *Cassis de Dijon*[101] (61978CJ0120, red line), then *Keck and Mithouard*[102] (61991CJ0267, darker and shorter purple line), and *Commission v. Germany* (*Beer purity*)[103] (61984CJ0178, dark blue line).

Several interesting observations follow from this. First, the findings clearly strengthen assumptions regarding the cases that were historically important. *Van*

[100] Case C-8/74, *Dassonville* (EU:C:1974:82).
[101] Case C-120/78, *Cassis de Dijon* (EU:C:1979:42).
[102] Case C-267/91, *Keck and Mithouard* (EU:C:1993:905).
[103] Case C-178/84, *Commission v. Germany (Beer Purity)* (EU:C:1993:905).

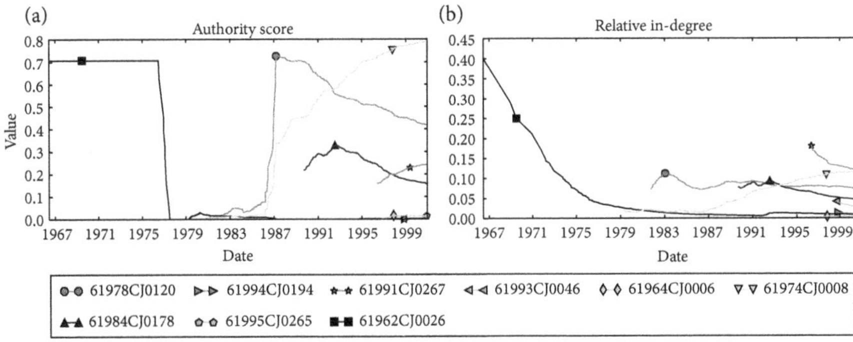

Figure 4.1 Authority scores and relative in-degree scores (vertical axis) for landmark free movement of goods cases over time (horizontal axis) with celex numbers

Gend (61962CJ0026, black line) was one of the less important cases in 2002 and, as such, not identified as an important case by the metrics outlined in the previous section (Section 4.A). However, the temporal approach reveals that it was a key case in the 1970s in the free movement of goods domain. This shows that adding a temporal perspective to a structural network analysis is essential to obtaining a comprehensive picture of the profile of a case. It shows, for instance, that historically *Van Gend* was not a symbolic case but a case with practical relevance. Its symbolic component, however, outlived its practical relevance. The inference is based on its citation pattern and supported by legal scholarship.[104]

Additionally, the comparison between the evolution of authority scores (figure (a)) and relative in-degree (figure (b)) shows that while authority scores can detect shifts between leading cases in a specific context, relative in-degree provides a more precise and comprehensive vision of the evolution of importance. For instance, focusing on *Cassis de Dijon* (red line), the evolution of its authority score seems to indicate a sharp increase of importance (along with *Dassonville*, although even sharper) before a clear decline. This perspective is contrasted with the evolution of its relative in-degree showing a steady importance over time. The natural evolution of relative in-degree is to decrease over time since the value is a ratio whose denominator grows as the network grows. Thus, a prolonged steady value for *Cassis de Dijon* reveals that—even though the authority score seems to indicate a decline in its authority—judges actively cited the case over an extended period when they had to decide cases included in the free movement of goods network.

In this regard, the evolution of *Dassonville* is rather spectacular since its value increases over time. *Dassonville* gained authority—as suggested by the authority score—and became even more frequently cited as time passed. Relative in-degree

[104] Weiler, 'Van Gend En Loos: The Individual as Subject and Object and the Dilemma of European Legitimacy', 12 *International Journal of Constitutional Law* (2014) 94.

also highlights the emerging importance of *Keck* (shorter and darker purple line), which seems to coincide with the two earlier cases and was not detected by measuring the authority scores. This analysis suggests that the evolution of importance of *Dassonville*, *Cassis de Dijon*, and *Keck* is related and they should be analysed together in order to obtain a comprehensive understanding of the evolution of free movement jurisprudence.

ii. Legal Versatility

Following the insights of the temporal perspective, we were interested in whether the group of landmark cases with unusual and unexpected citation patterns had a distinct legal quality which the network approach could tease out. We hypothesized that cases which the Court continues to cite have a wide-ranging application, meaning that they are legally relevant across different subject areas. By referring to a wide-ranging application, we are cognizant of a necessary distinction. First, some cases address a procedurally relevant point, for instance the Court's insistence on taking into account the actual conditions at the time of the Commission's notice in the infringement procedure, and can arise in any legal domain. Second, some cases solve multiple legal problems—either general (such as primacy, proportionality, or the status of general principles of EU law) or particular (such as defining measures that have an effect equivalent to quantitative restriction, and establishing that a specific article has direct effect).[105] We tried to capture these properties in the measure of case versatility.

We proceeded in two steps. In the first step, we mapped each case to its primary subject matter. For instance, for *Van Gend* this was the free movement of goods. Then, we explored whether the case had an influence spreading beyond its primary subject matter. Again, we used the Court's classification and our reclassification to track the subject matter of cases. We defined the versatility of case C as a function of its diffusion and diversity. Diffusion means that a case is cited by cases that span over a wide set of subject matters. It allows us to scrutinize whether case C, which has the subject matter c, is cited by cases A and B, which have the subject matter a and b. Diversity means that such a citation pattern is relatively regular, meaning that the distribution of citations across the subject matters is uniform and relatively stable over time. This simply means that case C is cited regularly by cases whose subject matter is a and b.

The process produced mixed outcomes. It showed that cases with continuous relevance could be divided into two types: those that are legally versatile and others that are not. This implied that there were several paths to 'immortality' but did not offer any conclusive answers regarding the special character of landmark cases. Non-selected cases largely followed the same pattern. It also demonstrated

[105] Here, the size of the legal domain is less relevant because sub-networks are independent.

that there were different types of cases with a different lifespan and that the network measures should take this property of the case citation networks into account.

Figure 4.2 illustrates these patterns using two cases selected by the Court. The first case, *Dassonville*, is continuously cited by subsequent cases that also fall into the category free movement of goods.[106] Occasionally, it is cited by cases whose subject matter is related to agriculture and approximation of laws of competition. This could be due to the noise in the categorization. The Court often assigns a subject matter to the case at the time of the decision or prior to the decision. It

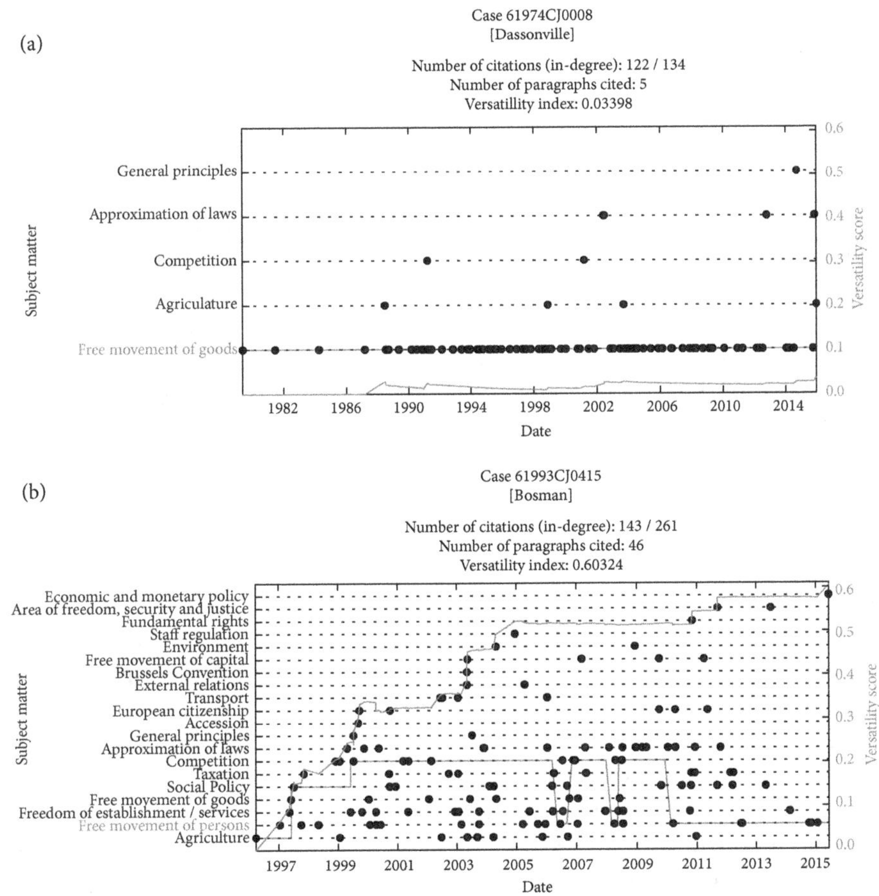

Figure 4.2 The versatility of two landmark cases selected by the Court of Justice, *Dassonville* (a) and *Bosman* (b)

[106] For more detail see the recent contribution by Schütze: in Schütze, '"Re-Reading" Dassonville: Meaning and Understanding in the History of European Law', *SSRN Electronic Journal* (2018), available at https://www.ssrn.com/abstract=3150391 (accessed 6 November 2018).

also assigns several subject matters—some general, others less so. One case can also fall within several categories and it may be difficult to establish the category into which the case primarily falls, even after reading the case. This creates errors in the categorization (i.e. false categorizations).

The versatility score of *Dassonville* is low. In contrast, *Bosman* (Figure 4.2, part b) has a high versatility score. It is regularly cited by cases outside its category, which is the free movement of persons. Both cases are among the most cited cases in the citation network of the Court, yet their patterns are completely opposite. In terms of methodology, this study shows that the network approach can differentiate between these patterns, which are revealing when assessing the legal properties of cases. It can do so comprehensively and systematically for all cases in the network.

C. What Networks Can Tell Us about the 'Real' Importance of Cases

This section (Section 3.C) addresses two points of criticism outlined in Section 3.B. First, that the network analysis approach treats all citations as equally important and does not discriminate between different types of references. Second, that since citation network analysis relies on explicit case citations, it can only be applied to courts with a developed and rigorous citation practice. Continental-style courts like the Court of Justice tend to repeat the wording and the arguments established in past cases without citing the source (so-called implicit citations).[107] While this is less true of more recent judgments, certainly in its earlier cases the Court often resorted to such implicit citations.

To address such challenges, we combined the network approach with text analysis. First, we constructed the citation network based on references to paragraphs of individual judgments as units rather than entire judgments. Our dataset consisted of 10,418 judgments and around 445,000 paragraphs. Since the Court did not number the paragraphs within judgments systematically until the 1970s, our first pilot study excluded all judgments that do not have numbered paragraphs. This is an important limitation, which could be corrected in the future by automatically numbering the paragraphs of all judgments.

Most cited paragraphs typically include a concept or a formulation indicating relevance in the process of construction of legal arguments. Our method went a step further in identifying the aspects of cases that are legally important—and the approach allowed us to acquire information concerning whether the case is

[107] M. de S.-O.-L'E. Lasser, *Judicial Deliberations: A Comparative Analysis of Judicial Transparency and Legitimacy* (2004); N. MacCormick and R. S. Summers, *Interpreting Precedents: A Comparative Study* (1997); Komárek, 'Reasoning with Previous Decisions: Beyond the Doctrine of Precedent', 61 *American Journal of Comparative Law* (2013) 149.

relevant for one or several legal aspects. For instance, if only one paragraph of a case is repeatedly cited, the case is most likely important for resolving one legal issue. If, by contrast, several different paragraphs of one judgment are cited, the case might be important for resolving more than one legal issue. This would also imply its higher versatility score as discussed earlier. However, in the present research set-up this could be directly verified because it contained a direct link to the legal text.

Second, we identified references to entire cases and used text similarity techniques to increase the precision of the reference. Typically, the Court uses numbered paragraphs to structure its judgments. When scholars discuss cases, they also refer to case paragraphs. Hence, we applied text similarity techniques to case paragraphs rather than sentences to find precise references. An instance of a reference to an entire case is when case A is citing case B. A case-to-case citation network—as employed by studies using the network approach thus far—is typically constructed on the basis of these references. By contrast, we broke the case-to-case citation networks down into a network of case paragraphs. For instance, we might find that case A, paragraph 10, cites case B, paragraph 5. Hereafter, by looking at the language of the Court, we can identify the relation between case A, paragraph 10, and case B, paragraph 5, *even if* case A does *not* cite case B explicitly by case name (B) or cites it by name but does not specify the paragraph. We labelled these references implicit references or missing citations and added them to the network along with the explicit citations. In other words, the language similarity technique is a technique used to identify additional (missing or implicit) citations and construct a complete and detailed network that reflects the legal importance of cases accurately. It gives every case its legal due.[108]

The similarity index that we used[109] treats case paragraphs as 'bags-of-words' in the sense that the order of the words is not important. The latter property largely reverses the effect of paraphrasing, a challenge in the detection of implicit citations. The Court often paraphrases the wording of the original formula to express the same content. The new versions of the formula are thus not identical, but are similar to the original formula.

Third, we assessed the relevance of cited paragraphs from a legal perspective. Because we infer implicit citations, the networks reflect the 'true' relevance of the case. The approach is illustrated using three cases: *Dassonville*, *Defrenne*, and *Francovich*.[110] Doctrinally speaking, *Francovich* stands for judicial innovation.[111]

108 Tarissan, Panagis, and Šadl (n. 82).

109 Tversky, 'Features of Similarity', 84 *Psychological Review* (1977) 327; Tarissan, Panagis, and Šadl (n. 82).

110 Case C-6/90, *Francovich* (EU:C:1991:428).

111 See e.g. M. P. Maduro *et al.*, *The Past and Future of EU Law: The Classics of EU Law Revisited on the 50th Anniversary of the Rome Treaty* (2010). It is also one of the most commented on cases in the history of the Court. See for instance Tridimas, who mentions the 'vast bibliography' resulting from the case: T. Tridimas, *The General Principles of EU Law* (2nd ed., 2006) 498.

It established a principle that did not originate from a written legal source of EU law and laid down the conditions under which it could be applied. The reasoning of the Court invoked the legal cornerstones of the European legal order: primacy, direct effect, the duty of cooperation of national courts, and the power to create new legal remedies, as well as respect for the principles of effectiveness and equivalence.[112] *Dassonville* is prominent among legal scholars with regard to one legal aspect in a well-defined area of EU law (free movement of goods).[113] Legal scholars typically situate and consider *Defrenne* in several areas of EU law. For instance, the case is relevant to the debates on the general principle of non-discrimination on grounds of gender (the principle of equal pay for equal work), the limitation of temporal effects of judgments of the Court in exceptional circumstances, and horizontal direct effect of the Treaty as fundamental characteristics of the EU legal order.[114]

The citation patterns, presented in Figure 4.3, clearly reflect these features of the judgments. The differences in legal substance are aptly represented by the fact that the *Dassonville* (a) sub-network consists almost entirely of one star, with incoming citations only to paragraph 5, whereas in *Defrenne* (b) and *Francovich* (c) the citations to several legal aspects produce a number of smaller clusters. The manifold character of *Francovich* is reflected in the high number of different paragraphs that are cited in subsequent cases.

To summarize, the findings of the objective-quantitative analysis are in line with legal observations of the selected cases. They indicate that the network

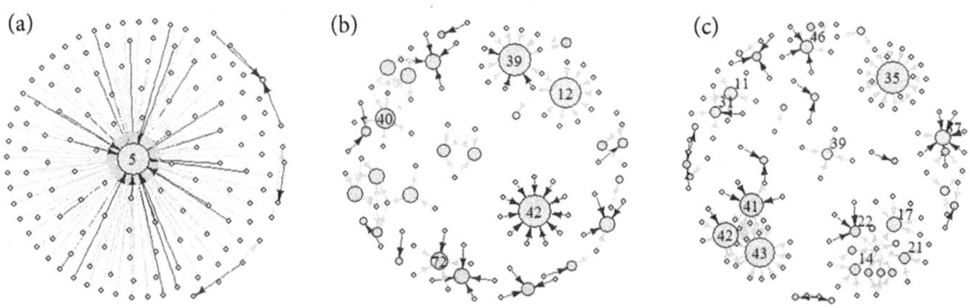

Figure 4.3 Different profile of cases based on the paragraph-to-paragraph citation network and the extraction of implicit citations

Note: Image **(a)** shows the network of citations to different paragraphs of *Dassonville*, image **(b)** shows the network of citations to different paragraphs of *Defrenne*, while image **(c)** shows the network of citations to different paragraphs of *Francovich*.

[112] See *Francovich* (n. 110) at 11 *et seq.*

[113] M. P. Maduro, *We the Court: The European Court of Justice and the European Economic Constitution: A Critical Reading of Article 30 of the EC Treaty* (1998); Weiler, 'Epilogue: Towards a Common Law of International Trade', in J. H. H. Weiler (ed.), *The EU, the WTO, and the NAFTA: Towards a Common Law of International Trade* (2000); Schütze (n. 106).

[114] P. Craig and G. De Búrca, *EU Law: Text, Cases, and Materials* (6th ed., 2015).

approach can approximate a legal study, and the 'true' character of the jurisprudence. Clearly, though, the findings cannot stand on their own. They require legal interpretation and contextualization.

D. Summary of Key Findings

Our re-imagined approach highlights three network techniques which can effectively address the claim that citation patterns invariably fail to reflect the *legal* importance of cases. The main advantage of all three methods is that they incorporate legal logic into research design and develop measures and techniques that reflect this logic. Our first example utilized 50 cases which the Court selected as landmark cases or historic case law at the time of 2004 enlargement. First, we demonstrated how measures of case centrality, one of the central concepts of network analysis, can be used to reflect the legal importance of cases. We argued that different metrics highlight different properties of the citation network and that complementary metrics can capture the legal relevance and the doctrinal importance of individual cases more accurately than a single measure of centrality. Second, our findings showed that the network approach can provide a nuanced picture of which cases are important in different domains of EU law. It can also assist in identifying specific periods of importance. Subsequently, when we organized the full network of cases decided by the Court between 1954 and 2002 into smaller networks by subject matter, the network metrics performed considerably better in detecting authoritative cases. In fact, the sub-networks rendered results that are 10 times more accurate.

Second, we addressed criticism that network metrics do not reflect the dynamic aspect of law. We used the temporal perspective and simulated the growth of the network to measure the evolution of legal importance of a case over time. Concretely, the evolution of two complementary measures of centrality—authority scores and relative in-degree—showed that authority scores can accurately detect the fluctuating importance of leading cases (old cases being supplanted by newer cases). We also saw that relative in-degree can offer a comprehensive view of the evolution of case importance. Surprisingly, some cases seemed to challenge the expected patterns.

Finally, we engaged with doubts about whether the network approach could reveal the real importance of cases, especially given that legal importance is not a unitary concept. This means, in rather simplified terms, that not all cases (not even all the important cases) are important for the same (legally relevant) reasons. We addressed this criticism by obtaining more granulated information from our dataset. This involved separating the network of judgments into the network of case paragraphs. We used text similarity techniques to identify implicit citations. This was a crucial step in identifying all legally relevant aspects of cases. We constructed a new metric which could reflect the legal versatility of a case. The findings demonstrated that the network approach could identify—based on citation patterns—the difference between individual cases which were also doctrinally relevant.

5. Conclusion: The Citation Network Approach and the Lure of Law

Our contribution has affirmed the relevance of the network approach for legal research. Part of this process required constructive engagement with two well-established modes of critique: one which finds fault with the network approach because it is quantitative, and a second which asserts that such methods cannot measure the law. We addressed the first objection by outlining the qualitative origins and aspects of the network approach. We also pointed to its interest in the substance of its object of inquiry—a dynamic requiring qualitative interpretation. This largely repudiated the claim of a fundamental incompatibility between network methodologies and the law. The second mode of objection was addressed via three case studies which combined to demonstrate that the citation network approach could successfully approximate legal reality (i.e. that it could accurately take into account the legal aspect of case citations). Primarily, the examples showed that the approach could accurately identify important cases and crucial moments in the development of the law. Furthermore, the approach could be adjusted to reflect the legally relevant aspects of cases and detect the doctrinal contribution of individual cases to EU law. The last case study considered explicit references to past cases as well as implicit references, meaning the repetition of legal formulas without case citations. These findings, we claim, largely neutralize the objection that network metrics fail to appreciate the necessary legal detail, capture legal development, or accommodate the practice of civil law courts.

The question of relevance is related to (but different from) the question of added value of the approach. The former asks whether the approach lends itself to legal study, the latter to what novel insights the approach might generate that legal method alone cannot produce. Added value refers to potential. In this contribution, we have dealt primarily with relevance because it appears more urgent. Put differently, objections to the network approach tend to pre-emptively dismiss any insights the method might produce on the grounds that they will be inaccurate or 'wrong' and thus irrelevant (i.e. the approach is *a priori* rejected). Quantitative methods will be targeted for disregarding legal logic and failing to touch the normative core of law. In this sense, the question of relevance is the primary question, which we addressed, and somewhat overshadows the question of contribution. Nonetheless, the examples we have presented also speak indirectly to the second question concerning the potential (the promise) of the approach.

There are obvious synergies between legal analysis and citation networks as a method or as a metaphor. Both forms of scrutiny are interested in the content of judicial opinions. They share the idea of webs, patterns, and relations.[115] Citation network analysis connects cases by mapping citations and orders cases into groups and sub-groups based on those citations. A legal scholar orders legal sources and legal categories, as well as sub-categories, arranging them into a coherent system.[116]

Legal scholarship sees law as a system of norms. For the most part, it rationalizes individual court decisions by looking at legal rules, principles, and doctrines. It reconstructs this system based on its underlying values and principles. Often the connections remain implicit. Legal analysis allows conclusions about these implicit connections, based on carefully selected examples, obtained in the process of interpretation. The lure of the legal methodology in EU law is in generating a narrative of legal development, either by rationalizing the Court's decisions (scholarship of celebration) or by criticizing the same decisions (scholarship of critique).[117] Legal analysis offers constant evaluation and criticism, and calls for improvement. In that latter sense, it is prescriptive.

By contrast, the network approach can capture only explicit (observable) relations between legal sources and legal language. It is descriptive. It can thus never replace doctrinal work. However, it can provide a comprehensive, objective, and transparent basis on which this work can proceed and a 'real life reference' to which the approach can relate. It opens legal arguments to contestations based on what *the Court* says and does—on facts rather than personal opinions and normative preferences. This is not, in principle, incompatible with the discipline of law as an argumentative discipline, at least not with the contextual approach to law.

To summarize, the first advantage of combining the legal approach with the citation network approach lies in the greater transparency of the research process. This includes the research design, which must explicitly justify the selection of legal material and its relevance for answering the legal questions at issue. The benefit continues when it comes to the range of arguments that can be made and defended. One could argue that while empirical research may reduce the range of possible arguments, it will strengthen those arguments that are possible. One implication is that one can also draw a clearer line between those arguments that follow from legal interpretation supported by empirical observations and arguments that follow from legal interpretation alone. This discussion differs from contestations about objectivity and its value in legal research—which provides

[115] A. Somek, *The Legal Relation: Legal Theory after Legal Positivism* (2017).
[116] Šadl and Olsen (n. 25).
[117] Somek, 'The Emancipation of Legal Dissonance', 09-02 University of Iowa Legal Studies Research Paper (2009).

scope for future research.[118] We can, however, affirm that producing evidence capable of countering accepted narratives and beliefs will support a dialectic process which is desirable as a goal in itself. The unpacking of legal beliefs and the discovery of new connections between cases could help to explain issues which thus far elude us.

The network approach does not present a threat to the normativity of legal doctrine or to the law more broadly. It does not tell the law to cease being a science about legal norms. The approach is agnostic about the idea of the law's autonomy—not least the question of whether the legal system is an autonomous system, free of politics.

Meanwhile, the shortcomings of the network methodology are apparent and almost self-evident. They are related to data sources and to the quality of data obtained from those sources. On the one hand the limitations issue from inconsistent referencing, errors in the official metadata (non-existent links and cases), the new citation format (ECLI:EU:), and the repetition of formulas without references to the original decision but instead references to several subsequent decisions. They stem from the practical challenges related to the Court's procedures, such as subtle changes in translations from the French text,[119] the changing structure of the judgments (the labelling of paragraphs), and the developments in the practice of citations. Finally, they are of a technical nature. The Court repeats the same statement within the text of judgments, first as a preliminary question, second as the 'answer' of the Court, and third in the decision of the Court in the operative part. Most of these shortcomings of data collection and validity (quality of the data) are potentially solvable. A deeper problem arises from the level of ontological resistance to opening legal methodology to empirical scrutiny. *If* this were to change, it would require a more thoughtful engagement with modes of objection. It would also rely upon good will brought to the process of translating these arguments into network metrics. Making a start along these lines was the aim of our contribution.

[118] Frankenreiter (n. 59).

[119] For an example of problems arising from translation, see McAuliffe, 'Behind the Scenes at the Court of Justice: Drafting EU Law Stories', in F. Nicola and B. Davies (eds), *EU Law Stories* (2017), available at https://www.cambridge.org/core/product/identifier/9781316340479%23CT-bp-3/type/book_part (accessed 8 November 2018).

5

Judicial Legitimacy in the European Union

Jan Komárek

1. Introduction

In a volume which, according to its title, promised to be *Judging European Judges*, Joseph Weiler expressed scepticism towards the use of the concept of legitimacy in that exercise. In his view 'there is simply not enough agreement to be able to use it in a broadly and meaningfully accepted way'.[1] This chapter is an attempt to suggest an opposite view and to show how the concept of legitimacy can be used to understand the place of the European Court of Justice (ECJ) in the EU political system.[2] In my view, as long as people are clear about *their* understanding of the concept, legitimacy can serve as a focal point around which scholarly, and hopefully also public, debate potentially revolves.[3] Indeed, the very disagreements about legitimacy's precise meaning have the potential to generate debate and invite engagement from different sides. This can facilitate mutual understanding—or at least clarification of mutually irreconcilable conflicting positions—and establish political legitimacy of a sort. The key is to have some sophisticated account of legitimacy at hand. Here one must agree with Weiler in his diagnosis of lawyers' use of the concept as a proxy to something else: 'factors that enhance or detract from the authority or authoritativeness of judicial decisions and of the Court'.[4] I will argue that legitimacy should be taken to mean much more than that—and that lawyers should take note.

The chapter therefore begins with some reflections on the concept of legitimacy, as it is used in the debates on the EU and its judicial system, particularly the ECJ, in Section 2. In Section 3, I will seek to present a framework for studying the ECJ's legitimacy which does justice to its dual role: to decide particular cases and at the

[1] Weiler, 'Epilogue: Judging the Judges—Apology and Critique', in M. Adams *et al.* (eds), *Judging Europe's Judges: The Legitimacy of the Case Law of the European Court of Justice* (2013) 235.

[2] By the 'European Court of Justice' I mean the highest court in the EU judicial system and use the abbreviation ECJ to refer to it; the (now) commonly used abbreviation CJEU refers to the whole judicial institution of the EU, which comprises, besides the ECJ also the General Court (and contained, for the period between 2 December 2005 to 1 September 2016, the Civil Service Tribunal).

[3] See C. S. Sternberg, *The Struggle for EU Legitimacy: Public Contestation, 1950–2005* (2013). This being said in addition to the fact that there is in reality much disagreement about many concepts used in the scholarly and political discourse (e.g. justice, democracy, rule of law—to name just few).

[4] Weiler (n. 1) 235.

Jan Komárek, *Judicial Legitimacy in the European Union*. In: *New Legal Approaches to Studying the Court of Justice*. First edition. Edited by Claire Kilpatrick and Joanne Scott, Oxford University Press (2020). © Jan Komárek.
DOI: 10.1093/oso/9780198871477.003.0006

same time to fulfil much wider functions in the EU political system. Section 4 then focuses on the perennial problem of judicial legitimacy in the Western legal tradition: how to legitimize creative moments of judicial interpretation of law, which are at the same time unavoidable and deeply problematic for what is sometimes called the liberal doctrine of politics? Section 5 looks in some detail on the recent turn to semantic pragmatism and its relationship to the democratic theory and discusses some of its shortcomings, and Section 6 concludes.

2. Approaching Legitimacy

A. Against the Normative/Descriptive Dichotomy

Most accounts of legitimacy distinguish between descriptive or sociological accounts of legitimacy, on the one hand, and normative, on the other.[5] Descriptive legitimacy concerns '*people's beliefs* about political authority and, sometimes, political obligations'.[6] Normative account, on the other hand, 'refers to some *benchmark* of acceptability or justification of political power or authority and—possibly—obligation'.[7] In both senses legitimacy is thought to be conducive of compliance, in addition to mere habit, self-interest, or fear of sanctions.[8]

The distinction between descriptive and normative accounts can sometimes obscure important issues, however, especially when what are being assessed are political institutions.[9] In this case we always need to ask who it is that the political institution must appear legitimate to. It makes a big difference if the subject of the legitimacy judgment is 'the individual' or 'we the people'. The first refers to the liberal repository of values such as liberty, individual rights, or (negative)

[5] In general, see Fabienne, 'Political Legitimacy', in E. N. Zalta (ed.), *Stanford Encyclopedia of Philosophy*, Spring 2014 Edition, available at http://plato.stanford.edu/archives/spr2014/entries/legitimacy/ (accessed 16 September 2020). For studies in law, see particularly Fallon, 'Legitimacy and the Constitution', 118 *Harvard Law Review* (2005) 1787 and Thomas, 'The Uses and Abuses of Legitimacy in International Law', 34 *Oxford Journal of Legal Studies* (2014) 729.

[6] Fabienne (n. 5), emphasis added.

[7] Ibid., emphasis added. Some authors break down normative legitimacy into legal and moral legitimacy. I am rather sceptical of the usefulness of the concept of 'legal legitimacy' understood as conformity with law, employed by both Fallon (n. 5), and Thomas (n. 5). In my view legality is a more appropriate term—and needs to be distinguished from legitimacy, as continuous discussions of this conceptual pair/opposition suggest. See particularly e.g. Thornhill, 'Legality, Legitimacy and the Form of Political Power: On the Construction of a False Antinomy', 3 *Journal of Power* (2010) 293, with further references to the classical debates concerning the distinction.

[8] Hyde, 'The Concept of Legitimation in the Sociology of Law', *Wisconsin Law Review* (1983) 379 presents a very sophisticated critique of such view.

[9] For Habermas, 'Legitimation Problems in the Modern State', in J. Habermas (T. Carty trans.), *Communication and the Evolution of Society* (1979) 179, '[o]nly political orders can have and lose legitimacy; only they need legitimation. Multinational corporations or the world market are not capable of legitimation'. I think when other actors and systems (such as multinational corporations or markets) are delegated public power and become autonomous to an extent unseen in the late 1970s when Habermas was writing these words, they also need to be legitimated as such.

freedom. The latter will draw on a different, republican, or communitarian register, where justice, democracy, or political freedom will most probably be the key value.[10] Those who defend the idea of the European Union as a union among the *peoples* of Europe will add another possible subject—the collectivity of already collective subjects.[11]

There is also a related, more practical problem with sociological legitimacy, if used in the political context.[12] It is difficult to ask 'we the people'—the political collective—for its opinion in a sociological survey, since what one obtains is an aggregate view of a number of individuals (even if all people in the given polity were consulted). The voice of 'we the people' is *always moderated*, be it through the way a sociological survey is structured or the electoral system, political representation, or even referendum (something arguably closest to an opinion poll) are organized.[13] The people, as any political collective (the nation, for example), exists only in public imaginary but not in the concrete (physical) reality.[14] Sociological surveys provide information on what selected respondents think, but their responses can never reflect *political* legitimacy in a deeper sense.[15] Political legitimacy of a collective subject (the state, the EU) can only be *construed* through a democratic procedure—it never exists on its own.[16]

In the context of European integration, the matter is further complicated by how much the identification of the relevant subject of legitimacy depends on how the nature of the EU is understood—a very contested question indeed.[17] This is the point raised by Fritz Scharpf, who argues that in a polity such as the Union '[f]rom the perspective of citizens compliance is exclusively demanded by *national* administrative agencies, tax authorities, and courts'.[18] From this Scharpf infers that 'we need to discuss the legitimating arguments that justify the

[10] Conceptually speaking these people may (at least sometimes) have the same concept in mind, but use different terms to denote it. On the importance of political vocabulary see e.g. T. Ball, J. Farr, and R. L. Hanson (eds), *Political Innovation and Political Change* (1989).

[11] On the idea of 'demoicracy', see Müller, 'The Promise of "Demoi-Cracy": Democracy, Diversity, and Domination in the European Public Order', in J. Neyer and A. Wiener (eds), *Political Theory of the European Union* (2011).

[12] Hyde (n. 8), discusses many other methodological problems with sociological legitimacy.

[13] This applies to the so-called aggregative conception of democracy, which is primarily concerned with collecting individual preferences of citizens, without any regard for the common good. For an overview of different conceptions of democracy, see D. Held, *Models of Democracy* (3rd ed., 2006).

[14] On these fictions, see Y. Ezrahi, *Imagined Democracies: Necessary Political Fictions* (2012).

[15] This seems to be forgotten by Moravcsik and Sangiovanni, 'On Democracy and "Public Interest" in the European Union', in W. Streeck and R. Mainz (eds), *Die Reformierbarkeit der Demokratie: Innovationen und Blockaden* (2002) 122, who seem to ascribe output democratic legitimacy (in their words 'what people really want') to what public opinion analysis would reveal.

[16] On this point see C. Möllers, *The Three Branches: A Comparative Model of Separation of Powers* (2013) 63–78.

[17] Besides Sternberg (n. 3), see a more theoretical account: Christodoulidis and Bankowski, 'The European Union as an Essentially Contested Project', 4 *European Law Journal* (1998) 341.

[18] Scharpf, 'Legitimacy in the Multi-level European Polity', in M. Loughlin and P. Dobner (eds), *The Twilight of Constitutionalism?* (2010) 97, emphasis added.

compliance of member states with EU mandates, and the conditions that allow member states to legitimate this compliance in relation to their own citizens'.[19]

This, however, is not how European citizens perceive the Union. First, Scharpf focuses too much on the question of enforcing compliance, where it can be national administrative and judicial institutions which are indeed in charge (although competition policy would be an exception even on such narrow view). The power, exercised by the Union, is perceived by citizens as stemming from the EU even in the absence of enforcement by the EU institutions.[20] Think of various public campaigns against different EU policies (anti-immigration, too much social Europe, too little social Europe, . . .), culminating in the Eurocrisis anti-austerity movement.[21] It does not matter that the cuts are executed by national governments after a formal rubber-stamping by national parliaments—it is the EU that is blamed.[22]

In sum, no 'descriptive' account of legitimacy can avoid normative questions—at best it can sweep them under the carpet. The normative and descriptive are deeply intertwined and attempts to have one without the other can be quite deceptive. In *Judging Europe's Judges*, mentioned at the start of this chapter, Michal Bobek rejects the scholarly critique of the ECJ, epitomized in Joseph Weiler's well-known complaint about the 'cryptic, Cartesian style' of the Court's reasoning.[23] In Bobek's view 'it is questionable whether all the ensuing practical implications of [the academic ideal of the ECJ's reasoning] are equally appealing to all the other cultures and audiences apart from the internationally minded (and Anglo-American dominated) legal academia'.[24] Instead, Bobek suggests that the key standard should be 'the practicability or feasibility of the Court's pronouncements on what national courts should do with respect to EU law in the national judicial domain'.[25] Bobek then takes the ECJ's judgment in *Zambrano*[26] to illustrate this point. He first notes that it was 'pilloried as the epitome of an illegitimate decision, expanding the scope of EU law through citizenship while giving no substantive reasons'. In Bobek's view, however, 'from the vantage point

[19] Ibid. 98.

[20] See in general S. B. Hobolt and J. Tilley (eds), *Blaming Europe? Responsibility Without Accountability in the European Union* (2014).

[21] See D. della Porta, *Social Movements in Times of Austerity* (2015) 138.

[22] A point raised, interestingly, by Scharpf himself, when he warned against the EU taking responsibility for Greece's public debt crisis, while imposing conditionality on it without a democratic mandate: Scharpf, 'Monetary Union, Fiscal Crisis and the Disabling of Democratic Accountability', in A. Schäfer and W. Streeck (eds), *Politics in the Age of Austerity* (2013) 138.

[23] Bobek, 'Of Feasibility and Silent Elephants: The Legitimacy of the Court of Justice through the Eyes of National Courts', in Adams *et al.* (eds), *Judging Europe's Judges: The Legitimacy of the Case Law of the European Court of Justice* (2013) 197. Bobek refers to Weiler, 'Epilogue: The Judicial Après Nice', in G. de Búrca and J. Weiler (eds), *The European Court of Justice* (2001) 225.

[24] Bobek (n. 23) 204. [25] Ibid. [26] Case C-34/09, *Ruiz Zambrano* (EU:C:2011:124).

of national courts, the decision is not devoid of an understandable reason, giving clear and transposable guidance to them.'[27]

It could be questioned whether the decision truly provided a 'clear and transposable guidance', given the number of references that followed *Zambrano*, where national courts desperately sought further clarification. But the real issue is whether—especially in relation to the citizenship case law of the ECJ—'feasibility' for national courts is the most important normative criterion, thus allowing the criticism of the reasoning contained in the decision to be dismissed as merely a lamentation by the 'internationally minded (and Anglo-American dominated) legal academia'. The ECJ's case law in this field (and in many others) has influenced both the EU and national legislation and is deeply implicated in the policy-making at both levels.[28]

One could even ask whether 'feasibility' as a standard has anything to do with legitimacy, if legitimacy means something more than just acceptance or compliance.[29] The 'something more', I suggest, refers to 'good reasons', which can justify compliance and acceptance and thus legitimate the exercise of public authority. Any examination and evaluation of such reasons is screened out from the functional, 'descriptive' analysis. Is the ECJ's authority accepted by national courts because it empowers them against other branches of government (or, in the case of the lower or ordinary courts, against their judicial superiors or constitutional courts), or is its authority recognized on another basis—such as the belief that the Court exercises its judicial function in conformity with the mandate provided by the Treaties or that it helps to protect important constitutional principles shared by the Member States and the Union?[30]

To move to a more abstract level of political theory: descriptive, 'sociological' accounts are tied to what Jeremy Waldron called a fundamentally *liberal* thesis about legitimacy of a social and political order. Such 'order is illegitimate unless it is rooted in the *consent* of those who have to live under it'.[31] In other words, people must enter into a social contract. The problem is, of course, that such consent/contract can never be actual, empirical consent and liberal theorists then quickly move to *reasons* for which people *would* give their consent. The social contract becomes a 'hypothetical contract' and the actual reasons for entering it,

[27] Bobek (n. 23) 207.

[28] See D. S. Martinsen, *An Ever More Powerful Court? The Political Constraints of Legal Integration in the European Union* (2015).

[29] Legitimacy as feasibility essentially says 'it works, therefore it is good!'. In such logic gas chambers (and the whole holocaust machinery) would be 'legitimate', since they were a 'feasible' method for killing millions of people. I doubt anybody would want to confuse feasibility with legitimacy in such context—even today, when almost everything seems to go in public discourse.

[30] Here I do not suggest that we know what such criteria precisely demand—I only raise the point that there are important differences between possible criteria, which the descriptive analysis does not engage with at all.

[31] J. Waldron, *Liberal rights: Collected Papers 1981–1991* (1993) 50, emphasis added.

grounded in actual people's beliefs about the legitimacy of the social and political order, turn into a theory—usually a theory of justice.[32]

I make this more theoretical point here because, as we will see, legitimacy of courts in the great part of the liberal theory still depends on some form of consent—however conceptualized and/or placed within different arrangements (such as representative institutions or, more fashionably, various deliberative fora). The centrality of consent (even if 'only' hypothetical) for political legitimacy also makes many conceptualizations of judicial legitimacy more problematic than we usually think.

B. Legitimacy as a Discursive Concept

Now, if even the descriptive notion of legitimacy is dependent on some notion of good reasons to acknowledge legitimacy, how do we know what these good reasons are? Habermas' theory of communicative action provides a helpful perspective, which will be used throughout this chapter: 'whether reasons are "good reasons" can be ascertained only in the performative attitude of a *participant* in argumentation, and not through the neutral *observation* of what this or that participant in a discourse holds to be good reasons'.[33] This is what Jürgen Habermas calls the 'reconstructive' notion of legitimacy.[34] The precise meaning (and application) of the criteria for legitimating public institutions is subject to a continuous (and in fact never-ending) democratic debate.[35]

In an important sense no such debate is 'innocent' in the sense that it would not influence its subject—the concept of legitimacy itself. Participants in discourses contribute with their understandings of legitimacy and the good reasons for its recognition and thus influence what others will possibly opine and say in return (if only by forcing them to nuance their own positions in case of their

[32] Horton, 'Political Legitimacy, Justice and Consent', 15 *Critical Review of International Social and Political Philosophy* (2012) 129, 132–137. For an overview of the role of consent for political legitimacy, see Simmons, 'Political Obligation and Consent', in F. G. Miller and A. Wertheimer (eds), *The Ethics of Consent: Theory and Practice* (2010) 305.

[33] Habermas (n. 9) 200. Habermas thus rejects the dichotomy between descriptive and normative legitimacy and adopts a 'reconstructive' approach, combining the two (see ibid. 204–205). It is of course possible to 'observe' which reasons different actors will mention as 'good' when making legitimacy assessments; this, however, leaves open the question whether the observer should recognize all such mentioned reasons as 'good' (as opposed to considering them as reasons for acceptance and obedience, which *explain*, but do not *legitimate* acceptance and obedience). The only way out from this dilemma is by taking a performative attitude, as suggested by Habermas.

[34] Ibid. 204.

[35] More recently Horton (n. 32) 145, suggested that 'we should locate political legitimacy in relation to the criteria that are operative in particular social, cultural and conceptual contexts, and which inform people's judgements about the legitimacy of their state'. In other words, related to the points made about the importance of consent for the liberal theory, consent is relevant, but it is given in the form of judgment based on the criteria that are relevant in a given polity.

disagreement).[36] This applies even more to legal institutions, since law (and its interpretation) is normative 'all the way down'. Relative to the position of legal doctrine in a particular legal culture, one may say that any contribution on the legitimacy of legal institutions has a potential to be transformative—or has the power to confirm the prevailing social imaginary of legitimacy.

Some participants contribute with notions of legitimacy that may seem quite under-theorized and some may even want to avoid a debate on the deeper questions concerning the normative foundations of their positions. As I have tried to explain, this does not mean that their contributions are neither normative nor bound to a particular theory of legitimacy. Their theory only remains unstated. Moreover, avoiding discussing foundations is itself a normative approach.[37]

This chapter is an attempt to uncover these deeper foundations, for the sake of our intellectual emancipation.[38] One may recall what John Maynard Keynes once observed on account of economic theory: 'The ideas of economists and political philosophers, both when they are right and when they are wrong, are more powerful than is commonly understood. . . . Practical men, who believe themselves to be quite exempt from any intellectual influences, are usually the slaves of some defunct economist'.[39] Later I will seek to show how some ideas that practical men of law hold about legal reasoning and legitimacy may keep them (and, by virtue of the effects of their contribution on the conceptualization of legitimacy in their legal culture, also us) in the slavery of sometimes defunct political or constitutional theorists.

C. Semantic Struggles over Legitimacy

One way of looking at discourses of legitimacy is to see them as 'semantic struggles'—struggles over which conceptual vocabulary will dominate the prevailing understanding of what makes the political order and its institutions (including courts) legitimate.[40] So, for example, the debate on the legitimacy of

[36] How this process works is explored by Ezrahi (n. 14).

[37] In the US constitutional theory parlance called 'anti-foundationalism', related to pragmatism. For a discussion, see Desautels-Stein, 'Pragmatic Liberalism: The Outlook of the Dead', 55 *Boston College Law Review* (2014) 1041, at 1087–1096.

[38] In the sense of critical theory explained by R. Geuss, *The Idea of a Critical Theory: Habermas and the Frankfurt School* (1981) 55–95.

[39] J. M. Keynes, *The General Theory of Employment, Interest and Money* (1953) 383.

[40] For the notion of 'semantic struggle', see Busse, 'Semantic Strategies as a Means of Politics: Linguistic Approaches to the Analysis of "Semantic Struggles"', in P. Ahonen (ed.), *Tracing the Semiotic Boundaries of Politics* (1993) 121. A good overview of different approaches to what is called here semantic struggles can be found in Norberg, 'Political Concepts', in M. Gibbons (ed.), *The Encyclopedia of Political Thought* (2015). For a critique of the focus on concepts and the linguistic dimension, not considered by Norberg, see Shapiro, 'Realism in the Study of the History of Ideas', 3 *History of Political Thought* (1982) 535 (emphasizing the role of ideologies).

the EU was for a long time dominated by the concept of democracy and its conceptual framework.[41] People disagreed, of course, on what kind of democracy the EU needs, but the debate was framed in the language of democratic theory, which offered a range of options and arguments that could be made (and excluded, or at least limited, others). Only relatively recently has the concept of justice entered the scene, making room for different sensibilities (and cynically speaking, making it—arguably—more plausible for the EU to be legitimated on its terms).[42]

Carl Schmitt was an early student of semantic struggles (and their competent practitioner) and developed what Kaarlo Tuori called the 'military science of concepts'.[43] In Tuori's reconstruction, we can distinguish 'three alternative conceptual strategies within the doctrinal battlefield' adopted by Schmitt in his critique of liberal democracy. First, 'we can hijack a positively-laden concept from the adversary'.[44] In the context of the EU, consider how democracy and the constitution, two central concepts of the post-war liberal political vocabulary, were reinterpreted in the course of the debate on the legitimacy of the EU that started after the 'Maastricht Moment'.

Democracy is said to produce externalities and thus needs to be reinterpreted in order to take account of those affected beyond its borders,[45] despite the necessity of borders (and exclusion) for democracy to be able to take decisions. In view of those who defend the idea of democratic externalities, the EU helps democracy and its normative commitments to be taken more seriously; it does not undermine them. Similarly, the concept of the constitution was expropriated from the state, where it was located (hence the once fashionable notion of 'constitutionalism beyond the state').[46] The following quotation illustrates nicely how this happens in the scholarly discourse. Joseph Weiler, the key proponent of the language of constitutionalism in the EU context thus approvingly refers to Miguel Poiares Maduro (giving him his blessing as 'one of the most brilliant of the new generation of European constitutional thinkers'):

> European integration not only challenges national constitutions . . . it challenges constitutional law itself. It assumes a constitution without a traditional political community defined and proposed by that constitution . . . European integration

[41] See Sternberg (n. 3).

[42] See J. Neyer, *The Justification of Europe: A Political Theory of Supranational Integration* (2012) and D. Kochenov, G. de Búrca, and A. Williams (eds), *Europe's Justice Deficit?* (2015).

[43] See K. Tuori, *Ratio and Voluntas: The Tension Between Reason and Will in Law* (2011) 109.

[44] Ibid. 112.

[45] This is what Alexander Somek calls 'The Darling Dogma of Bourgeois Europeanists', 20 *European Law Journal* (2014) 688. For a less polemical account, see e.g. Erman, 'The Boundary Problem and the Ideal of Democracy', 21 *Constellations* (2014) 535 or Whitt, 'Democracy's Sovereign Enclosures: Territory and the All-affected Principle', 21 *Constellations* (2014) 560.

[46] See J. H. H. Weiler and M. Wind (eds), *European Constitutionalism Beyond the State* (2003). For a critique, see Loughlin, 'In Defence of *Staatslehre*', 48 *Der Staat* (2009) 2.

> also challenges the legal monopoly of States and the hierarchical organisation of the law (in which constitutional law is still conceived of as the 'higher law').[47]

It is notable that in the same passage Weiler rejects the relevance of the constitutional thought of both Carl Schmitt and Hans Kelsen, stripping European constitutionalism of its scholarly tradition and (re-)setting it on completely new foundations.[48]

The debate on the EU constitution also illustrates the second possible strategy: 'neutralis[ation] of a positively-laden and strategically important concept'.[49] Thus it was said that even golf clubs have a constitution—and therefore calling the EU treaties 'a constitution' was not such a big thing.[50] Finally, as a third strategy 'one can attempt to transform a concept's value quality from positive to negative or vice versa'.[51] Consider how sovereignty or the nation state fared badly in the constitutional debate on the EU of the early 2000s. The EU is presented as a means to overcome the excesses of both—and therefore should not become the state nor gain full sovereignty.[52]

We can observe similar semantic struggles regarding the ECJ. Once popular was a debate as to whether the ECJ is a constitutional court—now revived in the context of its extended powers over fundamental rights adjudication after the EU Charter came into force. It is certainly an important matter that the ECJ regularly participates at triennial congresses of the Conference of European Constitutional Courts as an observer and prepares its own institutional report, and it is perhaps even more telling that in the analogous Association of the Councils of State and Supreme Administrative Jurisdictions of the EU, the ECJ has the status of a full member.[53]

[47] Weiler, 'In Defence of the Status Quo: Europe's Constitutional *Sonderweg*', in J. H. H. Weiler and M. Wind (eds), *European Constitutionalism Beyond the State* (2003) 7, 16, quoting from M. P. Maduro, *We the Court: The European Court of Justice and the European Economic Constitution—A Critical Reading of Article 30 of the EC Treaty* (1998) 175.

[48] Weiler (n. 47) 15–16, reducing Schmitt's theory to examining the question of who has the final word and Kelsen's to the idea of hierarchy of norms. A decade later, however, Weiler seems to have reconsidered some of his ideas: see Weiler, 'Prologue: Global and Pluralist Constitutionalism—Some Doubts', in G. de Búrca and J. H. H. Weiler (eds), *The Worlds of European Constitutionalism* (2012) 8.

[49] Tuori (n. 43) 112.

[50] The British foreign minister was reported to have said this by Kumm, 'Beyond Golf Clubs and the Judicialization of Politics: Why Europe Has a Constitution Properly So Called', 54 *American Journal of Comparative Law* (2006) 505, at 505.

[51] Tuori (n. 43) 112.

[52] The debate between Joseph Weiler and Federico Mancini is illustrative of this strategy: see Mancini, 'Europe: The Case for Statehood', 4 *European Law Journal* (1998) 29 and Weiler, 'Europe: The Case against the Case for Statehood', 4 *European Law Journal* (1998) 43.

[53] On these associations, see de Visser and Claes, 'Courts United? On European Judicial Networks', in A. Vauchez and B. de Witte (eds), *Lawyering Europe: European Law as a Transnational Social Field* (2013) 75, at 79–80.

The remark by the former President of the Court, Vassilios Skouris, at the FIDE conference in May 2014,[54] that 'the Court of Justice is not a human rights court; it is the Supreme Court of the European Union',[55] can also be read as a strategic move within a semantic struggle concerning the ECJ's legitimacy. As Leonard Besselink interpreted the message, the ECJ's main task is to uphold the supremacy of EU law, not the EU citizens' rights—and saying so in front of a plenary composed of EU law practitioners and academics may certainly influence their expectations as regards the ECJ. It is also quite important if an article published in the *Common Market Law Review*—according to one (and in fact the only) study the most influential journal at the ECJ[56]—claims that it is an 'institutional actor' acting 'as a leading policymaker in European integration'.[57]

The following Section seeks to put the ECJ's legitimacy on more solid theoretical grounds, combining some insights from political and legal theory with a more orthodox EU law scholarship.

3. Conceptualizing the ECJ's Legitimacy

A. Two Basic Elements of Adjudication and the Fundamental Contradiction

Adjudication by the ECJ, similarly to adjudication by most of the highest courts in the Western legal tradition, comprises two basic elements. First, deciding a particular case and, second, exercising judicial authority that reaches beyond that particular case.[58] These two basic elements of adjudication involve different subjects, who may view the main purpose of adjudication (and the 'good reasons' that legitimate it) quite differently: it can be a timely, legally correct decision achieved at proportionate costs in case of the former;[59] whereas when the effects

[54] Most readers will surely know that in this context FIDE has nothing to do with the game of chess and refers to the *Fédération internationale pour le droit européen*. On the importance of FIDE for EU law, see Bernier, 'Constructing and Legitimating: Transnational Jurist Networks and the Making of a Constitutional Practice of European Law, 1950–70', 21 *Contemporary European History* (2012) 399.

[55] Reported by Besselink, 'The ECJ as the European "Supreme Court": Setting Aside Citizens' Rights for EU Law Supremacy'. *Verfassungsblog* (18 August 2014), available at http://verfassungsblog.de/ecj-european-supreme-court-setting-aside-citizens-rights-eu-law-supremacy/ (accessed 22 September 2020).

[56] See Bouthinon-Dumas and Masson, 'Quelles sont les revues juridiques qui comptent à la Cour de justice de l'Union européenne?', 49 *Revue trimestrielle de droit européen* (2013) 781.

[57] Horsley, 'Reflections on the Role of the Court of Justice as the "Motor" of European Integration: Legal Limits to Judicial Lawmaking', 50 *Common Market Law Review* (2013) 931, at 941.

[58] M. Shapiro, *Courts: A Comparative and Political Analysis* (1981) makes a similar distinction between 'conflict resolution' and 'social control'. I use a different language because this text is addressed primarily to lawyers and constitutional theorists.

[59] For this 'three-dimensional' approach to civil procedure, see Zuckerman, 'Justice in Crisis: Comparative Dimensions of Civil Procedure', in A. Zuckerman (ed.), *Civil Justice in Crisis: Comparative Perspectives of Civil Procedure* (1999) 3.

of the decision reach beyond the particular case, time may be less important and formal legality may give way to other values, such as justice or freedom.[60] The key problem concerning the theoretical construction of judicial legitimacy in my view concerns this tension between the particular case and normative considerations in the context of its deciding on the one hand, and normative considerations that relate to the wider political and societal context of the case on the other.

At the institutional level, the question of judicial legitimacy reflects a tension which far transcends the context of courts and adjudication: that between individuality and communality—our 'desire to be autonomous and the desire to be a participant in a common venture'.[61] In law the tension was made famous by Duncan Kennedy, who saw it as a 'fundamental contradiction' of the liberal conception of law.[62] The contradiction was adopted by many 'crits' even though Kennedy later 'renounced' it,[63] and lies at the heart of Maarti Koskenniemi's revolutionary study of legal argument in international law.[64] More broadly speaking it has been articulated in various debates on justice (between 'liberals' and 'communitarians'),[65] on freedom (where it relates to the distinction between liberal or negative freedom and different versions of political or social freedom),[66] or on self-determination.[67] In post-war European constitutional law it is visible in the conception of rights, which are always balanced both against each other and also some fundamental common interest, although the core of the right must always be protected.[68]

Speaking of the role of positive theory of public law, Martin Loughlin somewhat sceptically observed that its objective 'can only be that of developing the most effective apparatus we can that acknowledges the power of these competing claims. And since this disjuncture between freedom and belonging can be neither eliminated nor reconciled, it can only be negotiated'.[69] One way of analysing judicial legitimacy is to see how this tension is negotiated in concrete institutional

[60] Whether formal legality actually conflicts with justice or freedom of course depends on how these concepts are interpreted. See e.g. Sadurski, 'Social Justice and Legal Justice', 3 *Law and Philosophy* (1984) 329 and also Thornhill (n. 7).

[61] M. Loughlin, *Foundations of Public Law* (2010) 11.

[62] See particularly Kennedy, 'The Structure of Blackstone's Commentaries', 28 *Buffalo Law Review* (1979) 205, at 211–213. On what the 'liberal conception of law' refers to, see the text at n. 81 *et seq.*

[63] Gabel and Kennedy, 'Roll Over Beethoven', 36 *Stanford Law Review* (1984) 1, at 15–16.

[64] M. Koskenniemi, *From Apology to Utopia: The Structure of International Legal Argument: Reissue with a New Epilogue* (2005).

[65] See S. Mulhall and A. Swift, *Liberals and Communitarians* (2nd ed., 1996).

[66] See A. Honneth, *Freedom's Right: The Social Foundations of Democratic Life* (2014).

[67] See Möllers (n. 16), especially ch. 2, 'Self-determination as the source of separated powers'.

[68] See e.g. Art. 52 of the EU Charter. On this structure of rights and the development of legal thought, see J. Bomhoff, *Balancing Constitutional Rights: The Origins and Meanings of Postwar Legal Discourse* (2013).

[69] Loughlin (n. 61) 11.

settings, since the tension cannot be displaced, no matter how much some proceduralists would want it so.[70]

B. The Centrality of a Court's Deciding a Particular Case

In the Western legal tradition there is still a wide perception that judicial function is primarily concerned with deciding a particular case, whether because it is so described in the constitution or it is conceptualized as such in the relevant legal culture.[71] It is of course true that today this is not the only function exercised by the courts. In the case of the highest and constitutional courts, this is often even not their dominant function as seen by the relevant legal culture.[72] There still seems to be agreement, however, that without a case (however defined) there is no adjudication. The power (and duty) to decide the case is what distinguishes (or is said to distinguish)—even in the most progressive conceptualizations—courts from political institutions (political in the sense that they derive their legitimacy from political contestation epitomized, but not limited to, democratic elections).[73] This view extends to international law where courts and other adjudicative institutions were originally set up as instruments for international dispute settlement (and not international 'law-making').[74]

Judicial decision in the particular case entails primarily two parties, who seek an authoritative decision of their dispute. It may concern other participants to the judicial process too, such as interveners or *amici curiae*. Thus, before the ECJ the particular case can involve various actors: an EU official contesting violation of staff regulations and possibly seeking compensation for it; or EU institutions and Member States (represented by their governments) that litigate the scope of their competences or seek redress for violations of EU law. Importantly, the ECJ insists that in the context of the preliminary ruling procedure there are no true parties, only participants. The participants include the parties from the main procedure before the referring court and a plethora of other actors, such as the Member State governments and EU institutions—most importantly the Commission, which always submits its observations (not pleadings).

[70] See e.g. Mulcahy, 'The Collective Interest in Private Dispute Resolution', 33 *Oxford Journal of Legal Studies* (2013) 59, who observes at 59 that 'litigation models in England send out conflicting messages'. In my view it cannot be otherwise.

[71] See Shapiro (n. 58) 17.

[72] On the highest courts, see e.g. reports collected in P. Yessiou-Faltsi (ed.), *The Role of the Supreme Courts at the National and International Level: Reports for the Thessaloniki International Colloquium, 21–25 May 1997* (1998). On European constitutional courts, see M. de Visser, *Constitutional Review in Europe: A Comparative Analysis* (2015).

[73] A. von Bogdandy and I. Venzke, *In Whose Name? A Public Law Theory of International Adjudication* (2014) 109.

[74] Ibid. ch. 1.

'Particular case' can refer to quite different occurrences: it may involve a genuine dispute between two parties (concerning the scope of their respective competences or their rights and duties). It may also concern a more vertical relationship of accountability between a public authority (the Commission) and its subject (in administrative or constitutional adjudication, where the Court reviews an act of EU public authority, including legislation), or it may entail disciplining and enforcement (concerning both the Member States or EU institutions through actions in infringement against one of the former, or actions in damages against the EU).

C. Courts' Precarious Legitimacy: Reconciling Consent with Creative Moments in Interpretation

The conceptualization of courts as institutions concerned with conflict resolution corresponds to the 'root concept of "courtness"' developed in the seminal study of courts by Martin Shapiro. It presupposes a conflict structured in triads: between two parties, who 'call upon a third for assistance in achieving a resolution'.[75] The social need for an institution that can decide in the case of conflict explains why it is hard to imagine the organization of public power without courts.

As Shapiro notes, '[t]he most fundamental device for maintaining the triad is consent'.[76] If the losing party was able to choose the law and the judge (by giving her consent to have the dispute decided by the given court applying a concrete set of pre-determined norms), then she is more likely to comply with the judgment and may not even see the judgment as something that was imposed on her. International arbitration is still relatively close to this model,[77] but in the domestic context the parties' consent has long been replaced by compulsory jurisdiction of courts deciding on the basis of democratically adopted law, which is obligatory and coercive to everyone in the law's sphere of application.

The ECJ's legitimacy is precarious in this respect, since in the disputes where the EU is a party the ECJ cannot be viewed as an 'independent third'—in particular when it is called upon to decide on the division of competences between the EU and its Member States, but also more widely, since it is often viewed as having integrationist tendencies.[78] This precariousness is not unique to

[75] Shapiro (n. 58) 1. Shapiro notes that the triad structure is also applied by a much wider array of social institutions whose goal is to settle conflicts, such as mediators or arbitrators.

[76] Ibid. 2.

[77] For the development in this area, see Schill, 'Conceptions of Legitimacy of International Arbitration', in D. D. Caron *et al.* (eds), *Practising Virtue: Inside International Arbitration* (2015).

[78] See G. Beck, *The Legal Reasoning of the Court of Justice of the EU* (2012); S. Sankari, *European Court of Justice Legal Reasoning in Context* (2013).

the ECJ, however, since whenever a court has the power to decide a dispute without the consent of both parties (as would be the case in international ac hoc arbitration, for example), it has to substitute legitimacy based on *their* consent to *its jurisdiction* by other means.

The shift from consent as a basis for judicial legitimacy is less profound than it could appear, however, and leaves the conceptual foundations of judicial legitimacy untouched: what has moved is *the place* where consent emerges, *not its centrality* for judicial legitimacy. In today's domestic context 'democratically adopted law' means law to which all equal and free citizens have actually, or at least hypothetically, consented (various democratic theories differ in how they conceptualize the idea of citizens' equality, freedom, and consent, but these will be the ingredients of most of them).[79] In international law, sovereign states' consent underpins all its sources, including international customs, general principles of law, or judicial decisions and legal doctrine.[80]

Consent is central to what Martti Koskenniemi calls the 'liberal doctrine of politics', according to which 'legal standards emerge from the legal subjects themselves. There is no natural normative order. Such order is artificial and justifiable only if it can be linked to the concrete wills and interests of individuals'.[81] As Patrick Riley notes, '[p]olitical philosophy since the seventeenth century has been characterized, above all, by voluntarism, by an emphasis on the consent of individuals as the standard of political legitimacy'—something that has applied to all strands of political philosophy, not only to liberalism.[82] While in the municipal political theory this voluntarism was overcome by putting the constraint of reason on it (in the form of constitutional democracy, or as the historian of European political thinking Jan Werner Müller calls it, 'constrained democracy'),[83] in international law and international relations it dominated conceptualizations of legitimacy for much longer.[84]

As already mentioned, consent is given to laws, rather than the particular court's jurisdiction (which is itself based on laws). Hence the central position of legislated sources of law and the much less stable position of general principles of law, customary law, or judge-made law in the *classical* positivist theory of law (such as those of Jeremy Bentham or John Austin), which corresponds to the

[79] See the text at n. 32.

[80] This is of course controversial; I follow I. Venzke, *How Interpretation Makes International Law: On Semantic Change and Normative Twists* (2012) 16–29 here. I should make it clear that I am much indebted to this work for developing my own thinking about legal reasoning, more than mere footnotes can indicate.

[81] Koskenniemi (n. 64) 21. On the liberal doctrine, with further references, see also ibid, ch. 2.

[82] P. Riley, *Will and Political Legitimacy: A Critical Exposition of Social Contract Theory in Hobbes, Locke, Rousseau, Kant, and Hegel* (1982) 1. As the title of the book suggests, Riley explores his argument in relation to writers who usually do not qualify as 'political liberals' in the standard accounts.

[83] See J. W. Müller, *Contesting Democracy: Political Ideas in Twentieth-Century Europe* (2011) 146.

[84] See n. 80.

liberal doctrine of politics as it emerged in the eighteenth and nineteenth century in the work of, for example, John Locke or Jean-Jacques Rousseau.[85] Duncan Kennedy calls this period the era of the 'classical legal thought', which saw 'law as "a system", having a strong internal structural coherence' and being committed 'to legal interpretive formalism'.[86]

However, as Ingo Venzke observes, in his study *How Interpretation Makes International Law*:

> the law's reach towards consent is severed when it comes to a provision's meaning. Semantic content is negotiated in the legal practice of interpretation. This is significant. Part of legal normativity is thus removed from formal pedigree and placed into the practice of interpretation itself. The practice of applying the law makes law. It sets free normative force.[87]

In the context of the particular case, the creative moment of interpretation is often captured as 'judicial discretion', which ensues from 'legal indeterminacy'. In general jurisprudence this is a problem that has been debated since the first challenges against the liberal positivist doctrine were raised—most notably by the free law movement in Germany[88] or *juristes inquiets* in France,[89] followed by sociological jurisprudence and legal realism in the US.[90] The intensity of the challenge was changing according to the political stakes involved, as well as the grounds for challenges, in particular relating to advances in the philosophy of language and semiotics.[91] It is important to keep in mind that the period of 'classical legal thought' was less formalistic than many accounts have it, and the extreme views about law's internal coherence and the normative self-sufficiency of its formal sources were held by hardly anyone.[92] Venzke's revelation as regards

[85] Koskenniemi (n. 64) 83–87. For the links between early political liberalism and legal positivism, see L. Green, 'Legal Positivism' in E. N. Zalta (ed.), *The Stanford Encyclopedia of Philosophy* (Fall 2009 Edition), available at http://plato.stanford.edu/archives/fall2009/entries/legal-positivism/ (accessed 22 September 2020), and in detail, Schofield, 'Jeremy Bentham: Legislator of the World', 51 *Current Legal Problems* (1998) 115.

[86] Kennedy, 'Three Globalizations of Law and Legal Thought: 1850–2000', in D. M. Trubek and A. Santos (eds), *The New Law and Economic Development: A Critical Appraisal* (2006) 19, at 25. On the 'classical legal thought', see also D. Kennedy, *The Rise and Fall of the Classical Legal Thought* (1998).

[87] Venzke (n. 80) 6.

[88] See e.g. Herget and Wallace, 'The German Free Law Movement as the Source of American Legal Realism', 73 *Virginia Law Review* (1987) 399.

[89] Belleau, 'The "Juristes Inquiets": Legal Classicism and Criticism in Early Twentieth-Century France', *Utah Law Review* (1987) 379. See also N. Hakim and F. Melleray, *Le renouveau de la doctrine française: les grands auteurs de la pensée juridique au tournant du XXe siècle* (2009).

[90] Among countless accounts, see W. Twining, *Karl Llewellyn and the Realist Movement* (2nd ed., 2012) and B. Leiter, *Naturalizing Jurisprudence: Essays on American Legal Realism and Naturalism in Legal Philosophy* (2007).

[91] For a brilliant intellectual history, see B. Frydman, *Le sens des lois: Histoire de l'interprétation et de la raison juridique* (3rd ed., 2011) 409.

[92] For a revisionist history of American legal realism's challenge to the 'classical legal thought' see B. Z. Tamanaha, *Beyond the Formalist-Realist Divide: The Role of Politics in Judging* (2010).

judicial power in international relations seems acute now because it is only relatively recently that the power of international adjudicators has been realized.[93]

The rise of judicial power—domestic and international—relates to the development in the Western legal tradition, which has provided courts with ever greater authority beyond the particular case: national highest and constitutional courts keep other branches of government accountable through judicial review. According to some influential conceptualizations, they are expected to update the meaning of the constitution and develop new constitutional rights through interpreting very broad constitutional provisions such the right to human dignity or equality, to name just two. This is the 'judicialization' of politics, most frequently analysed in relation to the constitutional review of legislation (and more broadly speaking, of politics).[94] This focus on constitutional review, however, obfuscates many important questions that relate to the legitimacy of all adjudication, not only that in the context of the review—especially when seen from the perspective of a particular case and subjects of legitimacy involved.

The ECJ is part of this development and it would be an intriguing question to explore to what extent it has facilitated the judicialization of politics in Europe and to what extent its own power has been extended thanks to the rise of the judiciary at the domestic level. This is not, however, the question I would like to examine here.[95] Instead, I would like to ask: how can this be legitimized—in the light of the liberal doctrine of politics, which still arguably dominates the Western political imagination, however reformulated it has been in the course of centuries? To state the same point in terms not so much connected with the critical legal theory: how can the creative moments of adjudication be reconciled with democratic theory, which at its heart insists that equal and free citizens should provide consent to their laws?

I shall emphasize that the question I am concerned with here is different from that, which dominates much of the writing on courts and the legitimacy of adjudication today, which is the question of the legitimacy of judicial review. I am not therefore primarily interested in theories that posit courts and constitutional adjudication as guarantees of democracy and thus legitimize their functioning.[96] My question is wider, as the creative moments in adjudication occur far more often than in the context of judicial review—and as will be seen, are problematic

[93] See K. J. Alter, *The New Terrain of International Law: Courts, Politics, Rights* (2014) and also von Bogdandy and Venzke (n. 73) ch. 2.

[94] See, among many sources, M. Shapiro and A. Stone Sweet, *On Law, Politics, and Judicialization* (2002).

[95] See Thornhill, 'The Formation of a European Constitution: An Approach from Historical-Political Sociology' (2012) 8 *International Journal of Law in Context* 354.

[96] For such conceptualizations of judicial review, see particularly J. H. Ely, *Democracy and Distrust: A Theory of Judicial Review* (1980) and Waldron, 'The Core of the Case Against Judicial Review' (2006) 115 *Yale Law Journal* 1346.

not only for democracy, but also for other liberal principles, particularly the rule of law.

My concern about legitimacy of adjudication also distinguishes the following analysis from many accounts of legal (in)determinacy and constraints on adjudication, in that I am interested in the indeterminacy and the absence of constraint that ensues from the sources of law that derive their legitimacy from the consent of the people—the heart of the classical liberal doctrine of politics. Why this distinction is important for our purposes can be illustrated by how a leading legal theorist defines legal indeterminacy:

> To say that the law is indeterminate is to say that the class of legal reasons (hereafter 'the Class') is indeterminate. Roughly speaking, the Class includes those reasons a court may properly give in justifying its decision. More precisely, the Class in some legal system consists of four components: (1) the legitimate *sources* of law (e.g., statutes, court decisions, morality, a constitution, etc.); (2) the legitimate methods of interpreting sources of law (e.g., intentionalism, originalism, purposive interpretation, structural interpretation, 'strict' and 'loose' readings of precedent); (3) the legitimate ways of characterizing the facts of a case in terms of their *legal* significance; and (4) the legitimate ways of reasoning with legal rules and legally described facts (e.g., deductive reasoning, reasoning by analogy).[97]

Leiter's concern is analytical, not normative: he wants to understand what it means for a member of the class of legal reasons to determine the outcome of a case; Leiter is rather indifferent to the question what counts as a *legitimate* legal reason, which is the core question for me in the following exposition.[98]

Finally, I should also point out that while I often invoke the category of 'liberal doctrine of politics', by no means do I endorse it. I use it as an analytical category, since in my view it helps to understand why so many conceptualizations of interpretation's creative moments are not satisfactory in the context of the EU, whose legitimacy is still very much related to this doctrine and its emphasis on will and consent, either in the form of a social contract among the EU citizens, or in the form of the international agreement among the Member States. The latter is what EU law decisively shares with international law—despite its 'constitutionalization'—and it also seems that it will be its dominant feature in the light of the 'new

[97] Leiter (n. 90) 9, emphasis in the original.

[98] This is not to suggest that Leiter would not understand this—see his comments in ibid. 115. This indifference makes much of the Anglo-American analytical jurisprudence (including Hart's) problematic, since it is not an interesting question to explore whether a previous judicial decision is a legitimate source of law.

intergovernmentalism' which characterizes the EU in the second decade of the 21st century.[99]

D. Consent and Will in the EU—But of Whom?

Venzke's conceptualization of judicial creativity is motivated by his concern for the role of consent in legitimating international norms. As he puts it:

> In the orthodox positivist picture of international lawmaking, a norm is considered binding because those subject to that norm have themselves created it in accordance with certain recognized procedures (commonly known as sources). The norm rests on their consent.[100]

The creative moment of interpretation severs the link to a source legitimated by consent (which in the modern liberal theory is conceptualized as a 'hypothetical' consent, not an actual one).[101] The question then is, how to legitimate the creative moment? As I have already mentioned, this problem is haunting international courts as much as their domestic counterparts. It materializes in different *problématiques*, or 'particular problematics'[102] of each, however. In international law, it is seen in the fact that states are at the same time authors of and subject to its rules. To keep these rules binding on their creators, international law must resort to arguments from justice, and turns into utopia, being kept in a perpetual internal contradiction, since it can always be challenged by the competing argument from states' consent and become apologetic—hence the title of Koskenniemi's work.[103]

In the domestic context, the particular problematics are different: the liberal subject (the citizen) is said to be free by giving her consent to general laws. Equal freedom for all citizens would, however, presuppose unanimity, otherwise the subject not giving her consent to a rule imposed on her would not be free but dominated by the majority. Democratic theory seeks to come to terms with this problem through the notion of general will and distinguishing between the decision rule, which resorts to majority instead of unanimity, and the legitimatory principle of the establishment (as opposed to functioning) of democracy, which remains based on an idea of unanimity, reinterpreted as either organic unity (in

[99] See C. J. Bickerton, D. Hodson, and U. Puetter (eds), *The New Intergovernmentalism: States and Supranational Actors in the Post-Maastricht Era* (2015).

[100] Venzke (n. 80) 6.

[101] See the text at n. 32.

[102] I take this English term from M. Lasser, *Judicial Deliberations: A Comparative Study of Judicial Transparency and Legitimacy* (2004).

[103] *From Apology to Utopia: The Structure of International Legal Argument*, see n. 64.

its most extreme form as ethnic nationalism)[104] or political community (republican statism).[105] In reality, uniformity, however conceived, is always a fiction, albeit 'necessary'.[106]

EU law uniquely combines the *problématiques* of both international legal thought and domestic democratic theory: its normativity oscillates between the legitimatory principle of the states' consent (the Member States as the 'Masters of the Treaty') and the consent of its citizens (a metaphysical utopia of justice in international law is replaced by the utopia of an actually existing EU citizenship and a meaningful, if only hypothetical, social contract among them).[107] Each, however, undermines the other; as seen in the context of international law, there is always a possibility that either conceptualization may be used strategically against the other. Germany can be at once the force for 'more Europe', invoking solidarity stemming from the bonds that exist among EU citizens irrespective of the absence of their states' consent (as in the case of reallocation of refugees between Member States against the will of some of the governments) and, on another occasion, it may resort to the intergovernmental logic and insist that democracy means primarily democracy for German citizens, for example when it comes to controlling the use of the European stability mechanism.[108]

The contradiction is truly existential: to insist that the EU is legitimated only through its states would relegate the EU to a similar status as other 'ordinary' international organizations. This is, however, still not what most governments want,[109] especially as the absence of a true body of EU citizens is an empirical reality that puts the EU's uniqueness on very unstable foundations. It is this empirical reality that prevents the EU from overcoming its inter-state foundations completely—no matter how hard some EU elites try.

This has several consequences. First, in contrast to domestic settings, given the absence of a true political body of EU citizens and the near impossibility of their mobilization *as European citizens* (in contrast to, for example, Greek citizens

[104] This is how Carl Schmitt posited the foundations of a constitutional order, in contrast to Kelsen. See Lindahl, 'Constituent Power and Reflexive Identity: Towards an Ontology of Collective Selfhood', in M. Loughlin and N. Walker (eds), *The Paradox of Constitutionalism: Constituent Power and Constitutional Form* (2008) 9.

[105] For a rich comparative intellectual history, with a proposal for a solution in the present condition, see P. Rosanvallon (A. Goldhammer trans.), *Democratic Legitimacy: Impartiality, Reflexivity, Proximity* (2011).

[106] Rosanvallon notes, at ibid. 13, that it has always been a problem that this fiction was never recognized as such. For an incisive study of such 'necessary political fictions', see Ezrahi (n. 14).

[107] Citizenship is another conceptual battlefield in the semantic struggle, being reinterpreted to suit the EU: see e.g. J. Shaw, *The Transformation of Citizenship in the European Union: Electoral Rights and the Restructuring of Political Space* (2007).

[108] See Everson and Joerges, 'Who is the Guardian for Constitutionalism in Europe after the Financial Crisis?', LEQS Paper No. 63/2013, available at http://www.lse.ac.uk/europeanInstitute/LEQS%20Discussion%20Paper%20Series/LEQSPaper63.pdf (accessed 22 September 2020).

[109] For reasons why, see Bickerton, 'A Union of Member States: State Transformation and the New Intergovernmentalism', in C. J. Bickerton, D. Hodson, and U. Puetter (eds), *The New Intergovernmentalism: States and Supranational Actors in the Post-Maastricht Era* (2015) ch. 2.

protesting against austerity imposed by the EU), 'their' voice is appropriated more easily than it is in the national context.[110] The claim made by Jean-Claude Juncker's chief of staff in 2016 that Juncker (at that time the President of the European Commission) was more legitimate than the then Italian Prime Minister Matteo Renzi illustrates this well.[111] The reason was purportedly that Juncker was the 'spitzenkandidat' of the most popular party in the 2014 European elections (no matter how little that actually played any role in the elections),[112] whereas Renzi had become prime minister through a backroom deal rather than a national election. As the Italian political scientist Sergio Fabbrini dryly commented, this of course overlooks the fact that in representative (as opposed to populist) democracies the legitimacy of the government and its head is derived from the parliament and not directly from voters.[113] In contrast to Hungary or Poland, where people went out onto the streets to protest against their populist governments that sought to speak in their name (and monopolize the people's voice in the partisan pronouncements of a single party), nobody will come to protest in Brussels.

Second, there is a fundamental, or one could say constitutive, ambiguity about the EU's governing subject, which makes the EU vulnerable to capture. In international law, no matter how much it has become 'post-Westphalian', the governing subject is still the sovereign states. In the domestic context, it is free and equal citizens. The EU's centre of legitimacy seems to be overcrowded: it is simultaneously nation states, their citizens ('peoples'), and EU citizens. In reality, however, it has become vacated: being able to point to so many sites, we have lost orientation.[114]

4. Legitimating Creative Moments in the Judicial Interpretation of Law

The absence of an unequivocal subject of legitimacy in the EU is crucial when we try to think of judicial legitimacy in democratic terms. Before turning to this

[110] I put 'their' in inverted commas since in my view there is no 'they' in the first place.

[111] Reported by *Politico* on 10 February 2016, available at http://www.politico.eu/newsletter/playbook/politico-brussels-playbook-germanys-nato-ambush-juncker-vs-renzi-trump-and-sanders-win/ (accessed 22 September 2020).

[112] See Hobolt, 'A Vote for the President? The Role of *Spitzenkandidaten* in the 2014 European Parliament Elections', 21 *Journal of European Public Policy* (2014) 1528.

[113] Fabbrini, 'Le conseguenze di una Commissione "politica"', *Il Sole 24 Ore* (7 February 2016), available at http://www.ilsole24ore.com/art/notizie/2016-02-07/le-conseguenze-una-commissione-politica-165729.shtml?uuid=ACyshYPC (accessed 22 September 2020).

[114] This is, in my view, nicely illustrated by the exclusion of EU citizens, even those permanently resident in the UK, from the vote on 'Brexit' (see illuminating comments by Veerle Heyvaert, 'Death of a citizen: Britain's referendum and EU nationals living in the UK', *LSE EUROPP Blog*, 4 March 2016, available at http://bit.ly/21MuwfO (accessed 22 September 2020)).

conceptualization, I want to give a short overview of how creative moments are approached by various theories of judicial legitimacy.

A. Resignation and Indifference or Nihilism and Denigration

The first approach is resignation: a simple recognition of the fact that the rules of law (however defined) can never fully determine the judicial decision. There is always an element of unconstrained choice for the decision-maker, stemming from the nature of norms. Such is the position of the two leading legal positivists of the twentieth century, Hans Kelsen and H. L. A. Hart.[115] There are many instances where the rule will give a clear guidance to the judge, and one of Hart's points was that such instances are far more numerous than various critical accounts (he aimed primarily at legal realists) assume.[116] At the same time Hart openly acknowledges that 'the open texture of law means that there are, indeed, areas of conduct where much must be left to be developed by courts or officials striking a balance, in the light of circumstances, between competing interests which vary in weight from case to case'.[117] Kelsen emphasizes the moment of volition in the act of interpretation, comparing the judge applying a statutory provision to the legislator who adopts statutes on the basis of the constitution, which serves as the higher norm grounding the statute, in a similar way as the statute provides a foundations to the judicial decision. Kelsen notes:

> Certainly there is a difference between these two cases, but it is only a quantitative and not a qualitative difference, consisting simply in the fact that the legislator is far less bound materially than the judge—in other words, the legislator enjoys far greater independence in creating law. But even the judge creates law, even he is relatively independent in this capacity. And precisely for this reason, it is a function of will to arrive at the individual norm in the process of applying a statute, provided that the frame of the general norm is filled in thereby.[118]

Neither Hart nor Kelsen would, however, conclude from this that the judicial activity is not legitimate. While Hart's views can be only inferred from his general theory of law (analytical jurisprudes would probably say that providing a normative theory of the legitimacy of legal institutions is not their job), Kelsen's

[115] On Kelsen's views on legal interpretation, see H. Kelsen (B. L. Paulson and S. Paulson trans.), *Introduction to the Problems of Legal Theory, A Translation of the First Edition of the Reine Rechslehre or Pure Theory of Law* (1992) ch. 6 and also Paulson, 'Formalism, "Free Law", and the "Cognition" Quandary: Hans Kelsen's Approaches to Legal Interpretation', 27 *University of Queensland Law Journal* (2008) 7. Hart's views can be found e.g. in his *Concept of Law* (2nd ed., 1994) ch. VII.

[116] On this question, see Schauer, 'Legal Realism Untamed', 91 *Texas Law Review* (2013) 749.

[117] Hart (n. 115) 135.

[118] Kelsen (n. 115) 83.

political theory, though for a long time rather neglected,[119] dealt with this question, most comprehensively in his debate with Carl Schmitt over the legitimacy of constitutional review: the 'who ought to be the guardian of the constitution' debate between two prominent continental jurists at the twilight of the Weimar Republic.[120]

An opposite approach was taken by some (not all!) legal realists and also by one of the intellectual fathers of legal positivism, Jeremy Bentham.[121] Arguably the most extreme of the former, Fred Rodell, in 1939 described judicial reasoning as nothing 'more than a circumloquacious statement of the result, rather than a reason for arriving at it'[122] in a book called tellingly *Woe unto you lawyers!*, characterized by one contemporary reviewer as 'a book to end all books on the law and the lawyers'.[123] This characterization of the book captures one of the key critiques of American legal realism (and later critical legal studies), its apparent nihilism[124]—a different kind of resignation than that we can find in Kelsen.

B. Denial

A rather different approach to judicial creativity is a strategy of denial. Ronald Dworkin's theory of law as interpretation, developed first as a critique of H. L. A. Hart's legal positivism in *Taking Rights Seriously*,[125] and later refined in *Law's Empire*,[126] is arguably the best available (and certainly the most influential) theory of this kind. The central principle of Dworkin's theory is integrity: 'propositions of law are true if they figure in or follow from the principles of justice, fairness, and procedural due process that provide the best constructive interpretation of the community's legal practice'.[127] Dworkin's theory can be said to be in denial of creative moments in interpretation in that Dworkin believes that there exists a 'one right answer', although no real judge can ever find it, and can only approximate it through interpreting the law guided by the principle of integrity.[128]

[119] See L. Vinx, *Hans Kelsen's Pure Theory of Law: Legality and Legitimacy* (2007).

[120] See L. Vinx, *The Guardian of the Constitution: Hans Kelsen and Carl Schmitt on the Limits of Constitutional Law* (2015). This of course gives only a partial picture, since, as stressed here, adjudication must be legitimated as regards both of its dimensions and Kelsen was not concerned with 'small scale adjudication', entailing only two parties, and therefore did not confront the contradiction discussed here.

[121] See the quotation at n. 177. [122] Cited from the 2nd edition (1957) 44.

[123] Lerner, 'Legalism and Legality', 2 *Journal of Politics* (1940) 336, at 342.

[124] See Singer, 'The Player and the Cards: Nihilism and Legal Theory', 94 *Yale Law Journal* (1984) 1.

[125] R. Dworkin, *Taking Rights Seriously* (1977). [126] R. Dworkin, *Law's Empire* (1986).

[127] Ibid. 225.

[128] Dworkin thus invents a hypothetical judge, Hercules, 'a lawyer with superhuman skill, learning, patience and acumen' who is capable of finding the single right answer in the hardest of cases before him (Dworkin (n. 125) 105, Dworkin (n. 126) 239).

At the same time, however, Dworkin's theory certainly departs from the classical liberal doctrine's commitment to people's consent provided by an act of volition, and invests judges with an impressive power: in his own words, '[t]he courts are the capitals of law's empire, and judges are its princes', although he adds that they are not the empire's 'seers and prophets' (this role falls to philosophers).[129] For some, Dworkin's critics, this marked the advent of legal imperialism, arguing that 'Dworkin's theory of law as integrity can best be understood as a fear of and attempt to escape from politics'.[130]

A version of denial can occasionally be found in judges' own descriptions of their work (which may be why Dworkin was so popular among them). It is also very often what appears to be the official judicial philosophy as we can reconstruct it from the text of judicial decisions—certainly those of the ECJ. As Thomas von Danwitz, the German judge of the ECJ, once insisted: 'The basic understanding of the judicial decision as an act of cognition, that is, as a decision-making process determined exclusively by the law, must not . . . be cast into doubt, the hunt for the motives behind the reasons must not be opened'.[131] This, however, does not mean that it is necessarily what the judges actually think—it is the legal culture that forces them to denial.

This is not peculiar to Europe—quite the contrary. For example, consider the current US Chief Justice John Roberts' characterization of judges as 'merely [umpires] calling balls and strikes', made before the Senate Judiciary Committee during the hearing on his nomination in 2005.[132] As Richard Posner ironically noted, in order for this analogy to work 'we must imagine that umpires, in addition to calling balls and strikes, made the rules of baseball and changed them at will'.[133] But still, the senators seemed to be satisfied with what Roberts said (whether they actually believed him is a different matter), which made the confirmation hearing somewhat defunct.[134] Roberts was saying what the senators *wanted* to hear,[135] nicely illustrating 'the paradox of American critical legalism'—'an odd combination of utter faith and utter distrust in law'.[136]

[129] All quotations from Dworkin (n. 126) 407.

[130] Hunt, 'Law's Empire or Legal Imperialism?', in A. Hunt (ed.), *Reading Dworkin Critically* (1992) 9, at 10.

[131] von Danwitz, 'Funktionsbedingungen der Rechtsprechung des Europäischen Gerichtshofes', 43 *Europarecht* (2008) 769, as quoted in von Bogdandy and Venzke (n. 73) 102.

[132] See R. A. Posner, *How Judges Think* (2008) 78. The transcript of the hearings is available at https://www.judiciary.senate.gov/imo/media/doc/GPO-CHRG-ROBERTS.pdf (accessed 22 September 2020).

[133] Posner (n. 132) 78–79.

[134] See particularly Dworkin, 'Judge Roberts on Trial', *New York Review of Books*, 20 October 2005, available at http://www.nybooks.com/articles/2005/10/20/judge-roberts-on-trial/ (accessed 22 September 2020).

[135] This can be explained by the particular context of the confirmation hearings, where, at least after the controversial hearings of Robert Bork, 'any nominee who wants to win confirmation must hide his or her judicial philosophy and morality from public scrutiny'. Lininger, 'On Dworkin and Borkin', 105 *Michigan Law Review* (2007) 1315, at 1316.

[136] D. Kennedy, *A Critique of Adjudication (fin de siècle)* (1997) 73.

C. Acknowledgement and Endorsement

A third approach to judicial creativity can be characterized as its endorsement: it openly acknowledges the creative moment in judicial decision-making and often warmly welcomes it. This is the position with which many (not all) legal realists are identified, and which is now most famously defended by Richard Posner, who was a federal judge for many years. Judicial creativity is justified on various grounds, none of them related to people's will. So, for example, judges may be believed to have a unique experience from judging real-life disputes; they are said to get a 'situational sense' that guides them to the 'right' decision.[137] What makes that decision 'right' is often not stated (although many legal realists believe in the normative power of judicial experience).[138]

For Posner the guiding norm seems to be wealth maximization. In one of the numerous statements of his theory of judicial legitimacy Posner states that judges:

> have a dual role: to interpret the interest-group deals embodied in legislation and to provide the basic public service of authoritative dispute resolution. They perform the latter function not only by deciding cases in accordance with preexisting norms, but also—especially in the Anglo-American legal system—by elaborating those norms. . . . The law they created exhibits, according to the economic theory that I am expounding, a remarkable . . . substantive consistency. It is as if the judges *wanted* to adopt the rules, procedures, and case outcomes that would maximize society's wealth.[139]

While the last sentence may sound as a descriptive statement, Posner makes clear throughout his writing that he takes wealth maximization to be a normative commitment too.[140]

The problem with this view, however, is that wealth maximization is a not a neutral concept and economics is much more political (as opposed to 'scientific') than some proponents of the law and economics movement, such as Posner, want to see it.[141] The only way to assess the outcomes of decisions made by public

[137] This is how Karl Llewellyn's jurisprudence may be crudely summarized. For a much more sophisticated account of legal realism, see Leiter (n. 90) ch. 1: 'Rethinking Legal Realism: Toward a Naturalized Jurisprudence'.

[138] This is probably most visible in K. Llewellyn, *The Common Law Tradition: Deciding Appeals* (1960).

[139] R. A. Posner, *The Problems of Jurisprudence* (1990) 355.

[140] Ibid. 374–392.

[141] See what Posner says at 362: 'If all this seems reminiscent of Langdell [the "arch-formalist" and father of the "classical legal thought"—at least in the legal realist imagination—see Tamanaha (n. 92)], it differs fundamentally in being empirically verifiable. The ultimate test of a rule derived from economic theory is not the elegance or logicality of the derivation but the rule's effect on social wealth'. Such views have been trashed for quite some time—see e.g. J. R. Hackney Jr, *Under Cover of Science: American Legal-Economic Theory and the Quest for Objectivity* (2007) 121 for a fascinating intellectual history.

authorities is through democratic politics. This is the general problem with this approach to judicial creativity. It seeks to replace democratic legitimacy with something else, but the 'something else' is always much less neutral than the proponent of the alternative theory wants to have it.

This applies to an approach to judicial legitimacy which seeks to replace democracy with reason and which therefore does not problematize creative moments in interpretation in the light of the liberal doctrine of politics, for which, as discussed earlier, consent and will is centrally important. This approach has its home in political theory in the idea of public reason and deliberative democracy. There is, of course, a huge body of literature dealing with both concepts, which cannot be even cursorily summarized here.[142] Central for my purposes, I think, is the idea that reason is apolitical, which gives it a special force in the context of the liberal theory suspicious of politics and its passions. Once this assumption about reason and rationality is displaced, however, they can no longer justify anything.[143]

5. Linguistic Turn—to Democracy?

Posner's writing over time exhibits a visible move from economism to pragmatism.[144] In *The Problematics of Moral and Legal Theory* Posner describes a judicial pragmatist as someone 'who wants to come up with the decision that will be best with regard to present and future needs'.[145] Note that Posner does not explicitly say what the 'best decision with regard to present and future needs' actually is, although he is certainly committed to a certain vision of society and its politics. He does not, however, put this vision to a critical deliberation and in this respect he departs from many pragmatists he invokes in his later works.[146]

This ambiguity regarding Posner's credentials as a 'true' pragmatist illustrates the problem with the term, which has been 'so recklessly overused in recent years that it has been rendered, by now, utterly banal or simply empty'.[147] Leaving American pragmatism aside for now (however important it is to have a complete mapping of strategies for dealing with the problems associated with interpretation's creative moments), I want to focus on what might be called semantic pragmatism.

[142] See J. Bohman and W. Rehg (eds), *Deliberative Democracy: Essays on Reason and Politics* (1997).

[143] See e.g. Boyle, 'The Politics of Reason: Critical Legal Theory and Local Social Thought', 133 *University of Pennsylvania Law Review* (1985) 685.

[144] See especially his *Law, Pragmatism, and Democracy* (2003), but already Posner (n. 139), contains 'A Pragmatist Manifesto' (ch. 15).

[145] R. A. Posner, *The Problematics of Moral and Legal Theory* (1999) 242. Notably, 'wealth maximization' is not ever mentioned in this book.

[146] On this point, see Solove and Sullivan, 'Can Pragmatism Be Radical? Richard Posner and Legal Pragmatism', 113 *Yale Law Journal* (2003) 687.

[147] Leiter (n. 90) 46.

In a way, this is the approach taken in this chapter, i.e. focusing on semantic struggles over judicial legitimacy. The focus on the language of political (and legal) argument implies that our attention turns to the practice of interpretation (hence the 'interpretative turn' in jurisprudence, which followed the earlier 'linguistic turn' in philosophy).[148] One implication of such a turn is to see interpretation as an inter-subjective enterprise. Actors make interpretations while having their addressees in mind, taking into account their possible reactions. They thus become constrained by those predicted reactions. Not everything goes—only that which can be accepted by the relevant audiences. The interaction between the interpreter and her audience(s) is governed by certain rules, which do not have a metaphysical grounding, but follow from the nature of language and linguistic communication.[149]

This is the approach of, for example, Habermas' theory of communicative action[150] or Robert Brandom's semantic pragmatism,[151] which was recently taken up by Ingo Venzke in his study of international courts' law-making through interpretation:

> Robert Brandom has perceptively argued that present interpreters are constrained both by past and future practices. They need to connect to the past in order to be understood and, if they want to be successful and wish to assert their authority, they need to consider in anticipation how their interpretations will be received. In this sense, the development of the law is interstitial. It stands between the past and the future.[152]

The constraint that Brandom has in mind does not come from the 'rule of law' as conceived by the liberal theory of law and politics, however—i.e. the rules adopted through a procedure that seeks to achieve consent.[153] The rule of law is part of the pragmatic constraint, but, as many semantic pragmatists argue, there is much more: it consists of things that escape people's conscious agency, such as the 'structure' or the way in which the human mind operates, studied by

[148] On the linguistic turn, see Surkis, 'When Was the Linguistic Turn? A Genealogy', 117 *American Historical Review* (2012) 700. On the 'interpretive turn' in jurisprudence critically, with a wealth of further references, see D. Patterson, *Law and Truth* (1996) chs 5 and 6 (engaging primarily Ronald Dworkin and Stanley Fish).

[149] Here we get to the terrain of the philosophy of language, linguistic theory and semiotics. Many assumptions adopted by Habermas or Brandom, that I take as my primary reference points here, are of course contested—as in any discipline.

[150] A very concise summary can be found in H. Baxter, *Habermas: The Discourse Theory of Law and Democracy* (2011) ch. 1.

[151] See R. Brandom, *Making it Explicit: Reasoning, Representing, and Discursive Commitment* (1998).

[152] Venzke (n. 80) 49, references to Brandom, 'Hegel's Account of the Structure and Content of Conceptual Norms', 7 *European Journal of Philosophy* (1999) 164 omitted.

[153] See the text at n 81 *et seq.*

phenomenologists,[154] and more recently by scholars who study law and legal reasoning through the prism of neuroscience.[155] We may call such constraints 'extra-legal', although this is not precise since many of them come from within the law, broadly conceived: for example, legal education, the process of selection of legal officials, or the rules (legal and non-legal) that determine how legal officials interact with the political system and the general public. Some legal realists call these constraints 'steadying factors', in the sense that they stabilize the interpretation and application of legal rules, albeit in ways that are very different to those imagined by legal formalists.[156]

Drawing on the pragmatist approach of Brandom and Habermas, Ingo Venzke comes up with the notion of semantic authority: 'an actor's capacity to influence and shape meanings as well as the ability to establish its communications as authoritative reference points in legal discourse'.[157] In his later work Venzke adds that an actor enjoys semantic authority 'even if others do not agree in substance',[158] which must mean that the authority is due to the status of the actor rather than the content of her particular communications. Venzke rejects the view that semantic authority depends on persuasion (quoting approvingly Hannah Arendt, who wrote that '[w]here arguments are used, authority is left in abeyance')[159] and focuses on what he understands as 'sociological legitimacy', raising normative questions only tentatively and giving their meaning 'a thoroughly pragmatic twist',[160] meaning that rightness ensues from the discursive practice and not some external standard.

This explains why Venzke is able to assert that he takes 'authority to be a phenomenon that can be justified as well as unjustified'.[161] However, he ultimately does search for semantic authority's 'evasive foundations',[162] based on the idea of democracy, 'the gold standard against which to assess the legitimacy of authority'.[163] This is later developed in another book, co-authored with Armin von Bogdandy.[164]

[154] See Boyle (n. 143).

[155] See especially S. L. Winter, *A Clearing in the Forrest: Law, Life, and Mind* (2001) and M. S. Pardo and D. Patterson, *Minds, Brains, and Law: The Conceptual Foundations of Law and Neuroscience* (2013).

[156] See Llewellyn (n. 138) 19 *et seq*. For an application of such realist approach to the reasoning of the ECJ, see Beck (n. 78).

[157] Venzke (n. 80) 63.

[158] Venzke, 'Semantic Authority' ACIL Research Paper 2016–03, available at https://ssrn.com/abstract=2723851, 7 (accessed 22 September 2020).

[159] I. Venzke, 'Semantic Authority, Legal Change and the Dynamics of International Law', 12 *No Foundations: An Interdisciplinary Journal of Law and Justice* (2015) 12, quoting H. Arendt, *Between Past and Future* (2006) 91, 96.

[160] Venzke (n. 159) 12–15.

[161] Venzke (n. 80) 64.

[162] Ibid. 245–261.

[163] Ibid. 247.

[164] See von Bogdandy and Venzke (n. 73) 135–155. A shorter version outlining the main argument invokes democracy explicitly: von Bogdandy and Venzke, 'In Whose Name? An Investigation of International Courts' Public Authority and Its Democratic Justification', 23 *European Journal of International Law* (2012) 7.

There are two interesting twists made throughout the development of the concept of semantic authority. First, while initially Venzke seems to side with those pragmatists who reject any firm foundations for claims to truth, he parts company with them when it comes to the practical consequences of such a move, since he then seeks to find such foundations through which he would be able to assess the normative legitimacy of actors holding semantic authority.[165]

Second, while doing this, he first discusses one such foundational idea, namely justice, but does so in the mode of an 'external' analysis,[166] in order to show how the concept can be used (and misused) in communicative practices—how the 'bittersweet taste of justice in legal discourse' can be felt.[167] After reviewing numerous contributions to the thinking about the normativity of international law on the basis of justice (taking account of both the idealist-constructivist side and that occupied by sceptics and realists), Venzke observes: 'The notion of communicative action situates itself between these two competing paradigms and focuses on the actions of socially embedded actors. In so doing, it seeks to explain and to provide a foundation for legitimate order that is situated in inter-subjectivity'.[168] The focus on communicative action then steers Venzke from justice towards the deliberative theory of democracy.

One can argue that the discourse of democracy easily collapses into the discourse on justice (and vice versa) and that each only puts emphasis on different normative concerns, which are, however, present in both.[169] One can also object to the specific conception of democracy used by Venzke and von Bogdandy, based on the provisions of the Treaty on the European Union on democratic principles.[170] As they acknowledge, this conception is thoroughly individualistic,

[165] The reluctance to draw from pragmatism guidelines for a practical, political action is what often distinguishes the present pragmatists (such as Richard Rorty or Stanley Fish) from the earlier ones (such as John Dewey). See Kloppenberg, 'Pragmatism: An Old Name for Some New Ways of Thinking?', 83 *Journal of American History* (1996) 100.

[166] The distinction, made famous by H. L. A. Hart, is of course problematic: see Barzun, 'Inside-Out: Beyond the Internal/External Distinction in Legal Scholarship', 101 *Virginia Law Review* (2015) 1203.

[167] Venzke (n. 80) 198–223. [168] Ibid. 214.

[169] This is nicely illustrated by Rainer Forst's comments on Jürgen Neyer's call to focus on justice, not democracy in the context of the EU (see Neyer (n. 42) and more explicitly Neyer 'Justice, Not Democracy: Legitimacy in the European Union', 48 *Journal of Common Market Studies* (2010) 903). Forst's theory of justice as justification is what Neyer takes as his theoretical basis. Forst comments on it in 'Justice, Democracy and the Right to Justification: Reflections on Jürgen Neyer's Normative Theory of the European Union', in D. Kochenov, G. de Búrca, and A. Williams (eds), *Europe's Justice Deficit?* (2015) 227–234, 233: Neyer's 'discussion rests on and reproduces the immanent relation between justice and democracy which a discourse theory of justice establishes and that he wished to avoid in his argument'.

[170] Arts 9–12 TEU. For a critique of the EU model of democracy, see e.g. Bellamy and Castiglione, 'Three Models of Democracy, Political Community and Representation in the EU', 20 *Journal of European Public Policy* (2013) 206.

'[s]ince positing a European people or a global nation is hardly persuasive'.[171] One may wonder whether this practical impossibility is a reason for rejecting the correctness of a theoretical construction, even more so as, a few lines earlier, they claim that those provisions 'unlike *any theory*, are the outcome of democratic politics',[172] amplified by '[t]he consent of the large majority of the Union's citizens'.[173] It is quite puzzling to deny the existence (and normative significance) of a collective body and at the same time invoke it in support of one's normative argument.

More importantly for our present purposes, however, by this conceptual move von Bogdandy and Venzke do not capture the whole range of judicial action. This is despite the fact that they nicely displace a one-dimensional understanding of international adjudication, focused on dispute settlement, and present a quite nuanced picture attentive to various functions of international adjudication.[174] Most of their normative reconstruction concerns law-making 'for the future' and its legitimacy based on their reconstruction of the democratic principle. Deciding the concrete case hardly gets mentioned, and neither does the problem judicial creativity poses in this context.[175]

There is, however, one more problem with the account of judicial legitimacy based on democracy: its failure to provide good reasons for accepting judicial authority exercised in the context of a particular case. This is because the creative moment in interpretation contradicts predictability and legal certainty, which are the cornerstones of the liberal principle of the rule of law.[176] The metaphor of 'dog-law', invented by the father of modern legal positivism Jeremy Bentham, still bites:

> It is the judges . . . that make the common law. Do you know how they make it? Just as a man makes laws for his dog. When your dog does anything you want to break him of, you wait till he does it, and then beat him for it. This is the way you make laws for your dog: and this is the way the judges make law for you and me.[177]

The problem can be further moderated by reinforcing other legitimatory elements: impartiality and independence, objectivity, or non-arbitrariness. These are,

171 von Bogdandy and Venzke (n. 73) 140. 172 Ibid. 137. 173 Ibid. 137.
174 Ibid. 5–17. 175 See only ibid. 105–106.
176 As with many other 'big ideas' used in this chapter, the rule of law has also been analysed in a vast amount of literature that resists summarization. Good starting points can be found in Fallon, '"The Rule of Law" as a Concept in Constitutional Discourse', 97 *Columbia Law Review* (1997) 1 (from the point of view of the liberal constitutional theory); B. Z. Tamanaha, *On the Rule of Law: History, Politics, Theory* (2004); and J. E. Fleming (ed), *Getting to the Rule of Law* (2011).
177 Bentham, 'Truth versus Ashhurst; or, law as it is, contrasted with what it is said to be' [1792], quoted from Dean Alfange Jr.: Alfange, 'Jeremy Bentham and the Codification of Law', 55 *Cornell Law Review* (1969) 58, at 65.

however, in contradiction to possible cures for creative elements that reach beyond the context of the particular case, making courts more 'accountable' and in sync with politics.[178] This is yet another illustration of the persistent problem with the fundamental tension—for which the theory of judicial legitimacy still needs to find a satisfactory solution.

6. Conclusion

This chapter has argued for a communicative concept of legitimacy, which is grounded in the concrete practices and understandings of those who make judgments about the legitimacy of particular political orders and institutions. It has sought to explain how some seemingly modest and untheoretical conceptions of legitimacy cannot escape such normative judgments, which are in turn grounded in some theory of legitimacy.

Judicial legitimacy is facing a fundamental tension that reflects our contradictory impulses. First, to be free from others—to have our space of 'negative freedom' protected from their interference. Second, however, we need others in order to fully realize our freedom, which is also 'social'. Courts face the same structural problem: the concern for particularity and justice to be provided to individual parties on the one hand, and the need to serve wider societal aims on the other.

Different conceptualizations of judicial legitimacy do not address this tension in a fully satisfactory matter, in my view. This chapter does not offer a viable alternative, but I hope the discussion here has at least clarified matters, and provided a basis for further thinking about judicial legitimacy in the EU and beyond.

[178] For an interesting overview of the recent debates concerning judicial accountability, see Kosař, 'The Least Accountable Branch', 11 *International Journal of Constitutional Law* (2013) 234.

Index

For the benefit of digital users, indexed terms that span two pages (e.g. 52–53) may, on occasion, appear on only one of those pages.
Tables and figures are indicated by an italic *t* or *f* following the page number. Notes are indicated by n. following the page number.